International Socialism 135

Summer 2012

Contributors

Colin Barker joined the Socialist Review Group in 1961-2, and has maintained almost continuous membership of the IS and SWP since then. He lives in Manchester.

Ian Birchall has just edited an issue of *Revolutionary History* devoted to solidarity action with the Algerian liberation struggle by European revolutionaries, and is currently working on a book about internationalism and the French left.

Joseph Choonara is the author of *Unravelling Capitalism: A Guide to Marxist Political Economy*.

Gareth Edwards is a socialist activist and works in a wholesalers in Portsmouth. He blogs at http://inside-left.blogspot.co.uk

Sai Englert is a student organiser for the Socialist Workers Party.

Jack Farmer is a deputy editor on *Socialist Review*.

Nigel Harris taught at University College London for forty years before retiring.

Shirin Hirsch is a postgraduate student at the University of Manchester.

Bea Leal is a socialist activist living in Norwich.

Jonathan Maunder is a member of the SWP in North London and is involved with the MENA Solidarity Network—www.menasolidaritynetwork.com

Marieke Mueller is postgraduate student at the University of Oxford.

Judith Orr is the editor of *Socialist Worker* and author of *Sexism and the System*.

Brian O'Boyle is the editor of *Socialist Worker* in Ireland, where he also works as an economist.

Jamie Pitman is a a student at Ruskin College in Oxford.

Jen Roesch was a participant in Occupy Wall Street and is a long-time activist in NYC where she is an organiser for the International Socialist Organization.

Julie Sherry is a journalist on *Socialist Worker*.

Dan Swain is a postgraduate student at the University of Essex.

Jim Wolfreys is a senior lecturer in French and European politics at King's College, London.

Sarah Young is a socialist and Unison activist based in Brighton.

Dave Zirin is the sports editor at the *Nation* Magazine and co-author of *The John Carlos Story: The Sports Moment that Changed the World* (Haymarket). Find out more at www.edgeofsports.com

Crunch-time for the eurozone?
Alex Callinicos

Nearly five years after it started, the global economic and financial crisis shows no signs of resolving itself. On the contrary, in Europe it is taking a more virulent form, as the eurozone inches towards some kind of moment of truth. The slow motion catastrophe in Europe threatens to kill off the chronically weak recovery in the US. This is part of a global levelling down process, as the Chinese economy, which has since 2009 provided the main motor of revival, itself runs out of steam. The *Financial Times* reported in mid-June:

> The *FT*/Brookings Tiger index [which is supposed to track the global economic recovery] showed world growth stalling after an initial rapid recovery from the 2008-09 economic crisis. Growth in the US was slowing, much of Europe is in recession, China's growth outlook has weakened, the reform processes in India have stalled and other large emerging economies have slowed dramatically.

> Prof [Eswar] Prasad [of Brookings] said: "The engines of world growth are running out of steam while the trailing wagons are going off the rails. Emerging market economies are facing sharp slowdowns in growth while many advanced economies slip into recession".[1]

1:   Giles, 2012.

One can analyse what's happening at three levels. The first and most immediate centres on Greece. Here politics is in command: will the popular revolt against the parties supporting the Memorandum of Understanding between the Greek state and its people's tormentors (the troika of the European Central Bank [ECB], the European Commission and the International Monetary Fund [IMF]) precipitate Greece into jumping or being pushed out of the eurozone? Most commentators agree the success of New Democracy, the main party of the Greek right, in squeaking narrowly ahead of Syriza (the Coalition of the Radical Left) in the general election of 17 June has merely bought a little time. The economist Nouriel Roubini tweeted that night: "In 6–12 months ND-Pasok gov will fall as economy will fall into a depression. Then new elections will lead Syriza to win & Grexit to occur".[2]

Much more on the politics below; the economics of the Greek agony is mainly about the impact of a "Grexit" and whether it would spread contagion to other vulnerable members of the eurozone: at present Spain is most in the firing line. This takes us to the second level of analysis. The eurozone crisis is the specific European form taken by the bursting of the financial bubble that gripped advanced capitalism in the middle of the last decade. What this involved was a great surge in bank lending, which financed a series of speculative booms, often centred on the property market. A recent analysis by the *Financial Times*'s Alphaville blog called "The Rise and Fall of European Banking" cites a Citibank study showing how European banks led the surge in cross-border lending (largely in this case within the European Union itself) in the last decade:

> Global bank assets increased *c*160 percent from 2002 to 2008. Over this period, EU banks' global assets increased *c*190 percent, with France leading the way (+250 percent). Several EU bank systems' global assets, including France, the UK, Sweden, Greece, Ireland, Denmark and Netherlands, increased over 200 percent over this period.[3]

But this process has, since the 2008 crash, gone into reverse. To quote Citibank again: "Europe ex UK is the exception to the post 2009 international bounce back theme. Naturally more exposed to the second leg of the global financial crisis—the euro sovereign and banking crisis—European ex UK banks have reduced their overseas exposures in

---

2: http://twitter.com/Nouriel/status/214422086968549377
3: Pollack, 2012.

the past year, three and five years." While US, British and Japanese banks have held on to their shares of global banking assets, those in continental Europe have seen their share fall.

This retreat reflects both the losses that these banks made when the bubble of the mid-2000s unravelled and also the losses they fear they may still make on their loans to the so-called "peripheral" eurozone economies. As we have repeatedly argued, the "rescues" of Greece, southern Ireland and Portugal have been all about saving the northern European banks that had lent so heavily to both public and private borrowers in these countries. The mechanism that has forced these countries into the arms of the troika has been financial markets forcing up the interest rates on government debt—swollen by the Great Recession and the costs of the initial bank bailouts—to unsustainable levels.[4]

But—as we have also argued—the price of the "rescues", austerity programmes designed to slash public spending, has forced already weak economies into a vicious downward spiral in which contracting output makes it harder to meet the debt reduction targets demanded by the troika. One effect has been further to weaken shaky banking systems. For example, a combination of economic and political fears has promoted what Alphaville call a "bank jog" in Greece, with a steady drain of deposits being withdrawn amounting by early June to a 35 percent fall in the ratio of bank deposits to Greek gross domestic product.[5]

The ECB has been plugging the gap through its programme of emergency liquidity assistance to the Greek banks, estimated at €60 billion in mid-May. But such measures increase the losses that the rest of the European Union would make if Greece did fully default on its debt. The Marxist economist Michael Roberts offers the following estimate of these losses:

Adding up what the Greek government owes to other EU governments from the two bailouts, what the central bank debts are to the Eurosystem and how much the ECB has already lent to Greek banks and holds in Greek government debt, we find that the eurozone is exposed to around €500 billion of potential losses, or near 5 percent of eurozone GDP...

Germany and France alone are exposed to around €150 billion each. And this is just exposure to sovereign debt. If the Greek private sector should also

4: See Callinicos, 2010a, Georgiou, 2010, and the analysis developed by the Research into Money and Finance group, now collected in Lapavitsas and others, 2012.
5: Cotterill, 2012, and Keohane, 2012.

default on its loans, French and German banks will take a sizeable hit (French banks have about €25 billion lent to Greek companies). When you add all this in, the total exposure is closer to €750 billion.[6]

If the default of tiny Greece could have such an impact, what about Spain, the markets' most recent target? The Spanish economy is nearly twice as large as those of Greece, Ireland and Portugal combined. Some €97 billion left Spain in the first three months of 2012, amounting to about a tenth of national income.[7] Much more directly than in Greece, the collapse in confidence centred on the banks, deeply implicated in the economically and ecologically destructive property bubble of the preceding decade.[8]

The fumbling right wing government of Mariano Rajoy, elected on an austerity ticket in November but desperate to avoid the full-scale troika treatment, tried to get the ECB to fund the rescue of Bankia, a conglomerate of seven failed *cajas* (regional savings banks) headed by an ex managing director of the IMF, Rodrigo Rato, through the back door.

When this didn't work, with markets pushing up interest rates on Spanish government debt to unbearable levels, Rajoy had no choice but to appeal for an EU bailout. The terms offered the Spanish state on 10 June were more favourable than those given its predecessors. Rather than being tied to an IMF programme, the €100 billion loan will go to the government body responsible for restructuring the Spanish banks. But German finance minister Wolfgang Schäuble has said that a team of troika inspectors will be checking Spain's books, so it remains to be seen whether the differences with earlier "rescues" are more than cosmetic.[9]

But it only took a few hours for the yields on Spanish government debt to start rising again to unsustainable levels, with Italian bonds soon suffering a similar fate. The Royal Bank of Scotland estimates that €134-180 billion is needed to recapitalise the Spanish banks, €155 billion to refinance sovereign bonds that fall due at the end of 2014, and €121 billion to cover budget deficits till then.[10] The €100 billion bailout fund, probably from the new European Stability Mechanism, will cover only a fraction of this enormous bill. On a broader front, quite apart from the escalating crisis in Greece, there are too many unexploded bombs in the European financial system. One particularly toxic factor is offered by the long-term financing operation through

---

6:   Roberts, 2012a.
7:   Jones, Jenkins and Johnson, 2012.
8:   For an excellent analysis of the Spanish bubble, see López and Rodriguez, 2011.
9:   Wiesmann, 2012b.
10:   Mallet, 2012.

which the ECB pumped around €1 trillion into the banking system. Banks used quite a lot of this money to buy their governments' bonds: Spanish banks, for example, have taken €83 billion of Spain's sovereign debt since December. This bought a bit of time but could act as what has been called a "doom loop", in which weak banks and governments drag each other down.[11]

Hopes of an eventual return to stability are based on the German government agreeing to a European banking union that would put the combined financial power of the eurozone behind any vulnerable national banking system. There have been signs of a slight softening in German policy, particularly in response to the overwhelming rejection of austerity in the elections in France and Greece. In early May first Schäuble backed higher wage increases and then the Bundesbank said higher inflation would be acceptable as part of a process of expanding the German domestic market and thereby making it easier for other eurozone economies to expand by exporting.[12] The somewhat less harsh packaging of the Spanish bailout might be another straw in the wind.

But these seem like relatively marginal adjustments. There is no sign of any willingness in Berlin and Frankfurt to offer more than cosmetic sweeteners to soften the savage austerity programme imposed on Greece. Chancellor Angela Merkel's strategy remains to use the pressures created by the eurozone crisis to force other member states into a fiscal union that would generalise and perpetuate the austerity regime that has been imposed on Greece, Ireland and Portugal as an emergency response to this crisis. Any steps towards a banking union will have to wait upon acceptance of this regime. Even discussion of palliatives such as allowing the eurozone bailout funds to buy Spanish and Italian government debt has proceeded at a paralysingly slow pace.

When meeting David Cameron in early June, Merkel said, "We need more Europe. We don't only need monetary union, we also need a so-called fiscal union. And most of all we need a political union—which means we need to gradually cede powers to Europe and give Europe control".[13] In fact, what she has in mind is nothing resembling a democratic political union based on the constituent power of the European people. Instead economic sovereignty is to be surrendered to a "Europe" consisting of unaccountable bodies such as the ECB and the European Council, in which the German state increasingly has the dominant say.

11: Jenkins, 2012.
12: Atkins, 2012.
13: Wiesmann, 2012a.

But the more immediate problem is that the banking crisis may overwhelm the deliberately paced game plan being pursued by Merkel and Schäuble. So far they have successfully relied on other European governments blinking first. But the situation is slipping out of the hands of the identikit mediocrities composing the European political elite in the neoliberal era. On the one hand, the financial markets may talk themselves into an uncontrollable panic, like the one that engulfed them after the collapse of Lehman Brothers in September 2008. Merkel herself has admitted, "We are certainly in a race with the markets".[14] On the other hand, the peoples of Europe—ignored so far in the deliberations of the troika and the Berlin cabinet—are threatening to upset all the calculations made at the top.

Before we turn to the latter, potentially decisive factor, a word about the third dimension of the crisis, which concerns its fundamental causes. Elsewhere in this issue Joseph Choonara demonstrates the central role played by the inability of the advanced capitalist economies to overcome the sharp fall in the rate of profit that they suffered during the 1960s. But pointing to problems of profitability as an ultimate cause of the crisis does not, as caricatural critiques of this interpretation sometimes suggest, require ignoring the destabilising role of financial markets. Marx himself in volume three of *Capital* closely connects the tendency of the rate of profit to fall with the fluctuations of financial markets, whose bubbles serve to allow the process of capital accumulation temporarily to overcome its limits. He writes: "The so-called plethora of capital is always basically reducible to a plethora of that capital for which the fall in the profit rate is not outweighed by its mass"—in other words, falling profitability creates a situation where there is too much capital relative to the mass of surplus value extracted from workers.[15]

The idea that crises represent a plethora of capital was developed by the so-called banking school of British political economists, early 19th century critics of the quantity theory of money that still forms a core assumption of neoliberal ideology. One of them, John Fullarton, argued that the origins of crises lie in the fact that "the amount of capital seeking productive investment accumulates in ordinary times with a rapidity greatly out of proportion to the increase of the means of advantageously employing it". Hence the excess capital is splurged on increasingly speculative investment, leading to bubbles, panics and busts. He concludes, in a passage quoted by Marx:

14: Peel, Mallet and Wigglesworth, 2012.
15: Marx, 1981, p359.

From more recent events, indeed, one might almost be tempted that a periodical destruction of capital has become a necessary cond any market rate of interest at all. And, considered in that point of these awful visitations, to which we are accustomed to look forward with much disquiet and apprehension and which we are so anxious to avert, may be nothing more than the natural and necessary corrective of an overgrown and bloated opulence, the *vis medicatrix* [medical power] by which our social system, as at present constituted, is enabled to relieve itself from time to time of an ever-recurring plethora which menaces its existence, and to regain a sound and wholesome state.[16]

Fullarton's diagnosis resembles the analysis developed by FA von Hayek during the Great Depression, which he argued was a result of overinvestment made possible by easy credit.[17] Hayek's contemporary followers criticise the bank bailouts and fiscal stimuli because they have prevented the purge of unprofitable capital needed to restore the system to health. In other words, state intervention has prevented the large-scale destruction of capital that would overcome the problems of overaccumulation and profitability that produced the crisis in the first place. Indeed, capitalists aren't investing the extra profits they were able to squeeze out of workers at the height of the slump in 2008-9, thereby adding to these problems. In March, the *Financial Times*'s Lex column reported: "Four years after the financial crisis, companies globally are awash with cash: $1.7 trillion among US companies, €2 trillion in the eurozone, and £750 billion in the UK".[18]

The trouble with leaving the system to correct itself through the destruction of capital is, as Keynes pointed out during the 1930s, that the result can be, as it was then, deep and protracted slump. Paul Krugman has taken up Keynes's banner, arguing that the US and the EU are caught in a new depression that austerity is making worse.[19] His criticisms of the "austerians" are highly effective, but Krugman presents overcoming the crisis as something as simple as flicking a light switch, through higher government borrowing and spending to stimulate effective demand. This ignores the much deeper problems in the accumulation process, and, in particular, as Roberts points out, that of profitability: "Even though

---

16: Fullarton, 1844, pp162,165; second passage quoted in Marx, 1973, pp849-850. See, on the banking school, Itoh and Lapavitsas, 1999, chapter 1.

17: Hayek, 1935.

18: Lex, 2012.

19: Krugman, 2012.

corporate profits have recovered in the US from their trough in mid-2009, the rate of profit is still below the most recent peak of 2005 and the 'neoliberal' peak of 1997. So corporations continue to hoard their cash and business investment growth is too weak to restore jobs and incomes to pre-crisis levels".[20]

Capitalism therefore remains caught in a structural dilemma: the large-scale destruction of capital threatens a much deeper slump, but without it the crisis of profitability will continue. The ineffective posturing of the Western economic and political elites is ultimately an expression of this dilemma. In the eurozone, currently the most dangerous arena of the crisis, there is absolutely no sign of any resolution.

The second coming of the European radical left

One reason why the eurozone crisis threatens to become unmanageable has nothing directly to do with these structural contradictions. Quite simply, austerity is producing an increasingly powerful political backlash. This became visible in the late spring and early summer of 2012 in a succession of political upheavals. Most obvious were the victory of the Socialist Party (PS) in the French presidential and legislative elections, and the spectacular advances scored by Syriza in the Greek parliamentary elections of May and June 2012. But there have been other significant political events—for example, the collapse of the coalition government in the Netherlands, leading to fresh elections in September.

The same pattern appears in all these cases: the centre is squeezed and there is polarisation further to the right and left. The most spectacular case of the centre being squeezed is provided by Greece, where the main parties of Greek capitalism for the past generation—New Democracy (ND) and Pasok (the Panhellenic Socialist Movement)—were punished for their role in implementing the Memorandum by being reduced to a third of the popular vote on the election of 6 May. Their combined vote rose to about 42 percent in the follow-up poll on 17 June, still a minority of the elec-

---

20: Roberts, 2012b.

torate, while that of the radical left was a stunning 32 percent. Syriza's score of nearly 27 percent is unparalleled since the Italian Communist Party was at the height of its power in the 1970s.

Thus we see here also the polarisation under way: the backlash against austerity is favouring parties of the radical left and the extreme right—the Front de Gauche and the Front National (FN) in France, Syriza and Chrysi Avgi (Golden Dawn) in Greece, the Socialist Party and Geert Wilders's PVV Party for Freedom in the Netherlands. Elsewhere in this journal, Jim Wolfreys analyses the French elections. He emphasises how Nicolas Sarkozy's populist racist policies have helped to create a much wider terrain on which the FN under Marine Le Pen's leadership can operate. Particularly in the light of the FN's high scores in the presidential and legislative elections, this is a threatening development. The picture is pretty ugly elsewhere as well. Chrysi Avgi, an openly Nazi paramilitary organisation, succeeded by exploiting state racism and popular disgust with the Memorandum parties, to win 7 percent of the vote in both elections, in a country where a tenth of the population died under the German occupation in 1941-4. Wilders pulled the rug from under the Dutch coalition in order to win broader support for his own distinctive brand of authoritarian neoliberal Islamophobia.[21]

Unfortunately the growth of the far right is a familiar feature of the European political scene. Indeed, this encourages a stereotypical conception in which history mechanically repeats itself, with economic depression favouring the triumph of fascism. Of course, in reality the 1930s saw immense class battles, particularly in 1934-6: it was their defeat, particularly thanks to the Popular Front policies of the Communist International, that made the continent-wide triumph of fascism possible.

Similarly, what we see in Europe is a process of social and political *polarisation*, in which crisis and austerity promote collective resistance and political radicalisation as well as the growth of the fascist and populist right. The re-emergence of the radical left is indeed the new feature in the situation, and therefore it requires particularly concentrated attention. *Re*-emergence: Between the late 1990s and the mid-2000s, a number of formations of the radical left emerged in Europe to challenge the social liberalism of mainstream social democracy. But, as the movements against neoliberal globalisation and the war on terrorism began to recede around 2005, so many of these formations suffered setbacks, quite often self-inflicted.[22]

21: Van der Zwan, 2011.
22: Callinicos, 2008.

Now they seem to be enjoying a second wind. The process isn't a uniform one. Die Linke, which in recent years has probably been the most high-profile party of the radical left in Europe, suffered a serious setback in the North Rhine Westphalia state elections at the end of May, when it lost all its seats. Rifondazione Comunista has been reduced to a marginal force in Italy since its disastrous participation in the centre-left government of 2004-6. Two other of the older formations, the Left Bloc in Portugal and the Red Green Alliance in Denmark, are still very much players, though the Left Bloc saw its parliamentary representation halved in last year's general election. And, in Britain, George Galloway's astonishing by-election victory in Bradford West at the end of March brought Respect back into the game with a bang.

The new front-runners—the Front de Gauche and Syriza—conform to the general pattern. They are both coalitions whose constituent forces are rooted in the complex histories of their countries' lefts. The Front de Gauche unites the French Communist Party (PCF) with Jean-Luc Mélenchon's Parti de Gauche, a left wing breakaway from the PS, and an assortment of far-left groupuscules and social movement activists. Syriza's dominant force is Synaspismos, a party that brings together most of the different elements of the Eurocommunist tradition in Greece, but its allies comprise a variety of far-left organisations of Maoist and Trotskyist provenance.

Is it possible to generalise about the politics of these formations? I have already tried to do so:

> Over-simplifying a little, it is essentially some version or other of left reformism… It's not surprising that left reformist parties are making the running against austerity. They are filling a space left by the rightward shift of mainstream social democracy. Parties like Labour and the French Socialists are now called "social liberal" because of their embrace of neoliberalism.

> Figures such as Mélenchon, the Syriza leader Alex Tsipras, and, in this country, George Galloway are able to reach out to traditional social-democratic voters by articulating their anger in a familiar reformist language. Ed Miliband and François Hollande are trying to recalibrate their parties' messages to relate to this anger, but their unwillingness to break with social liberalism leaves a big space to their left.[23]

23: Callinicos, 2012b.

This characterisation has come in for some criticism for failing to capture the novelty of these formations and the role played by the revolutionary left in them. Underlying these objections may be a deeper failure to understand the nature of reformism. It has become quite common on the far left to identify reformism with the mainstream social democratic parties and to argue that the latter's capitulation to neoliberalism represents their transformation into straightforwardly bourgeois formations without any connection to the workers' movement. This is a double mistake.

In the first place, reformism can't be equated with a specific set of political parties. It arises from a structural tendency for workers' struggles to limit themselves to fighting for improvements within the existing system. This tendency then gives rise to the trade union bureaucracy, in other words, to a specific layer of full-time officials whose function is to negotiate the terms of workers' more or less grudging accommodation with capitalism; their influence within the labour movement reinforces the tendency for the economic class struggle to be self-limiting. Social democratic *parties* emerged as the political expression of the trade union bureaucracy. But the underlying tendency can exist in the absence of such parties: the fact that the Democrats are as much an openly capitalist party as the Republicans doesn't mean that there is no reformism in the US, and, predictably enough, its privileged site is the labour bureaucracy, as the experiences of Occupy Wall Street (see Jen Roesch's article elsewhere in this issue) and the defeats in Wisconsin show.

Secondly, the social-liberal parties have yet to break with their moorings in the workers' movement. These links may have weakened as the PS, New Labour and the like have made themselves at home in a bourgeois political sphere increasingly dominated by corporate media and finance, but they still exist, allowing these parties to tack leftwards to rebuild their popular base. Hence the ability of the corrupt and apparently moribund PS to defeat Sarkozy and win a presidential and legislative majority for the first time since 1988; hence also the victory of the German Social Democratic Party (SPD), which a couple of years ago was under heavy pressure from Die Linke, in alliance with the Greens in the North Rhine Westphalia elections.

But, as noted above, social democratic revivals don't have to squeeze the radical left. And the development of social liberalism is crucial to the new parties' ability to appeal to working class voters disgruntled by their old parties' betrayal of their traditions. In many cases the radical left leaders are perfectly explicit about what they are doing.

Galloway inflicted a thumping defeat on the Labour Party under Ed Miliband by campaigning as "Real Labour". Oskar Lafontaine, the most dynamic figure in Die Linke, has been perfectly open that his project is to reconstruct German social democracy on a more left wing basis, with the aim of eventually forcing the SPD into coalition on Die Linke's terms. Mélenchon has explicitly modelled his own strategy of that of Die Linke. This means that he is much less willing to contemplate participating in a PS-led coalition than the PCF, whose parliamentary and municipal representation is heavily dependent on Socialist Party support. But this is because Mélenchon is playing a longer game than the venal apparatchiks of French Communism are now capable of—and not because he has renounced reformism.

But the new radical left parties aren't mechanically repeating the pattern through which classical social democracy developed. They don't have the luxury of the gradual, organic accumulation of forces enjoyed by Labour or the SPD in the late 19th and early 20th centuries. Their relationship with the trade union bureaucracy varies considerably. And organised revolutionaries are often able to find a space to operate, sometimes even to help found the new formations. This reflects a fluid situation in which reformist politicians sometimes find it in their interest to ally with the far left. Thus Lafontaine, sometime SPD chair and German finance minister, has on occasion openly given his support to the biggest far-left tendency in Die Linke, marx21.

This situation naturally poses the question of how the revolutionary left relates to the radical left parties. This has provoked the most debate in the case of Greece. Syriza is simply one strand in what is, in relative terms, the largest radical left in Europe. The other two main strands are represented by the Communist Party of Greece (KKE), historically the most powerful organised force in the workers' movement, and Antarsya (the Front of the Anti-Capitalist Left), a coalition of far-left groups of which the most significant are the New Left Current (NAR) and the Socialist Workers Party (SEK), the Greek sister organisation of the British SWP. Antarsya's decision to stand in the 17 June elections, after a low score of 1.2 percent on 6 May, which was predictably squeezed down to 0.33 percent five weeks later, provoked a hubbub of condemnation, This has been particularly intense in those parts of the blogosphere inhabited by armchair strategists whose confidence in pronouncing about Greece seems in inverse relation to their proximity to the country.

These storms in an internet teacup are a minor expression of a much larger and more generous and internationalist impulse to express solidarity with the Greek people and the struggle against austerity. We can see this impulse, for example, in a statement of support for Syriza by four poststructuralist philosophers, Étienne Balibar, Wendy Brown, Judith Butler and Gayatri Spivak.[24] Probably in many cases such sentiments are connected with a sense that, after years of crisis in which the radical left appeared to be a marginal force, now the situation is turning. Syriza and Tsipras are thus not merely the main vehicle for popular rejection of the parties of the Memorandum; they have become invested with the hopes of the left internationally. This is a heavy burden to carry.

Properly to assess what can be expected of Syriza requires attention to the specificities of recent Greek history. Nowhere else in western Europe have social and political struggles been as sustained for so long and at such a level of intensity as they have been in Greece—starting with the resistance to the German Occupation, continuing through the Civil War of 1946-9 and the mass movements against the monarchy in the late 1950s and 1960s and the military dictatorship of 1967-74, and into the republic established in 1974.[25]

Greek capitalism achieved relative stability during the 1980s, underpinned by entry into the European Community, but punctuated by frequent explosions of worker and student militancy. Hence the dominant political force for the past 30 years has been Pasok, led till his death in 1996 by Andreas Papandreou, a figure invested with the prestige of the struggle against the dictatorship, whose radical rhetoric masked much more conservative policies. His governments nevertheless delivered substantial reforms that served to accommodate a highly combative workers' movement. This social compromise was facilitated by the accumulation of foreign debt—long before Greek capitalism joined the euro in 2001, it was kept afloat by recycled petrodollars and Eurodollar loans.

Pasok was thereby able to dominate the trade union bureaucracy, but its position was always contested by strong forces further to its left. The KKE has deeply shaped the broader radical left, both because of its strong base among industrial workers and school students in particular, and through its broader influence. It is a profoundly Stalinist organisation whose illegality till the fall of the dictatorship bound it closely to Moscow. As with other Communist parties, the identification with the Soviet Union as the apparent antithesis of Western capitalism and

24: www.left.gr/article.php?id=2422
25: Mazower, 1993, is an outstanding study of the founding episode in this process, the Occupation and the popular struggles it provoked.

its role in the resistance to the Nazis and to the colonels allowed the KKE to attract many of the best working class militants. Elsewhere, the post war years saw a gradual weakening of the links with Moscow that allowed these parties increasingly to evolve into versions of social democracy.[26]

In the case of the KKE, this process was delayed by post-war repression, and then partially blocked by the rise of Pasok. This didn't stop the KKE developing powerful opportunist tendencies—it even served in an "ecumenical" government with ND, the Greek Tories, in 1989-90. But the form this has typically taken is a rhetorical ultra-maximalism masking a deeply cautious practice whose aim is to conserve the KKE's industrial and electoral base. Sectarian denunciations of the rest of the left have served to legitimise this practice.

Its main elements stemming from pro-European sections of the KKE, Synaspismos and its electoral alliance Syriza has been much less consistent in its political stances. Its much shallower social base has given Synaspismos much greater room for manoeuvre, and its far-left partners in Syriza allow it to project a very radical image when it suits, though these organisations have little influence on the determination of policy. Recent splits in Synaspismos to the left and the right—the departure respectively of the former Synapismos chair Alekos Alavanos and of what is now the Democratic Left (Dimar), led by Fotis Kouvelis—may have produced a greater degree of internal stability, but it is probable that the very plasticity of Syriza helped its vote to jump from 4.6 percent in October 2009 to 16.78 percent on 6 May 2012 and an astonishing 26.89 percent on 17 June. In other words, its political ambiguity allows people to read into Syriza what they want to believe. This interpretation is supported by the fact that for a while before the May general election, it was Dimar that was riding high in the polls.

But the political earthquake that the two Greek elections represent is determined by more fundamental factors. First, Greece is suffering an economic depression fully on the scale of the 1930s, causing immense human suffering. Second is, as we have noted, the massive popular rejection of the old parties: Pasok, in government either alone or in coalition since 2009, has suffered particularly badly (ND, though also hit, has benefited from the efforts of its leader, Antonis Samaras, to unite the fragmenting right against the threat of Syriza). Last but not least are the intense class battles that Greece has experienced ever since the youth

---

26: See O'Lincoln, 1985, for a lucid case study of this process.

revolt of December 2008—17 general strikes in the past two years, generating a radicalisation in the struggle as workplaces have been occupied and bitter local disputes fought out.[27]

All this has pushed Syriza to the forefront of Greek politics. It was narrowly pipped at the post by ND on 17 June, but no one expects the coalition Samaras will form to have an easy life. What will Syriza do if it eventually succeeds in forming the government of the left for which it is campaigning? One can begin to answer this by looking at its programme. As presented by Syriza's main economic spokesman, Yiannis Dragasakis (formerly a leading figure in the KKE and a junior minister in the ecumenical government of 1989-90), it embraces a series of reforms—for example, rejection of the Memorandum, freezing spending cuts, tying servicing of the debt to economic growth, recapitalising the banks under "public administration and social control", reform of the tax system and a clampdown on the black economy that has allowed the Greek rich to export vast amounts of capital.[28]

The general thrust of this programme is to challenge the logic of austerity. But it contains a fundamental contradiction. Dragasakis writes:

> It is not our choice to exit the euro, but neither can we consent to the continuation of policies that offer no guarantee for the survival of our society and our country. Syriza proposes to the Greek people, and also to the people of Europe, the only pragmatic option that consists of a new, honest and binding agreement with the institutions and the people of Europe, one that will allow us to achieve three goals.
>
> The first is to relieve the people who are suffering, the victims of this crisis. The second is stabilisation and recovery. And the third is the implementation of a programme of radical reforms and transformations, through which an effective reintegration of our country to the European future and to the international division of labour.[29]

So the changes Syriza is seeking are to be negotiated with the EU. This is true, in particular, in the case of the crucial issue of the debt, where Dragasakis proposes:

27: Garganas, 2012.
28: Dragasakis, 2012.
29: Dragasakis, 2012.

writing off a large portion of the accumulated debt, with provisions for servicing of the remaining debt to be linked to the rate of development, and suspensions of payments on the interest until the economy rebounds. This adjustment will be pursued within the framework of a common European solution for the public debt of all EU countries, and in the event that this does not prove feasible, on the basis of bilateral negotiations.[30]

Tsipras himself has struck a similar note, assuring the readers of the *Financial Times* a few days before the election of 17 June: "I will keep Greece in the euro".[31] The problem with this is obvious: not only does the eurozone have neoliberalism hard-wired into its structure (particularly through the limits on government borrowing and the power of the ECB), but the dominant forces within it, far from relenting in the case of Greece, are determined to institutionalise austerity on a permanent and Europe-wide basis. As a leading figure in Antarsya, Panagiotis Sotiris, points out,

> The result is that the left promises saving society and breaking with austerity without dealing with the very mechanisms that led to the current social devastation. Such a position does indeed seem realist: a change of policies within the contours of the current situation. However, how realist is it to suppose that loan funds and solvency injections that have been offered under the condition of extreme austerity and "structural adjustment" will continue to be available if the austerity policies are abandoned?[32]

Writing before the June election, Costas Lapavitsas predicted:

> Syriza will have a clear choice [after 17 June]. It could abandon its pre-election stance and participate in a government that accepted troika policies. This would be catastrophic for Syriza politically but also for the country. Default and exit would not be avoided in the end, and the political beneficiary could well be the fascist right.

> Or Syriza could refuse to participate in a compromise government and take whatever political actions necessary to support its programme. If that were to happen, there would be rising tension with the core countries of

---

30: Dragasakis, 2012.
31: Tsipras, 2012.
32: Sotiris, 2012.

the EU, and Greece could soon be out of the monetary union. Greece would have to take its lumps, but Europe would also come face-to-face with the folly of a monetary union that is threatening the stability of the entire continent.[33]

Stathis Kouvelakis, who along with Lapavitsas has argued powerfully that defeating austerity will require Greece to leave the eurozone, sees Syriza

engaging in a protracted battle which would almost certainly lead to results that go beyond the current objectives put forward by Syriza.

This would conform I think to a quite familiar pattern in history of processes of social and political change, where the dynamic of the situation, boosted of course by the pressure of popular mobilisation, pushes actors (or at least some of them) beyond their initial intentions. This is what scares most the dominant forces in Greece and in Europe and explains their hysterical campaign against Syriza and the perspective opened up by its possible coming to power.[34]

The thought seems to be that the very logic of the struggle would drive a Syriza government in the right direction. But history has taught us that this logic expresses itself through the play of political forces and that there is absolutely nothing inevitable about this play working out the right way from a revolutionary perspective. So, to the extent that Syriza in government were to implement measures against austerity this would need very powerful pressure from below both to keep it on track and to defend it from the furious reaction these measures would provoke, as Kouvelakis correctly implies, from Greek and European capital. But struggles—particularly with such high stakes—don't just happen: they depend on the conscious agency of organised political actors.

What conclusions follow from this analysis? First, the revival of the radical left is a welcome development that begins to offer in the bourgeois political arena an alternative not only to the austerity demanded by the mainstream parties but also the populist and fascist right. But, secondly, the radical left parties do not represent a development that is somehow off the register of the politics of the workers' movement as it has developed over the past two centuries. They may not recapitulate the history or structures of the traditional social democratic parties, but they also haven't

---

33: Lapavitsas, 2012.
34: Kouvelakis, 2012.

transcended the opposition between reform and revolution. They represent a particular kind of left reformism, shaped by the development of social liberalism, the weakening of the working class movement, and sometimes the influence the far left can have within them.

Thirdly, because these formations belong to a variant of left reformism, their political trajectory is unlikely simply to reflect the parallelogram of social and political forces. The more successful they become, the greater the pressure on them to act, as Sotiris notes, "realistically", ie as responsible managers of capitalism. Therefore when Tsipras writes in the *Financial Times* that "Syriza is the only political movement in Greece today that can deliver economic, social and political stability for our country", this can't be explained away just as spin: it reflects the logic of assuming the government of a capitalist state.[35] Of course, the polarisation of classes can reach a point where a reformist government finds itself directly confronting capital, as Popular Unity under Salvador Allende found itself doing in Chile in the early 1970s. But this example—and in particular the way in which Popular Unity sought to restrain the self-organisation of workers and the rank and file of the military in the months before the coup of September 1973—underlines how foolish it would be to assume that Syriza will get it right on the night.[36]

Fourthly, it is therefore necessary for revolutionary socialists, who understand the necessity of a decisive confrontation between the workers' movement and capital, to organise independently. This is not the same as a politics of abstract sectarian denunciation of the reformists' inevitable betrayals. It is simply a recognition of the harsh realities of class struggle to insist that revolutionaries must organise to help counter the immense power that capital can bring to bear on reformist parties and governments. It is crucial, however, that they do so in a way that doesn't isolate them from the movements that have begun to develop around the radical left parties. On the contrary, revolutionaries must strongly identify with these movements and work for their success.

What this means in mundane organisational practice inevitably varies tremendously, according to local conditions, depending crucially on the state of the class struggle, the nature of the radical left formations, and the strength and social implantation of the far-left. Sometimes this can mean that revolutionaries can be an organic part of these formations: the activists of marx21 in Germany helped found Die Linke and play a

35: Tsipras, 2012.
36: Gonzalez, 1984.

role in its leadership. Sometimes this type of approach doesn't work out too well, as it proved in the case of the SWP and Respect in Britain. The challenge in this kind of case is not to give up but to find a new way of working productively together. Sometimes, as this suggests, it makes more sense for revolutionaries to organise independently. In France, the leverage they might have had has been hugely reduced by the paralysis and partial disintegration of the Nouveau Parti Anticapitaliste, a situation that is at least in part of a result of the party's failure when it was strongest, at the time of its launch in 2009, actively to engage with the Front de Gauche, and to force Mélenchon and the PCF to respond to its unity initiatives, rather than let itself be outmanoeuvred and eventually marginalised.[37]

What about Greece? The organisations forming Antarsya bring together activists who play a significant role in both the workers' and the students' movements. Their coming together has greatly increased their ability to influence the explosive social struggles that have developed in the past few years. The judgement of these organisations is that affiliating instead to Syriza would greatly restrict their capacity for independent action. Participating in elections is an opportunity to present a more coherent alternative programme than that offered by Tsipras and Dragasakis—a programme (which in fact closely resembles that put forward by Kouvelakis and Lapavitsas, who now support Syriza) centring on a default from below, nationalising the banks, and leaving the eurozone.[38] But this political differentiation goes along with practising the politics of the united front, Antarsya militants fighting side by side with those of Syriza and the KKE (which, though electorally squeezed, remains a very powerful force on the ground). This is a coherent and realistic approach. It may, of course, prove wrong. Revolutionaries, being human, make plenty of mistakes. But the dogmatic certainty with which it is denounced in many quarters is, to be frank, ridiculous.

The intensity of the debates around Greece nevertheless underline that we have entered a new phase in the crisis. Till the past few months the situation has been dominated by the slow, remorseless working out of the economic logic of financial crisis and depression. Now, with the reaction developing around both the far right and radical left, the politics of the crisis is opening up. This carries great dangers, but it also raises great hopes, as we can see most clearly in Greece. Situations are developing

37: Callinicos, 2012a.
38: For a defence of this kind of programme, see Callinicos, 2010b.

where the anti-capitalist left can have a real influence on events. The choices they make matter, which is why it is important to be clear about what they involve.

Egypt: the revolution in danger

The Arab revolutions have reached a dangerous stage. This is clear in Syria, as Jonathan Maunder shows elsewhere in this issue. But it is also true in Egypt. We go to press days after the final round of the Egyptian presidential election, which Mohamed Morsi of the Muslim Brotherhood's Freedom and Justice Party claims to have won. It is now clear that the ruling Supreme Council of the Armed Forces (SCAF) is mounting what is widely described as a "soft coup". This began when it ensured that Ahmed Shafiq, Hosni Mubarak's last prime minister, stood effectively as its presidential candidate. But it was dramatically reinforced on 14 June, when the Constitutional Court dissolved the parliament elected in November and December last year. SCAF followed this up three days later with a "constitutional declaration" taking back the powers to make laws and control the budget that it conceded to parliament in January and assuming the right to veto a new constitution.

The first round of the presidential elections at the end of May revealed both the strengths and weaknesses of the Egyptian revolutionary movement. The strengths: A tremendous campaign by Hamdeen Sabbahi, leader of the left-Nasserist Karama party, which powerfully articulated the demands of the revolutionaries and the workers' movement, narrowly failed to push him ahead of Shafiq and into the second round runoff with the front-runner, Morsi.

Sabbahi came first in Cairo and Alexandria. His performance, combined with that of the liberal Islamist Abdel-Moneim Abul-Fotouh, led Hani Shukrallah to conclude: "For the first time in our history, we can with a fair degree of confidence say that while a quarter of us want the Brotherhood and another quarter want restoration, nearly half of us want the revolution realised; not at all a bad place from which to start putting that revolutionary house in order".[39] The massive street mobilisations that followed the mild treatment of Mubarak and his officials in their trial for the repression directed at the rising of 25 January 2011 were another sign of the enduring power of the revolution.

The weaknesses: The revolutionary vote was split between Sabbahi and Abul-Fotouh. Moreover, there was no presence helping to drive Sabbahi's campaign from the organised secular left. Not only was this a badly missed opportunity in itself, but it reflected a very powerful propensity of the broader revolutionary movement to boycott elections. The urge to boycott is motivated by justified anger at the continuing repression mounted by SCAF and at the Brotherhood's eagerness to work with Egypt's military rulers. But it also reinforces the dangerous gap that has been opened by a revolutionary movement that mobilises primarily through street protests and the much larger numbers of workers, urban poor and peasants (the revolution has hardly reached the Egyptian countryside) who may at best offer the young activists their passive sympathy. Undoubtedly SCAF has noted and is exploiting this confusion.

The second round of the presidential elections saw yet another boycott, this time led by Sabbahi. But the implied logic, that there is no difference between Shafiq and Morsi, is badly flawed. Shafiq is the open candidate of counter-revolution. The Brotherhood, by contrast, is a bourgeois party with deep social roots built up in opposition to Mubarak, which hoped the revolution would lift it into the role of manager of Egyptian capitalism. But it is now in SCAF's firing line: the dissolution of parliament directly targets the Brotherhood, which ineffectually dominated the People's Assembly. If Morsi does indeed become president, hedged in by a military reasserting its dominance, and with the pressures for austerity measures becoming stronger, these contradictions will probably become severe.

Putting the "revolutionary house in order" therefore requires a revolutionary left that combines a principled opposition to SCAF with the understanding that building a road to the majority of the working class means working with everyone threatened by the counter-revolution.

39: Shukrallah, 2012.

References

Atkins, Ralph, 2012, "Bundesbank Signals Softening on Inflation", *Financial Times* (9 May), www.ft.com/cms/s/0/54fa4006-99ed-11e1-accb-00144feabdc0.html

Callinicos, Alex, 2008, "Where is the Radical Left Going?", *International Socialism 120* (autumn), www.isj.org.uk/?id=484

Callinicos, Alex, 2010a, "The Second Bank Bailout", *International Socialism 119* (summer), http://www.isj.org.uk/?id=655

Callinicos, Alex, 2010b, "Austerity Politics", *International Socialism 128* (autumn), www.isj.org.uk/?id=678

Callinicos, Alex, 2012a, "France: Anti-Capitalist Politics in Crisis", *International Socialism 134* (spring), http://www.isj.org.uk/?id=794

Callinicos, Alex, 2012b, "The Politics of Europe's Rising Left", *Socialist Worker* (19 May), www.socialistworker.co.uk/art.php?id=28461

Cotterill, Joseph, 2012, "Plug-Pulling in Athens", Alphaville blog (16 May), http://ftalphaville.ft.com/blog/2012/05/16/998501/plug-pulling-in-athens/

Dragaskis, Yiannis, 2012, "The Crisis in Greece: The Economic Programme of Syriza-EKM", Global Research website (12 June), www.globalresearch.ca/index.php?context=va&aid=31378

Fullarton, John, 1844, *On the Regulation of Currencies* (John Murray).

Garganas, Panos, 2012, "Greece: The Struggle Radicalises", *International Socialism 134* (spring), www.isj.org.uk/?id=793

Georgiou, Christakis, 2010, "The Euro Crisis and the Future of European Integration", *International Socialism 128* (autumn), www.isj.org.uk/?id=682

Giles, Chris, 2012, "Global Recovery Has Stalled Again", *Financial Times* (17 June), www.ft.com/cms/s/0/fb7b2ab8-b882-11e1-a2d6-00144feabdc0.html

Gonzalez, Mike, 1984, "The Coup in Chile and the Left", *International Socialism 22* (winter).

Hayek, FA von, 1935, *Prices and Production* (RKP).

Itoh, Makoto, and Costas Lapavitsas, 1999, *Political Economy of Money and Finance* (Macmillan).

Jenkins, Patrick, 2012, "Spain's Balancing Act to Avert Doom Loop", *Financial Times* (11 June), www.ft.com/cms/s/0/26b9135a-b3da-11e1-8fea-00144feabdc0.html

Jones, Claire, Patrick Jenkins and Miles Johnson, 2012, "Spain Reveals €100bn Capital Flight", *Financial Times* (31 May), www.ft.com/cms/s/0/25c39204-ab01-11e1-b875-00144feabdc0.html

Keohane, David, 2012, "On the (Marginal) Advantage of the Greek Bank Jog", *ft.com/alphaville* (8 June), http://ftalphaville.ft.com/blog/2012/06/08/1034951/on-the-marginal-advantages-of-the-greek-bank-jog/

Kouvelakis, Stathis, 2012, "An Open Letter Regarding the Greek Left", www.socialistworker.co.uk/art.php?id=28641

Krugman, Paul, 2012, *End This Depression Now!* (Norton).

Lapavitsas, Costas, 2012, "Costas Lapavitsas Answers Your Questions on Greece and the Eurozone Crisis", *Guardian* (13 June), www.guardian.co.uk/world/greek-election-blog-2012/2012/jun/13/costas-lapavitsas-greece-eurozone-crisis

Lapavitsas, Costas, and others, 2012, *Crisis in the Eurozone* (Verso).

Lex, 2012, "UK Corporate Tax: A Missed Opportunity", *Financial Times* (21 March), www.ft.com/cms/s/3/f7f625f6-736c-11e1-94ba-00144feab49a.html

López, Isidro, and Emmanuel Rodriguez, 2011, "The Spanish Model", *New Left Review*, II/69, www.newleftreview.org/II/69/isidro-lopez-emmanuel-rodriguez-the-spanish-model

Mallet, Victor, 2012, "Rajoy Fights to Avoid 'Living Dead' Tag", *Financial Times* (10 June), www.ft.com/cms/s/0/211a7a4a-b314-11e1-83a9-00144feabdc0.html

Marx, Karl, 1973, *Grundrisse* (Penguin), www.marxists.org/archive/marx/works/1857/grundrisse/

Marx, Karl, 1981, *Capital*, volume 3 (Penguin), www.marxists.org/archive/marx/works/1894-c3/index.htm

Mazower, Mark, 1993, *Inside Hitler's Greece* (Yale University Press).

O'Lincoln, Tom, 1985, *Into the Mainstream: The Decline of Australian Communism* (Stained Wattle Press).

Peel, Quentin, Victor Mallet and Robin Wigglesworth, 2012, "Merkel Stands Firm on Tackling the Crisis", *Financial Times* (14 June), www.ft.com/cms/s/0/7d1842e2-b642-11e1-8ad0-00144feabdc0.html

Pollack, Lisa, 2012, "The Rise and Fall of European Banking", Alphaville blog (7 June), http://ftalphaville.ft.com/blog/2012/06/07/1032941/the-rise-and-fall-of-european-banking/

Roberts, Michael, 2012a, "Greece: Heading for the Exit?", The Next Recession blog (17 May), http://thenextrecession.wordpress.com/2012/05/17/greece-heading-for-the-exit/

Roberts, Michael, 2012b, "Krugman and Depression Economics", The Next Recession blog (27 May), http://thenextrecession.wordpress.com/2012/05/27/krugman-and-depression-economics/

Shukrallah, Hani, 2012, "Minerva's Owl Flies at Dusk: A Quick Reading of Egypt's Presidential Vote", *Ahram Online* (1 June), http://english.ahram.org.eg/News/43096.aspx

Sotiris, Panagiotis, 2012, "Greece: The Impossibility of Realism", www.thepressproject.net/detailsen.php?id=21258

Tsipras, Alex, "I Will Keep Greece in the Eurozone", *Financial Times* (12 June), www.ft.com/cms/s/0/4c44a296-b3b3-11e1-a3db-00144feabdc0.html

Van der Zwan, Maina, 2011, "Geert Wilders and the Rise of the New Radical Right", *International Socialism 131* (summer), www.isj.org.uk/?id=743

Wiesmann, Gerrit, 2012a, "Merkel Insists on Two-Speed Europe", *Financial Times* (7 June), www.ft.com/cms/s/0/725ec0bc-b091-11e1-8b36-00144feabdc0.html

Wiesmann, Gerrit, 2012b, "Troika to Supervise Spanish Loan", *Financial Times* (11 June), www.ft.com/cms/s/0/5c1d283a-b3e2-11e1-8fea-00144feabdc0.html

France after Sarkozy:
Confronting the politics of despair

Jim Wolfreys

In 1981 the joyous celebrations that greeted François Mitterrand's election as president, on a radical reform programme, were an expression of widespread hope of significant change. Almost exactly 31 years later the mood following François Hollande's victory over Nicolas Sarkozy could not have been more different. Hollande won on a modest promise of "fair austerity". The joy expressed at his success can largely be attributed to the fact that he is not Sarkozy, something Hollande was keen to trumpet as a virtue throughout the campaign, presenting himself as the unremarkable guarantor of a "normal" presidency. Hollande went out of his way to give assurances to financial markets that nothing would really change since he was "not dangerous", reminding them that under the Jospin government (1997-2002), the Socialists had "liberalised the economy, and opened up the markets to finance and privatisation".[1]

His victory nevertheless represents a sea change in European politics, breaking the Sarkozy-Merkel austerity axis and undermining the myth that there is no alternative to public spending cuts and wage freezes. This was the primary significance of the election result. It was not, however, the primary focus of the campaign. Indeed, as far as the mainstream candidates were concerned, austerity was the dog that didn't bark in this election, prompting the *Economist* to claim that France was "a country in denial",

1:    *Economist*, 2012.

and warning that it may find itself at the centre of the next euro crisis.[2] Public debt in France stands at the equivalent of 90 percent of GDP. So feeble, however, are the political justifications for austerity that not even the timidity of Hollande's proposals could undermine the basic common sense of his argument—that it is not working, that there should be more attention paid to growth and that the rich should pay more tax.

Despite the apparent differences between the two principal candidates' economic policies, the campaign exposed the lack of economic solutions emanating from either camp. Their attention was generally focused on the major preoccupations of the Sarkozy presidency—"national identity", immigration, law and order, and Sarkozy himself. His defeat was the first of a sitting president since 1981. Having won a convincing victory in 2007 his popularity had fallen to a record low, the result of disillusionment with both his record and his conduct in office. To this extent, Hollande's victory was predictable. The most notable aspects of the first round poll, therefore, were the scores achieved by Front National (FN) candidate Marine Le Pen (6.4 million votes) and by the Front de Gauche candidate Jean-Luc Mélenchon (4 million votes). This article will focus primarily on these developments, following an assessment of the impact of the Sarkozy presidency.[3]

Ultimately, there was a broad consensus between Sarkozy and Hollande on the question of the budget deficit. Sarkozy wanted to pay it off by 2016; Hollande proposed to take a year longer. Seven years earlier, during France's referendum on the new constitutional treaty for the European Union, Hollande and Sarkozy had posed together as the champions of a neoliberal Europe, spearheading the campaign to welcome the imposition of "free and undistorted competition" as the underlying principle of a modern economy.[4] In the intervening period it was not so much Hollande who differentiated himself from his rival, but Sarkozy who differentiated himself from pretty much everyone. His term of office became a grotesque psychodrama, evolving from a narcissistic "bling-bling" presidency, helplessly in thrall to wealth and celebrity, into an increasingly individualistic "hyper-presidency", combining authoritarianism, cronyism and crass opportunism in what could be mocked as a kind of kitsch Bonapartism were it not for the fact that Sarkozy was also the most brutally racist French president of modern times, putting the ruthless stigmatising of

2:   *Economist*, 2012.
3:   An analysis of the Socialist Party's evolution is beyond the scope of this article. It will be dealt with in a forthcoming piece on social democracy for this journal.
4:   See Wolfreys, 2005.

Muslims, Roma people and immigrants at the heart of his policy agenda. In word and deed Sarkozy went further than any other mainstream politician in legitimising the Front National and making racism respectable. His attempt to use racist demagoguery to compensate for policy failures managed to alienate even his own supporters, many of whom grew increasingly concerned that he was besmirching the highest office of state and blurring the distinction between his Union pour un Mouvement Populaire (UMP) and the extreme right.

In the wake of the election the resources of mainstream parties continue to appear limited, divided between a neoliberal right which lacks the confidence or the means to build a positive consensus for its economic outlook beyond political and economic elites, and Hollande's social liberal centre-left whose appeal exists by default—the product of disaffection with austerity and popular identification with values of solidarity and "fairness", values which remain aspects of the residual lexicon of social liberalism but are no longer part of its function or practice. While Sarkozy's defeat is a setback for those who argue there is no alternative to austerity, Hollande's victory is based on a repudiation of the effects of neoliberalism that will not be satisfied by his oxymoronic promise of austerity with a human face, or "fair rigour". This is borne out by the abstention rate of close to 43 percent in the first round of the June 2012 parliamentary elections, the highest ever recorded, indicating that Hollande may have been able to mobilise voters keen to see the back of Sarkozy (80 percent of the electorate voted in the presidential election), but was not offering enough to build on that mobilisation beyond his victory in the presidential election on 6 May.

In such a context, the record score for a Front National granted unprecedented legitimacy by both Sarkozy and Hollande marked, contrary to the ignorant complacency of many analyses,[5] a dangerous new phase in the development of post-war French fascism, whose threat has never been greater. The campaign also represented a new stage in the emergence of the French radical left as a viable alternative to social liberalism. The crystallisation of anti-austerity sentiment around the figure of Jean-Luc Mélenchon is a significant development, with the momentum on "the left of the left" shifting to the Front de Gauche from the Nouveau Parti Anticapitaliste (NPA) which, along with its previous incarnation, the Ligue Communiste Révolutionnaire, had been the dominant force on the radical left since 2002.

5:    Typical of attempts to downplay the significance of the Front's 6.4 million votes was Jon Henley's election blog for the *Guardian*—Henley, 2012a.

The disintegration of the Sarkozy phenomenon

The son of a minor Hungarian aristocrat, Sarkozy developed a love/hate relationship with the French elite. Forced to repeat his final year at an exclusive well-to-do Parisian secondary school and unable, because of his poor command of English, to graduate with a degree from the elite Institute of Political Studies—the traditional breeding ground for the French political establishment—he rose through the ranks of the Gaullist right to become leader of the UMP during Jacques Chirac's second term as president in 2004. The following year he became interior minister, for a second time, and made no bones about his desire to blame the inhabitants of France's poorest areas for the deprivation they suffered and much else besides. His notorious vow to clean out the impoverished urban fringes, or *banlieues*, with a power hose was a major contributory factor to the three-week uprising which swept these areas in November 2005.[6] His outspoken attacks on urban youth were combined with sideswipes at his political rivals—Chirac and his prime minister, Dominique de Villepin, portrayed as ineffective peddlers of compromise.

Sarkozy's combativity also served a political purpose, one that was to become increasingly important for the French right. His highly personalised, hyper-active bullishness served as a substitute for a world view capable of marshalling widespread positive affiliation to the free market.[7] Without the means or the will to elevate the figure of the entrepreneur as a potential solution to economic crisis, Sarkozy focused instead on pointing the finger at those he held responsible for it—a weak political elite, unable to impose its will on a resilient labour movement, and, above all, the "dangerous classes" represented by the urban poor and, in particular, those of "immigrant origin", the descendants of those who had found work in France during the years of post-war expansion, with special attention reserved for those of Muslim faith.

Following his election as president in 2007 Sarkozy promised a "break" with the past, an end to the compromises that had seen successive governments fail to drive through neoliberal reform. Vowing to "liquidate the legacy of May 1968" he was seen by many as the "neoliberal enforcer" that conservative commentators had long identified as the missing link in French political life. Sarkozy's appeal was partly based on his self-consciously cultivated "outsider" status. He did not belong to the conventional political elite. This manifested itself in

6:   See Wolfreys, 2006.
7:   For an analysis of some of the consequences of the Gaullist right's adoption of a neoliberal outlook, see Brustier and Huelin, 2011.

his aggressive bombast, his trenchant, often racist, rhetoric and his open infatuation with wealth, fame, glitz and glamour.

Much to the horror of aristocratic party grandees like Villepin, Sarkozy responded to his 2007 victory as if he had won a game show. During a special concert on election night at the Place de la Concorde, a nationwide television audience was treated to a self-indulgent parade of variety acts, the highpoint reached perhaps with former Playboy model and Eurovision contestant Jeane Manson's rendition of "Oh Happy Day!" ("Oh Happy Day, that Nicolas Sarkozy was born…").[8] Sarkozy himself made a speech about how he would represent "all of France and leave no one by the side of the road",[9] and then headed off to the exclusive Fouquet's restaurant on the Champs-Élysées accompanied by various celebrities (among them actor Jean Reno and the "French Elvis", Johnny Halliday), a select band of political allies (Villepin's foreign secretary Philippe Douste-Blazy had to endure the humiliation of being turned away from the restaurant) and, above all, a fairly large gathering of leading entrepreneurs. One study estimated that the value of the companies represented at Fouquet's rose by 7 billion euros in the months following Sarkozy's election.[10] The next day Sarkozy travelled by private jet to the tax haven of Malta where he holidayed on a yacht as the guest of a billionaire friend. His reputation as "the president of the rich" began to take hold on the night of his election.[11] His subsequent decision to award himself a 140 percent pay rise did nothing to help matters.

Sarkozy was to discover that his "outsider" status was not compatible with the role of president. This applied on a personal as well as a political level. Episodes which he may have imagined to be refreshingly irreverent were perceived as disrespectful of the office. Due to receive the title of Honorary Canon of the Basilica of St John Lateran at the Vatican a few months after his election, Sarkozy turned up late, with a stand-up comedian in his entourage, and proceeded to check his mobile phone for texts during the audience with the pope.[12] In an exchange with a hostile member of the public on a walkabout at an agriculture exhibition in Paris, Sarkozy was caught on television telling him, "*Casse-toi, alors, pauvre con,*" roughly translated as, "Sod off, then, you twat".[13] Running in parallel to

---

8:   TF1 News, 6 May 2007, http://lci.tf1.fr/politique/2007-05/sarkozy-concorde-vous-trahirai-4886749.html
9:   Chrisafis, 2007.
10: Coulomb and Sangnier, 2012.
11: See Pinçon and Pinçon-Charlot, 2011.
12: *L'Express*, 2007.
13: *Le Nouvel Observateur*, 2008.

such outbursts was the ongoing soap opera of the new president's private life, from his heavily publicised divorce from his first wife, Cécilia, to the whirlwind romance and hastily organised marriage to singer/model/heiress Carla Bruni.

Politically, the new government's priorities were established from the start with the virtual abolition of inheritance tax, establishing a pattern that would see 84 billion euros worth of tax breaks granted during the Sarkozy presidency—the equivalent of 4 percent of GDP—the vast majority benefiting companies and better off households.[14] Sarkozy avoided the kind of humiliating defeats at the hands of the so-called "social movement" that had punctuated the Chirac presidency. Like Chirac, he was also able to force through attacks on pensions, along with measures facilitating the marketisation of higher education. He did not, however, bring about the much-heralded "break" that would tame the "social movement", still less "liquidate the legacy of May 1968". For some commentators, his method amounted to a game of smoke and mirrors, consisting of:

> opening up a number of projects at the same time with the aim of drowning potential opposition under a deluge of dossiers (suffocation), while discretely conceding, often in a completely opaque manner, substantial advantages if resistance proved too strong (conciliation). At the end of the process, there remained only a media-friendly display of pseudo-reforms, the sole beneficiaries being the most influential pressure groups to the detriment of the collective interest and at the price of a rise in the public sector deficit.[15]

State racism

Emblematic of Sarkozy's presidency was his obsession with "national identity" and immigration. Here his attempts to outdo the FN at its own game backfired badly. The creation in 2007 of a ministry which conflated immigration, integration and national identity had set the tone from the outset for what would prove consistently racist administration. Sarkozy draped himself unashamedly in the colours of French colonialism with a speech in Dakar that detailed at length the "problems" of Africa, notably the failure of "African man" to "enter into history". His advice to an audience of intellectuals was that if they really wanted to deal with the problem of starvation in Africa, then they should grow their own food.[16] Such fatuous and

---

14: Peillon, 2012.
15: Cahuc and Zylberberg, 2012, p9.
16: A full "unofficial" translation of the speech can be found at http://bit.ly/KqqR2y

ignorant assertions were an important reminder of the neo-colonial ideology underpinning government policy.

Whereas previous administrations may have been accused of pandering to racism in order to pick up votes from the FN's electorate, Sarkozy's presidency went further, actively pursuing an unrelenting agenda of xenophobia and stigmatisation. Unable to take on the labour movement and inflict lasting defeat on it, Sarkozy prioritised attempts to sow divisions along ethnic and racial lines, mostly directed against France's 5 to 6 million Muslims, who became the target of an unprecedented campaign of vilification. Annual quotas of immigrants to be deported were established. Roma camps were dismantled. Interior minister Claude Guéant publicly declared that some civilisations were superior to others on the grounds that French civilisation respects women more than "others" such as, by implication, Islam.[17] As establishment figures lined up to indulge the misogyny of former IMF managing director and presidential hopeful Dominique Strauss-Kahn, such claims bore all the hallmarks of the state racism of France's colonial era. Like Muslim women in 1950s Algeria, those in 21st century France were to be liberated from the yoke of the veil. Complicity across the spectrum of the left, to varying degrees, in shoring up the myth of progressive Republican secularism merely served to bolster discriminatory attitudes towards France's Muslim population.

Part of Sarkozy's appeal in the first half of a decade in which he became the mainstream's dominant figure, between 2002 and 2012, was that he had grasped the relationship between racist demagogy and authoritarianism that underpinned the electoral success of the FN. Following Jean-Marie Le Pen's poor showing in the second round of the 2002 presidential election, when he barely improved on his first round score, Sarkozy moved to position himself as the figure capable not just of making speeches about the dangers of immigration, but of acting upon them. Once again Sarkozy was to discover that he could not be an "outsider" and a president at the same time. The scapegoating of immigrants is based on the notion that they are somehow to blame for social problems like unemployment and crime or the scarcity of resources like decent housing. The failure to stem the rise of the FN over the past 30 years is derived in part from a failure to counter this myth. The credibility given to it by Sarkozy meant that FN racism was further legitimised, but in the process he also exposed his own impotence: since immigrants are no more to blame for poor housing or unemployment than for inclement weather or wasp bites, no amount of

---

17: *Le Monde*, 2012b.

"tough" measures will be enough. Ultimately, the real outsider will always be able to propose something more. And so it proved.

Following the ban on schoolgirls wearing the hijab, the presence of mothers covering their hair on school trips was called into question. After the ban on wearing the burqa and the niqab in public, Marine Le Pen called for the wearing of the hijab on public transport to be outlawed. And so it went on. In 2010 she compared the sight of Muslims praying in the street to the Nazi occupation of France. Within a year the government had banned prayers in the street. In February 2012 Le Pen had whipped up a storm over the the ludicrous claim that all meat being sold in the Paris region was halal produce but not labelled as such. By early March Sarkozy was arguing that this was the number one preoccupation of the French.[18]

More surreal developments were to follow with a controversy generated over separate swimming pool hours for women. This arose when right wing politicians seized upon a decision by the Socialist mayor of Lille, Martine Aubry, to allow women-only sessions at a municipal swimming baths. Since some of the women in question were Muslim, what had occurred was perceived as a concession to "communalism", anathema to the increasingly zealous defenders of the Republican principle of secularism. The story arose because a local pool had been running a longstanding programme for obese women. A number of Muslim women from a local estate had joined the weekly aquagym class, and had asked that the porthole shaped windows to the outside be covered and that the instructors be female. The women in the class were from a variety of backgrounds, some Muslim, some Catholic, some atheist. Covering the windows was not a question of religion, said one woman who attended the class, "but modesty".[19] These requests were granted, but one for a separate class for Muslim women was denied.

When the local UMP leader questioned Aubry over what he saw as an attack on the Republican principle of equality, she defended the obesity programme in these terms: "Let's make a little detour (from our Republican principles) so that these women win and achieve their emancipation".[20] Eventually, however, the municipal authority bent to Republican orthodoxy. "It's the obligation to ensure the neutrality of public services that's at stake," said a city hall source. "We even had a request from bearded men for a slot

18: Lemarié, 2012.
19: Saberan and Bretton, 2012.
20: Her statement was put up on Lille's municipal website, 1 July 2003—www.maire-info.com/article.asp?param=3234

reserved for men. If we start off like that, we don't see why not dwarves, and people with one leg or no hair?"[21] From 2008 the windows were uncovered and most of the time at least one of the two instructors was male. Around a third of the women left the class.

The issue was revived during the presidential campaign as part of an attempt by the UMP to portray the Socialists as "communalists" who would encourage cultural isolationism. The president of the social centre in question, a former Socialist deputy, had written in 2011 to UMP leader Jean-François Copé, complaining about the party's continual attempt to create a furore over the issue: "Why this conspiracy against an hour of women's aquagym? Because some of the women are of foreign origin? But this is racism!"[22] At the height of an election to determine the presidency of the world's fifth largest industrial power, during the biggest economic crisis since the Great Depression, nothing symbolised the political distortions of the Sarkozy era more than his outburst on the subject during a campaign speech in the Loiret. "On the territory of the Republic," he declared, "we want—sorry, Madame Aubry—the same swimming pool opening hours for men and women".[23] Unable to provide solutions to any of the major problems facing its population, Republican state power has chosen instead to preoccupy itself with what Muslim girls and their mothers wear on their heads, with how their food is labelled, with where they pray and with whom they can do aquagym classes. During the traditional televised debate between the two presidential candidates, Hollande was at pains to stress that, should he become president, he too would ensure that the sanctity of mixed Republican swimming pools was upheld.[24]

Early in the campaign, in March 2012, Sarkozy had called for immigration to be cut by half. "There are too many foreigners on our territory," he declared. "The functioning of our system of integration is getting worse and worse because we can't find them a home, a job, a school".[25] Such rhetoric continued throughout the campaign, intensifying between the two rounds. Hollande was labelled a "communalist" candidate following unfounded claims that 700 mosques had called for Muslims to vote for him.[26] Sarkozy went out of his way to insist that the FN was

---

21: Saberan and Bretton, 2012.
22: Veron, 2012.
23: Veron, 2012.
24: *Les Echos*, 2012.
25: Tassel, 2012.
26: Equy and Cerez, 2012.

a fully legitimate part of French political life.[27] The unchecked legiti-misation of the organisation was accelerated by figures such as leading Socialist Arnaud Montebourg, who argued that there was now a "con-sensus" between the Socialists, the UMP and the FN over immigration: all accepted that there was a need for a certain number of immigrants to France and for limits to be imposed beyond this minimum. Pointing out that under Sarkozy more undocumented migrants had been regularised than under Jospin, Montebourg continued: "When Sarkozy argues that immigration should be stopped, I don't point the finger at him".[28]

The resurgence of the Front National

As ever, it was the FN that benefited most from such developments. When three children and a teacher were murdered at a Jewish school in March, following the killing of three soldiers, two of them Muslims, the week before, all by a lone Islamist, Mohamed Merah, Sarkozy warned against making political capital out of the atrocities before announcing snap meas-ures to clamp down on terrorism, including more stringent policing of internet browsing.[29] This underlined an important aspect of the role of racism in contemporary France. Along with its basic function of sowing divisions among those suffering the consequences of social inequality, the promotion of the notion that "French values" are under threat and must be protected serves as a justification for directing resources towards law and order rather than towards social provision, bolstering the penal authority of the state.[30]

Whatever Sarkozy could do, however, Marine Le Pen could outdo. At a 6,000-strong FN meeting in Paris, with the crowd chanting, "This is our home!" Le Pen shouted, "Yes, this is your home. And you're right to have had enough of these Franco-Algerians like Mohamed Merah!" At a meeting in Nantes she asked, "How many Mohamed Merahs in the boats and planes that arrive full of immigrants every day in France? How many Mohamed Merahs among the children of these non-assimilated immi-grants?" She did not concern herself with mere anti-terrorism measures, vowing instead to "bring radical Islam to its knees".[31]

A constant refrain of the French right since the 1970s has been the desire to reinvent itself "without complexes", in other words, a right

27: *Le Figaro*, 2012b.
28: Mathiot, 2012.
29: Husson and Ferran, 2012.
30: Tissot, 2004.
31: *Le Nouvel Observateur*, 2012.

not inhibited by "political correctness" or by the experience of wartime collaboration with the Nazis. This was one of the aims of the so-called *Nouvelle Droite* (New Right), a group of think tanks which emerged in the 1970s and 1980s which united various elements of the mainstream and extreme right in a strategy of "Gramscism of the right", an attempt to challenge the left's alleged hegemony on cultural issues.[32] In reality, this is something accomplished with far greater ease by the FN, since it has fewer qualms about openly embracing racism, but its task has been made far easier by mainstream legitimation of its ideas. In particular, the pursuit of Islamophobic policies in the name of "Republican secularism", embraced by government and opposition alike, has allowed the FN to appropriate secularism as one of its "values", linking it to the immigration question: "Secularism will be easier to apply once immigration is stopped." To this end, the FN proposes the creation of a ministry of "immigration and secularism".[33]

This is consistent with the strategy pursued by the FN for the past three decades: rather than attempt to contest France's Republican past, the Front embraces it, all the better to relativise its own counter-revolutionary, fascist legacy. The audience at Marine Le Pen's Paris rally, for example, heard from an FN speaker who saluted Napoleon's army, Clemenceau's defence of Dreyfus, and the Resistance as part of its own tradition. By contrast, at an FN convention in February 2012, Jean-Marie Le Pen read from a poem by the collaborator Robert Brasillach, editor of the collaborationist newspaper *Je suis partout*, who took a pro-Nazi and vehemently anti-Semitic line during the war. Le Pen's justification for such acts is that the FN assumes France's historical legacy in its entirety. When it comes to secularism, the Front is happy to embrace it, not for its own sake but because it offers it an opportunity to present itself as the most zealous secularists, those who will assert the authority of the Republican state against "outsiders".

Much has been made of the role of Marine Le Pen, who replaced her father as FN leader in 2011. Attitudes towards her tend to be based on the notion that she represents a "softer" or "gentler" image for the Front. The *Guardian*'s election blog, for example, carried articles by Jon Henley in this vein during the election campaign which could have been written by the FN press office. "The Front National is different", ran

---

32: See Fysh and Wolfreys, 2003.
33: *Le Monde*, 2012a.

the quote in one headline. "The knee-jerk racists are out".[34] Yet the list of FN candidates for the parliamentary elections revealed a party whose representatives retain close links with the various currents of violent, negationist, Catholic fundamentalist and "revolutionary nationalist" elements that form part of the organisational core of the FN.[35] Marine Le Pen understands the importance of cultivating these links. In January 2011 she went to Vienna to attend the annual ball of a secret neo-Nazi society, Olympia, dedicated to the propagation of anti-Semitism, pan-Germanism and Holocaust denial. She was a guest of the Austrian Freedom Party, an organisation that, like the FN, has its roots in pro-Nazi fascist currents that attempted to refashion the tradition to fit the post-war period.[36] This remains the FN strategy under Marine Le Pen. Her immediate reaction to the biggest ever vote for a fascist candidate in French history was to assert the party's outsider credentials, calling on people to join the FN's May Day demonstration, a tradition inaugurated by her father both as a deliberate challenge to the left and as an attempt to establish the Front as a party with a capacity for extra-parliamentary mobilisation. Sarkozy's call, following the first round presidential vote, for his own May Day march in defence of "real work", that consciously drew on the language of the Vichy regime, revealed the desperation of a mainstream whose efforts to set the agenda on issues of racist authoritarianism had merely left it tailing the FN.

Le Pen uses the same bullish provocations as her father, declaring herself the only "anti-system candidate", the candidate of "the forgotten, the middle classes, the popular classes". During the campaign she attacked the parties of both left and right who, she argued, had given power over to the "dictatorship of the banks—a gilded fascism which doesn't speak its name".[37] "This is just the beginning," she declared in response to the FN's score on 22 April, reappropriating a slogan from May 1968. "Let's keep up the fight".[38] Her decision, once again in the tradition of her father, to support neither Sarkozy nor Hollande in the second round of the presidential election, underlines that the Front's outsider status is more important to it than the prospect of alliances of any kind with the mainstream right. Such alliances may yet take place, but they will be the result of the disorientation of the mainstream, and the reactionary radicalisation

34: Henley, 2012b. See also Henley, 2012c.
35: Du Roy, 2012.
36: Gauquelin, 2012.
37: Mestre, 2012. See also Le Pen, 2012.
38: Le Figaro, 2012a.

of sections of Sarkozy's UMP, rather than any supposed "moderation" on the part of the FN. In 2002, when Jean-Marie Le Pen came second in the presidential election, a wave of anti-FN mobilisations dominated the entire fortnight between the two rounds, ensuring that his vote barely improved on his first round score. The most significant change affecting the extreme right in the subsequent decade has been the accelerated integration of racism, demagogy and intolerance into mainstream rhetoric and policy. The FN's respectability derives from this, rather than its change of leader.

The rise of the radical left

The candidate who offered the most vociferous and consistent opposition to the FN during both the presidential and parliamentary elections was Jean-Luc Mélenchon. He castigated Marine Le Pen at every opportunity. What message did he have for her? "I want to make your life rotten, until its last day. You make me feel ashamed... You're scared of me in the way that vampires are scared of the light".[39] Announcing that he would confront her in the northern constituency of Hénin-Beaumont in the June parliamentary elections, he said, "I hope that most citizens want to be represented in the National Assembly by someone whose response to the crisis is social and not ethnic".[40] To a population faced with ongoing factory closures he said, "If you don't want to do anything and take it out on the Arabs who work in the factory, then vote for Madam Le Pen! If you want to take it out on thuggish bosses and prevent redundancies then vote for the Front de Gauche".[41]

An indication of the momentum that built around his dynamic, confident presidential campaign was the way his 11 percent score, representing 4 million votes, was perceived as a disappointment by many activists, their hopes raised by polls putting them on level pegging with the FN and the prospect of finishing third. But Mélenchon nevertheless achieved what no radical left candidate had managed since its emergence as a meaningful electoral force in 1995—creating a single pole of attraction uniting the vast majority of voters across the spectrum of the "left of the left", from Communists and disaffected Socialists to revolutionaries. As one analysis put it in 2003, France since 1995 has experienced:

39: De Boni, 2012.
40: *Le Figaro*, 2012c.
41: *Le Monde*, 2012c.

a revival of collective protest at social inequality which is reconfiguring the relationship between a burgeoning associative network, the labour movement and the political left. But it remains a movement whose own lack of political and organisational focus has so far hampered its ability to mount a meaningful challenge from beyond the mainstream.[42]

The absence of forces able to give voice to the aspirations of the movement and to maintain a strong political profile beyond the electoral terrain, and in periods when struggle ebbs, has been a weakness affecting the radical left across most of Europe. A number of figures have emerged at various points to crystallise opposition to neoliberalism in France. For now the initiative in this ongoing and fluid process of recomposition rests with Mélenchon.

Part of the explanation for his success in 2012 lies with the highly impressive campaign conducted by the Front de Gauche, an alliance of former Socialists (who had left the party to form the Parti de Gauche in 2008), the Communist Party, and a number of smaller groupings forming part of the associative network constituting the so-called "social movement". With early polling putting the Front de Gauche's standing at around 5 percent, a series of huge demonstrations of the Front's mobilising capacity propelled its message into public consciousness in a manner that no other campaign had managed in a generation. Over 100,000 people joined a march and rally at the Bastille on 18 March, the anniversary of the establishment of the Paris Commune in 1871. The slogans of the day, calling for a "citizen's insurrection" at the polls, were given a resonance by the scale of the event, itself notable for the prominence of the traditional symbols of the French left—red flags, clenched fists, the Internationale, the references to the heroic struggle of the Commune, as well as the Marseillaise and even some tricolour flags.

The campaign became a phenomenon. Around 20,000 people turned up at Mélenchon's meeting in Lille, 70,000 were present at a huge open air meeting in Toulouse, 100,000 were in Marseille and around 50,000 attended an indoor rally in Paris shortly before the first round vote. Mélenchon, a junior minister between 2000 and 2002 under the Jospin premiership, developed a detailed set of radical left measures focused on wealth distribution and ecological renewal. Proposals to cap earnings at £300,000 were presented with none of the defensiveness that sometimes holds back the left. "We have to smash this prejudice that the rich are

---

42: Wolfreys, 2003.

useful just because they're rich," he told the *Guardian*.[43] According to the Front de Gauche, over 400,000 copies of the 95-page programme were sold during the campaign. Mélenchon is a powerful speaker, steeped in the oratorical traditions of French Republican socialism. His speeches struck a chord by articulating widespread and deep-seated anger at austerity, racism and neoliberal idolisation of the rich. "This country produces more than it has ever produced," he told the audience at his final election rally:

> You owe them nothing—they owe you everything!... This system is on its last legs... Look at these people with no imagination who keep trying to prolong the old world. The puffed up representatives of this kind of *ancien régime*, so sure of themselves, who scoff at you. They don't understand that we have understood—the model they propose no longer speaks a human language. Because a human language is not their lamentable calculation of suffering and misfortune. It's not their narrow-minded determination to haggle over every single euro we need for our small pleasures. It's not this odious calculation of misfortune that we should carry out for them someday and ask: how much does the ignorance cost that comes from all the teachers' posts you've got rid of? How much do the 564 deaths at work cost? The 43,000 people who are disabled for life at work? How much does the daily suffering cost—of imagination kept in check, deformed by greed? You no longer speak a human language. A human language is made up of words of love, words of fraternity, words of poetry! This is how a human language is spoken.[44]

It has been argued that part of Mélenchon's success can be attributed to the defeat inflicted on the impressive movement that developed in the autumn of 2010 against Sarkozy's pension reforms, reflecting a displacement of hopes invested in struggle onto the promise that they may be realised by electoral means.[45] Such arguments, however speculative, may well apply to sections of the Front de Gauche electorate, but they imply too rigid a distinction between the arena of struggle and that of elections. During the period of struggle opened up in France by the huge public sector strikes of 1995, the role of the street and the workplace has been emphatically reasserted in a developing movement that has scored some important victories and discovered various organisational forms with which to advance these struggles. The movement has regenerated a belief in the change that

43: Chrisafis, 2012.
44: Mélenchon, 2012.
45: Sabado, 2012.

collective action and solidarity can bring. A nurse involved in the 1995 strikes articulated this sense of possibilities:

> If I felt concerned again it's because this time it was about essential, political demands... It was the rejection of a capitalist society, the rejection of money. People were mobilised more against that than against the Juppé social security plan... At the end of the demos, people stayed where they were, as if they were waiting for something else.[46]

At times this thirst for fundamental social and political change has found electoral expression, initially with the Trotskyist candidate Arlette Laguiller, who won over 5 percent of the vote standing for Lutte Ouvrière in 1995, and then with the Ligue Communiste Révolutionnaire's Olivier Besancenot, who achieved similar scores in 2002 and 2007. In 2012 Mélenchon best articulated this desire for political change as part of a campaign that developed its own dynamic, one that cannot be reduced solely to a narrow electoral project characterised by a passive relationship between those who were mobilised by the campaign and its figurehead. His success has also been influenced by the fact that the NPA has failed to provide a durable political home for the activists who gathered so enthusiastically around the party when it was formed in 2009. The NPA has suffered splits and divisions, while Lutte Ouvrière has become an increasingly marginal influence on the radical left.

In Hénin-Beaumont, Mélenchon failed to win through to contest the second round of the parliamentary election against Marine Le Pen, his vote squeezed, like that of many Front de Gauche candidates, by a nationwide increase in support for the Socialist Party. He nevertheless achieved a creditable score of 21 percent. More importantly, his attempt to link the fight against the FN, and the gathering mood of anger at austerity and its effects, to the heritage of the labour movement and its traditions of struggle and anti-fascism, gave confidence to activists on the ground. As one NPA member in Hénin-Beaumont put it:

> It's about saying, "No, things don't always need to be this way. We can get beyond capitalism. There is a collective force that can be mobilised, and no, there's nothing inevitable about the extreme right gaining an influence in this area." There's a hope in this campaign that's inspiring. I've lived here for

---

46: Quoted in Béroud and Capdevielle, 1998, pp96-97.

11 years. We've done lots of painstaking anti-fascist activity—it's been hard sometimes. Now there's more of a sense of our mass, collective strength.[47]

Mélenchon, like many on the radical left in France, believes in the Republican model of citizenship, according to which shared values, rather than shared ethnicity or culture, are the key to a successfully integrated society. As we have seen, however, over time "universal values" like secularism can be moulded into a national heritage, becoming part of the ethno-cultural vision of a Guéant, a Sarkozy or a Le Pen. Historically, the Republican model has created a blind spot for the French left when it comes to confronting the FN and fighting racism, hampering its ability to defend Muslims when they are stigmatised, for example, for wearing a piece of cloth over their hair. Mélenchon himself supported the ban on Muslim schoolchildren wearing the hijab and in 2010 was critical of the decision by the NPA (hotly contested within the party itself) to present a regional election candidate, Ilham Moussaïd, who wore the hijab. She did not, he argued, represent the majority.[48] Moreover, those who wore the hijab should not complain of stigmatisation, since they were "inflicting a stigma on themselves".[49]

During the presidential election campaign Mélenchon presented a robust defence of the Republican tradition and its alleged capacity to integrate immigrants. This was given great prominence at his rally in Marseille. At the Front de Gauche's final meeting of the campaign he condemned the way the FN was diverting anger at the banks onto immigrants, "persecuting people and inciting a war of religion" by castigating "our companions in work, love, family—our children, grandparents, cousins— by attacking Muslims, once again, as previous generations attacked Jews".[50] The Republican tradition cannot simply be dismissed for its complicity in promoting Islamophobia. It forms part of a series of contradictions, centred on the role of the state, that are characteristic of the Mélenchon phenomenon. These contradictions are not fixed or static, however; they are part of a dynamic which is unfolding as resistance to austerity and neoliberalism develops. Which elements come to the fore in this process depends on the relationship between the forces gathered under the banner of resistance and their collective ability to shape events in the face of "the market".

47: *Socialist Worker*, 2012.
48: Wolfreys, 2010.
49: Andrieu, 2010.
50: Mélenchon, 2012.

Mélenchon referred throughout the campaign to the relationship between the vote and the struggle. The bigger the Front de Gauche score, "the stronger you will be in the workplace". After the election workers would be able to tell their employers, who "only understand force": "Carry on like that, and we'll call on Mélenchon and his friends." The more the bosses were afraid, the more they would concede. "They are right to fear us," he argued. France's 6 million manual and 7 million white collar workers "hold the future in their hands if they only become aware of themselves and their interests... Spread this word around you and don't ever be diverted: the rich have a class consciousness and they never forget it. Have a class consciousness, a sense of the general interest".[51]

The political trajectory of the Mélenchon phenomenon is not predetermined. It will be shaped by all kinds of elements in the months and years to come. How the rest of the radical left relates to the phenomenon can have an important influence on this process. A Mélenchon victory in Hénin-Beaumont, for example, would have had a significant impact on breaking the sense that the FN is on an upward trajectory and that its role in public life cannot be contested. He was pipped to second place by the Socialist candidate, who won 1,059 more votes. The four far-left candidates who stood in the election received a total of 656 votes. The exceptional circumstances of that election, in particular the very real prospect of a radical left candidate inflicting a defeat on Le Pen, could have prompted them to put their energies into a united campaign against the FN. Had they done so the outcome might well have been very different. Positive engagement with the Front de Gauche by the revolutionary left, welcoming the emergence of a significant radical left electoral force while not shying away from legitimate differences and concerns, can be part of a process of deepening and clarifying political understanding within the movement. Under a Socialist president who, as one report put it, "will have no choice but to disappoint",[52] this will be an important part of the social conflicts to come.

The Socialists won an overall majority in the June 2012 parliamentary elections, leaving the UMP is some disarray, notably over how to relate to the FN. In Hénin-Beaumont, Marine Le Pen narrowly lost to the Socialist candidate in the second round stand-off, her first round score only 190 votes up on her presidential score there. Mélenchon's first round score had increased by around a thousand votes on his presidential vote in the town. Overall, the Front de Gauche won around 700,000 more votes in

---

51: Mélenchon, 2012.
52: Von Rohr, 2012.

2012 than the Communist Party had won in the 2007 parliamentary elections, but it gained five fewer seats than the Communists had won alone. This, as Mélenchon noted, was the price of "autonomy",[53] since the Front de Gauche had no electoral agreement with the Socialists. The Greens, who made an alliance between the two rounds of the election, won more seats than the Front de Gauche, with fewer votes.

There was criticism that Mélenchon had narrowed the campaign down by focusing on opposition to the FN, revealing, as one analysis put it, "the limits of virulent anti-fascism".[54] François Delapierre, the director of Mélenchon's presidential campaign, however, dismissed the idea that the FN has become less extreme: "In reality, it's a fascist party which wants to reconfigure the political landscape around confrontation with immigrants and their children".[55] Mélenchon was equally trenchant. Arguing that the basic function of racism today is to divide people at a time when they are uniting against neoliberal austerity, he identified the threat of the FN as twofold. It represents both a menace to democratic institutions and a danger "in terms of possible ways out of the crisis." He claimed that those who complained he was putting undue focus on the FN were themselves reducing a social and ideological question to a moral question: "Either they win authority over the masses or we do," he argued. "And the question will be—is it the banker or the immigrant who's responsible for the crisis? That's what's at stake here…and in the wider world. So the struggle must be implacable and to the end".[56]

In the wake of the parliamentary election, Communist Party leader Pierre Laurent argued that the conditions were not right for the party to participate in a Socialist government. He noted the Socialists' continued orientation around Hollande's presidential programme, spurning the opportunity to engage with the Front de Gauche, and added that "we remain available if these conditions evolve".[57] Mélenchon claimed that the Front de Gauche would become "the spokespeople for the expectations of the social movement, without concession or naivety or impatience".[58] The extent to which it is able to do this will depend on its capacity to build a formation that is open to all elements of the radical left, one which sees its primary task not to win constitutional change (the call for

53: *L'Humanité*, 2012a.
54: Dupin, 2012.
55: Alliès, 2012.
56: *Socialist Worker*, 2012.
57: *L'Humanité*, 2012b.
58: *L'Humanité*, 2012a.

a Sixth Republic is a central element of its programme) but to advance the struggles against austerity that will take place outside the electoral arena. If Laurent's message implied that the situation was fluid as far as the Communists' relationship with the Socialist government was concerned, Delapierre's analysis points to the pitfalls of becoming associated with it:

> If Hollande confirms his acceptance of austerity, things can also happen. We saw in Greece how socialists disassociated themselves from the line taken by Pasok and Papandreou. But either way, it's outside the so-called social democratic parties that the search for an alternative to the domination of capital is finding expression. It's this analysis that motivated our departure from the PS, and it's been totally reinforced by the political cycle which is coming to an end.[59]

Although hopes that Mélenchon might have beaten Le Pen in both presidential and parliamentary elections were dashed, he did more than any other candidate since the FN's emergence as a political force directly to confront the party on the electoral terrain. Exposing the tension between the hard core elements of the FN and its wider periphery will take more than such confrontations alone, however. In the same way, giving electoral expression to the social movement will only be meaningful if the movement is backed at every turn in the struggles to come, building on and deepening the radical left critique of austerity that proved so effective in the presidential campaign.

Next to Mélenchon, Hollande looked a profoundly uninspiring figure. When he tried oratory or passion his words came out in an unmodulated bark that sounded more like someone hailing a cab than a call to arms. Hollande's campaign, however, gathered momentum under the impact of the Mélenchon phenomenon, with his pledge to introduce a 75 percent tax rate on annual incomes over 1 million euros coming to the fore, along with promises to restore the retirement age back to the age of 60, from 62, for anyone having worked for 41 years, to create 60,000 education posts over five years and to renegotiate the European fiscal compact, giving greater emphasis to growth. As the head of a think tank linked to the Socialist Party acknowledged, however, the 75 percent tax rate is "just a symbolic measure". The Socialist Party, he went on, "has modernised, and does understand the need to improve competitiveness and control the deficit".[60]

59: Alliès, 2012.
60: *Economist*, 2012.

The last time the Socialists were in office they were able to implement neoliberal reforms by incorporating the Greens and the Communists into Jospin's "plural left" project. For the moment Mélenchon's success has exerted sufficient influence on the Communist Party for it to resist such temptations. Whether that continues to be the case, and whether the Front de Gauche is able to succeed where others have failed and build a durable radical left formation, rooted in struggle and capable of directly confronting the threat of the Front National, remains to be seen. Those who speak for "the markets" insist that France needs to drive down its labour costs. In 2000 they stood 8 percent below those in Germany. Today they are 10 percent higher.[61] Significant social confrontations are likely to form as much a part of the Hollande presidency as that of his predecessors in a political environment that, as the 2012 elections demonstrate, continues to polarise. At stake is the ability of the radical left to create a positive, combative, effective alternative both to austerity and to the politics of despair represented by the Front National.

61: *Economist*, 2012.

References

Andrieu, Gérald, 2010, "Mélenchon: la candidate voilée du NPA relève du racolage", *Marianne* (4 February), www.marianne2.fr/Melenchon-la-candidate-voilee-du-NPA-releve-du-racolage_a184635.html

Alliès, Stéphane, 2012, "La page du Sarkozysme n'est pas complètement tournée" interview with François Delapierre, Parti de Gauche website (15 June), www.lepartidegauche.fr/actualites/actualite/la-page-sarkozysme-n-est-pas-completement-tournee-16083

Béroud, Sophie, and Jacques Capdevielle, 1998, "En finir avec une approche culpabilisée et culpabilisante du corporatisme", in Claude Leneveu and Michel Vakaloulis (eds), *Faire Mouvement. Novembre-Décembre 1995* (PUF).

Brustier, Gaël, and Jean-Philippe Huelin, 2011, *Voyage au Bout de la Droite. Des Paniques Morales à la Contestation Droitière* (La Decouverté).

Cahuc, Pierre, and André Zylberberg, 2010, *Les Réformes Ratées du Président Sarkozy*, (Flammarion).

Chrisafis, Angelique, 2007, "Cheering crowds hail Sarkozy's triumph", *Guardian* (7 May), www.guardian.co.uk/world/2007/may/07/france.angeliquechrisafis2

Chrisafis, Angelique, 2012, "Jean-Luc Mélenchon: the poetry-loving pitbull galvanising the French elections", *Guardian* (6 April), www.guardian.co.uk/world/2012/apr/06/jean-luc-melenchon-campaign-interview

Coulomb, Renaud, and Marc Sangnier, 2012, "Media coverage of Impacts of Political Majorities on French Firms: Electoral Promises or Friendship Connections?", PSE Working Paper, 2012-08, http://marcsangnier.free.fr/divers/coulomb_sangnier_media.pdf

De Boni, Marc, 2012, "Mélenchon veut 'pourrir la vie' du 'vampire' Le Pen", *Le Figaro* (24 February), www.lefigaro.fr/politique/2012/02/24/01002-20120224ARTFIG00641-melenchon-veut-pourrir-la-vie-du-vampire-le-pen.php

Du Roy, Ivan, 2012, "Rassemblement Bleu Marine: bienvenue au musée des horreurs de l'extreme droite," *Basta!* (6 June), www.bastamag.net/article2452.html

Dupin, Eric, 2012, "Mélenchon KO: le Couple du Front de Gauche en Grand Peril", ESSF website (11 June), www.europe-solidaire.org/spip.php?article25510

Economist, 2012, "The French Election: An Inconvenient Truth" (31 March), www.economist.com/node/21551461

Equy, Laure, and Gaël Cerez, 2012, "Appels de Ramadan et des 700 mosquées à voter Hollande, l'intox," *Libération* (26 April), www.liberation.fr/politiques/2012/04/26/l-intox-des-appels-de-tariq-ramadan-et-des-700-mosquees-a-voter-pour-hollande_814519

Fysh, Peter, and Jim Wolfreys, 2003, *The Politics of Racism in France* (Palgrave).

Gauquelin, Blaise, 2012, "Marine Le Pen valse à Vienne avec des pangermanistes", *L'Express* (27 January, updated 3 February), www.lexpress.fr/actualite/monde/europe/marine-le-pen-valse-a-vienne-avec-des-pangermanistes_1076264.html

Henley, Jon, 2012a, "Marine Le Pen's 17.9% is not a breakthrough for the far right", *Guardian* website, www.guardian.co.uk/world/french-election-blog-2012/2012/apr/25/marine-le-pen-french-elections-2012

Henley, Jon, 2012b, French election blog 2012, *Guardian* website, www.guardian.co.uk/world/french-election-blog-2012/2012/may/02/french-elections-front-national-different

Henley, Jon, 2012c, "Marine Le Pen has presented a more acceptable face for the Front National", French election blog 2012, *Guardian* website, www.guardian.co.uk/world/french-election-blog-2012/2012/may/02/marine-le-pen-acceptable-face

Husson, Geoffroy, and Benjamin Ferran, 2012, "Sarkozy veut punir l'accès aux sites Internet terroristes", *Le Figaro*, 22 March, www.lefigaro.fr/actualite-france/2012/03/22/01016-20120322ARTFIG00730-sarkozy-veut-punir-l-acces-aux-sites-internet-terroristes.php

L'Express, 2007, "Sarkozy reçu par le pape" (20 December), www.lexpress.fr/actualite/monde/sarkozy-recu-par-le-pape_468799.html

Le Figaro, 2012a, "Marine Le Pen: 'ce n'est qu'un début'" (22 April), http://elections.lefigaro.fr/flash-presidentielle/2012/04/22/97006-20120422FILWWW00224-marine-le-pen-ce-n-est-qu-un-debut.php

Le Figaro, 2012b, "République/Le Pen: compatible (Sarkozy)" (27 April), http://elections.lefigaro.fr/flash-presidentielle/2012/04/27/97006-20120427FILWWW00317-republique-le-pen-compatible-sarkozy.php

Le Figaro, 2012c, "Législatives: Mélenchon se présente face à Le Pen", (12 May), http://elections.lefigaro.fr/presidentielle-2012/2012/05/12/01039-20120512ARTFIG00335-legislatives-melenchon-se-presente-face-a-le-pen.php

L'Humanité, 2012a, "Pour le Front de gauche, 'ce n'est pas un bon résultat'" (18 June), www.humanite.fr/jean-luc-melenchon/pour-le-front-de-gauche-ce-nest-pas-un-bon-resultat-499000

L'Humanité, 2012b, "Pour Pierre Laurent, les conditions ne sont pas réunies pour que les communistes participent au gouvernement" (18 June), www.humanite.fr/politique/pour-pierre-laurent-les-conditions-ne-sont-pas-reunies-pour-que-les-communistes-participen

Le Monde, 2012a, "Eva Joly et Marine le Pen mettent la laïcité au coeur de la campagne" (16 January), www.lemondedesreligions.fr/actualite/eva-joly-et-marine-le-pen-mettent-la-laicite-au-coeur-de-la-campagne-16-01-2012-2185_118.php

Le Monde, 2012b, "Claude Guéant persiste et réaffirme que 'toutes les cultures ne se valent pas'" (6 February), www.lemonde.fr/election-presidentielle-2012/article/2012/02/05/claude-gueant-declenche-une-nouvelle-polemique_1639076_1471069.html

Le Monde, 2012c, "Hénin-Beaumont 'n'est pas le fief électoral de Mme Le Pen', affirme M. Mélenchon" (12 May), www.lemonde.fr/politique/article/2012/05/12/henin-beaumont-n-est-pas-le-fief-electoral-de-mme-le-pen-affirme-melenchon_1700421_823448.html

Le Nouvel Observateur, 2008, "Sarkozy à un visiteur: 'casse toi, pauvre con'" (23 February, updated 23 June), http://tempsreel.nouvelobs.com/societe/20080223.OBS1979/sarkozy-a-un-visiteur-casse-toi-pauvre-con.html

Le Nouvel Observateur, 2012, "Le Pen: 'Combien de Merah dans les bateaux pour la France?'" (25 March), http://tempsreel.nouvelobs.com/election-presidentielle-2012/20120325.OBS4544/le-pen-combien-de-merah-dans-les-bateaux-qui-arrivent-en-france.html

Le Pen, Marine, 2012, Speech in Lyon (extract) (7 April), www.youtube.com/watch?v=fe-5tW5HSes

Lemarié, Alexandre, 2012, "Halal: l'affirmation erronée de M. Sarkozy", *Le Monde* (6 March), www.lemonde.fr/election-presidentielle-2012/article/2012/03/06/halal-l-affirmation-erronee-de-m-sarkozy_1652325_1471069.html

Les Echos, 2012, 3 May, www.lesechos.fr/economie-politique/election-presidentielle-2012/document/0202043651099-la-video-integrale-et-le-script-du-debat-tv-entre-francois-hollande-et-nicolas-sarkozy-319170.php

Mathiot, Cédric, 2012, "Immigration: Montebourg et le 'consensus' PS-UMP-FN", *Libération* (24 April), www.liberation.fr/politiques/2012/04/24/immigration-quand-montebourg-evoque-un-consensus-ps-ump-fn_814026

Mélenchon, Jean-Luc, 2012, Speech in Porte de Versailles, Paris (19 April), www.placeaupeuple2012.fr/discours-de-jean-luc-melenchon-a-paris/

Mestre, Abel, 2012, "Marine Le Pen, la 'candidate antisystème' contre le 'fascisme doré'", *Le Monde* (9 April), www.lemonde.fr/election-presidentielle-2012/article/2012/04/07/marine-le-pen-la-candidate-anti-systeme-contre-le-fascisme-dore_1682247_1471069.html

Peillon, Luc, 2012, "Le quinquenat des privileges," *Libération* (6 March), www.liberation.fr/politiques/01012394140-le-quinquennat-des-privilegies

Pinçon, Michel, and Monique Pinçon-Charlot, 2011, *Le president des riches. Enquete sur l'oligarchie dans la France de Nicolas Sarkozy* (La Découverte).

Sabado, François, 2012, "Le Front de Gauche: Et Maintenant," *Tout est à nous*, 32 (May), www.npa2009.org/content/front-de-gauche%E2%80%89%E2%80%89-et-maintenant

Saberan, Haydée, and Laure Bretton, 2012, "Sarkozy bassine Aubry en remuant une histoire de piscine", *Libération* (12 April), www.liberation.fr/politiques/2012/04/12/sarkozy-bassine-aubry-en-remuant-une-histoire-de-piscine_811413

Socialist Worker, 2012, "Jean-Luc Melenchon: 'Blame the bankers not the migrants'" (12 June), www.socialistworker.co.uk/art.php?id=28750

Tassel, Fabrice, 2012, "Sarkozy désintègre l'immigration", *Libération* (8 March), www.liberation.fr/societe/01012394606-sarkozy-desintegre-i-immigration

Tissot, Sylvie, 2004, "Le repli communautaire: un concept policier. Analyse d'un rapport des Renseignements Généraux sure les 'quartiers sensibles'" (October), Les Mots Sont Importants website, http://lmsi.net/Le-repli-communautaire-un-concept

Veron, Michel, 2012, "A Lille, Aubry a-t-elle vraiment réservé des créneaux de piscine à des musulmanes?", *L'Express* (30 March), www.lexpress.fr/actualite/politique/aubry-a-t-elle-vraiment-reservee-des-creneaux-de-piscine-a-des-musulmanes_1098551.html

Von Rohr, Mathieu, 2012, "A New French President Predestined to Disappoint", *Spiegel* website (6 May), www.spiegel.de/international/europe/as-president-hollande-will-have-no-choice-but-to-disappoint-french-a-831667.html

Wolfreys, Jim, 2003, "Beyond the mainstream, la gauche de la gauche", in Jocelyn AJ Evans (ed), *The French Party System* (Manchester University Press).

Wolfreys, Jim, 2005, "How France's Referendum Caught Fire", *International Socialism* 107 (summer), www.isj.org.uk/?id=121

Wolfreys, Jim, 2006, "France in Revolt: 1995-2005", *International Socialism* 109 (winter), www.isj.org.uk/?id=156

Wolfreys, Jim, 2010, "Ilham Moussaïd: A proud tribune of the oppressed", *Socialist Review* (March), www.socialistreview.org.uk/article.php?articlenumber=11187

The life and times of
Occupy Wall Street

Jen Roesch

Occupy Wall Street (OWS), and the Occupy movement that rapidly spread across the country in late September 2011, marked a watershed moment in the re-emergence of mass struggle and radical politics in the United States.[1] In a matter of weeks, decades of accumulated bitterness and discontent found political expression and began to reshape national politics. Prior to Occupy the media had been focused on the right wing Tea Party, which most narratives portrayed as a grassroots rebellion against "big government". Almost overnight the national conversation was refocused on the idea of the "99 percent vs the 1 percent". This message helped the movement gain mass support and provided a left wing focus for people's simmering anger.

Coming out of a period in which most struggles in the US had been quickly defeated, the early gains of the movement were rapid and impressive. The occupation of Zuccotti Park in lower Manhattan began with no more than a couple of hundred campers, but quickly swelled to as many as 600 campers nightly and a regular presence of a couple of thousand people through the day and evening. The occupation movement spread like wildfire with activists setting up encampments in more than 500 cities. And in the early weeks protesters across the country were able to fight off eviction attempts by local mayors and police forces. In fact, at the height of the

---

1:    The Occupy movement was previously discussed in this journal in Trudell, 2012.

movement, each act of police repression only served to draw even more forces into the struggle. In the autumn of 2011, tens of thousands of people across the country became actively involved in the movement and hundreds of thousands joined in mass protests.

For a while it seemed to many participants as if the movement just needed to set itself ever more ambitious goals in order to move forward. Success seemed to follow success. However, when mayors across the US decided to move decisively against the encampments in early November, they were able to evict them en masse in short order. It would have been asking too much to expect the encampments to withstand the swift, overwhelmingly violent repressive force that mayors and police departments unleashed on the protesters. Despite mass sympathy for the movement, the social forces were simply not yet deep or organised enough to provide an effective resistance to the state's assault.

The first response of movement activists was defiance, summed up in the bold slogan "You can't evict an idea whose time has come". This confident posture seemed justified as tens of thousands in New York City (NYC) protested just days after the clearing of Zuccotti and activists on the West Coast prepared for a shutdown of the ports in early December. However, six months after the mass eviction of the encampments, it is clear that the movement has not been able to regain its feet. Throughout the winter activists had looked to the spring as a potential reawakening of the movement, with a particular focus on the call for a "general strike" on May Day. While there were some impressive mass marches, particularly in NYC where up to 30,000 people protested, the call for a general strike unsurprisingly went unheeded. More importantly, the movement has not been able to find a way to translate residual sympathy into active engagement in any kind of sustained way.

Today the future direction—and even the existence—of the Occupy movement, as such, is an open question. If activists and the left are to learn from this last wave of struggle, it is important to take this opportunity to assess the experience of the last eight months and the debates that have emerged. Most analysis of the Occupy movement has overwhelmingly centred on what are seen as its unique organisational and tactical forms. Many commentators and participants have focused on the way in which Occupy arose outside of the traditional forms of the left, movement organisations and the unions. They look for an explanation of its dizzying success in its tactical audacity, its rejection of hierarchical structures and its independence from existing organisations, which are seen as bureaucratic and ossified.

This article will argue that such a focus is too narrow to adequately understand the dramatic rise of the movement. Moreover, this focus on the "new" leaves us ill-equipped to understand the challenges facing us today and how to move forward. In reality, the picture is much more complex than the dominant narrative of the movement admits. It is true that Occupy emerged independently of the official trade union and left organisations (though there were both labour and left activists involved in its early formation). Movement activists quite consciously saw themselves as rooted in the developing "movement of the squares" internationally and shared many of the dominant assumptions of that movement: a rejection of political parties; a commitment to horizontal democracy; and a focus on the reclamation of public space and the construction of mass experiments in cooperative living.[2]

It is also the case that Occupy's tactical and organisational forms gave it a political space and a flexibility that allowed it to develop quite quickly and broadly. The occupation of public space created a gathering point for new people to enter the movement, to debate with one another and to cooperate in advancing struggles. The lack of demands meant that people entering into the movement could articulate their own grievances within the common framework provided by the slogan "We are the 99 percent". And the focus on direct democracy, epitomised by the mass general assemblies, helped to give people a sense that they had a voice in the shape and direction of the struggle.

But these factors alone are not enough to account for the movement's growth. From the very beginning the fate of OWS was bound up with its interactions and connections with longer-standing organisations and struggles. This is most true of the unions, which provided early support and resources. But the movement's ability to connect with longer-standing struggles, particularly those rooted in working class and multiracial communities, also proved decisive. In all of this, longer-standing activists, including members of the organised left, played a role in helping to build a bridge between the newly emerging movement and these existing organisations and struggles. To adequately understand the development of Occupy, it is necessary to grasp both these dynamics in their interaction.

Rather than seeing the Occupy movement as representing something distinctly unique that can only be analysed on its own terms, it is more useful to understand it as one expression of a growing resistance. Its antecedent can be found in the "movement of the squares" internationally, but there

---

2:    For more on the politics of the "movement of the squares", inspired by the occupation of Tahrir Square in Egypt and which spread from Madrid to other cities in Spain, Italy and Greece, see Durgan and Sans, 2011, and Jones, 2012.

were equally important preludes to be found within the US working class itself. First and foremost was the struggle against Wisconsin governor Scott Walker's attempt to completely smash the public sector unions in that state. This was the first taste of mass working class action after decades of retreat. Then, just weeks before OWS began, Verizon telecommunications workers up and down the East Coast had gone on strike and gained massive support.

Viewed in this light, the Occupy movement can be seen as one aspect of the process of rebuilding working class political and organisational capacity. The movement made a decisive contribution to reframing the political debate in the US and legitimising militant action. But if we are to move forward, we need a sober assessment both of the movement's strengths and its weaknesses. This article will attempt to provide such an account of the movement's development and outline some of the key debates facing it today.

The rise of OWS

No one could have predicted the movement's success. OWS was not the first attempt to occupy public space in lower Manhattan. In June 2011 activists with New Yorkers Against the Budget Cuts had maintained an encampment in the shadow of City Hall to protest at Mayor Bloomberg's proposed austerity budget. Over the course of a couple of weeks a core of 100 or so campers dwindled to about half that size. Activists from that struggle were the first to take up the call from *Adbusters* magazine to occupy Wall Street on 17 September. Throughout the late summer, 50 to 100 activists met in General Assemblies (GAs) and began planning.

The movement's beginning on 17 September was inauspicious. *Adbusters* had set a goal of flooding Wall Street with 20,000 protesters. Local activists were more modest in their expectations, but were still hoping for 5,000 to 10,000. Instead, fewer than 1,000 people showed up that day and about 700 people participated in the first GA in Zuccotti Park. As a small core of protesters set up tents and sleeping bags, it was unclear how long an encampment would be able to sustain itself or what impact it might have.

Several factors helped to give social weight to the initially small protest and to catapult it to national attention. The first was a march of 1,000 multiracial protesters in memory of Troy Davis—an innocent black man who had been executed in Georgia the day before. This protest was marked by a militancy that would come to characterise OWS-related actions. The crowd snaked its way through lower Manhattan, evading the police at several turns, and made its way to OWS where it joined in chants of "We are all Troy Davis". Not only did this connect OWS with a more multiracial, working class audience, but it also immediately established a pattern of local struggles looking to OWS for support. This helped to give the movement a social content and local relevance that it might not have had otherwise.

Activists immediately seized the initiative to build these types of connections. In particular, the newly formed Labour Outreach Committee organised support for ongoing labour struggles in NYC, including at some of the most potent symbols of the 1 percent: Sotheby's art auction house and the Central Park Boathouse. They also began reaching out to some of the larger unions in NYC for support. This support would become critical to Occupy's survival in its first weeks.

The key turning point, however, was the New York Police Department's incredibly brutal and completely unwarranted assault on peaceful protesters. On Saturday 24 September, activists attempted an unpermitted march up Broadway to Union Square. For some reason, the police had decided to draw a line in the sand, and attacked and penned in protesters, arresting more than 100. When one officer, Anthony Bologna, pepper-sprayed a group of female protesters who were already captured in a net, the video went viral and drew mass sympathy for the protesters. Suddenly OWS became mainstream news. And as viewers tuned in, they listened as protesters told stories of what had brought them to the encampment. The stories of homes foreclosed on, skyrocketing student debt, debilitating medical bills, lost jobs and more all resonated with a public still reeling from the impact of the economic crisis.

By the second week the encampment had assumed a mass character. Working class New Yorkers began streaming down to Zuccotti. People came before or after work. Students and those without jobs came and joined in the daily marches to the stock exchange and other activities. Many would carry signs expressing their particular grievance or individual tragedy. The numbers in the park swelled as impromptu discussions broke out in every corner. A "people's library" was set up and quickly became a centre of political discussion as guest speakers came to address the crowd. People would come and set up a table to promote a particular issue. Visitors would help out in the library or the kitchen or sanitation committee. And the nightly GAs grew to 1,000 or more.

By 29 September the Transport Workers' Union (TWU) became the first union to officially offer support for OWS. Other major unions quickly followed suit. On 5 October, a few days after police arrested 700 protesters on the Brooklyn Bridge, a coalition of union and community groups organised a demonstration of more than 20,000 in downtown Manhattan. Meanwhile the Occupy movement spread rapidly across the country with literally hundreds of encampments set up within weeks. The high point came on 15 October, one day after the successful defence of Zuccotti, when up to 100,000 people gathered in Times Square and many more thousands protested across the US as part of a global day of action.

The early weeks of the Occupy movement had an almost giddy quality. The movement was marked by a high degree of spontaneity and experimentation, which was in turn sustained by mass involvement. In the first weeks of the occupation tens of thousands of people came down to Zuccotti Park. Mass numbers engaged in discussions and participated in both planned and impromptu marches that took off from there every day. A significant minority of those people got actively involved in the more than a hundred working groups—with upwards of 5,000 people meeting in the various groups each week. The movement quickly grew beyond the bounds of the park and working groups spread to a public atrium where hundreds of people could be found meeting at any given time.

This meant that the movement very quickly developed its own momentum and seemed to go from success to success. Actions that seemed ill-conceived and that were not well planned still managed to succeed. For example, the largest action that took place during the first two months was the 100,000-person demonstration in Times Square on 15 October. However, this was initially called simply as a "dance party" at Times Square and was meant to be an add-on to a day of action against the banks. No one expected it to turn out the numbers it did. Of course, in retrospect, it is possible to identify concrete reasons for each of these successes. For example, the Times Square demonstration came the day after a successful defence of Zuccotti that saw thousands mobilised, in no small part by trade unions,[3] to prevent the forcible clearance of the camp. This gave a profile to the action it would not otherwise have had and built on people's sense of confidence. But to most participants, the belief was that anything could catch and the more ambitious and bold the better.

This meant that there was very little political discussion within the movement and that real differences between activists were minimised. Despite meetings that were several hours long, most discussions were dominated by tactical and logistical questions. This doesn't mean that there were no political debates. For example, there were critical early discussions about the importance of being explicitly anti-racist and the need to build

---

3:    "The AFL-CIO [union federation] sent email blasts to their members asking them to go to the park to defend it early Friday morning, and pressured the mayor behind the scenes to back down"—Singsen, 2012.

solidarity with labour, working class communities and the oppressed. But these were the exception to the rule.

The movement deepens

By late October, though, it became clear that the movement would need to deepen its roots in order to sustain itself and move forward. Wider layers of activists were beginning to discuss how to translate Occupy's tremendous resonance into concrete gains. And the question of how to defend the camps against possible eviction became increasingly dominant as mayors across the country began to take a harder line.

It was in this context that another turning point took place. On 25 October riot police and members of 17 other law enforcement agencies attacked Occupy Oakland with a qualitatively greater degree of brutality than had yet been levelled against the movement. They used tear gas canisters, flash grenades and rubber bullets against protesters. Scott Olsen, a 24 year old veteran, was struck by a tear gas canister and taken to hospital in a critical condition. Both the scale of the brutality and the particular character of Occupy Oakland gave the movement there an added political and social weight. Whereas OWS was camped in downtown Manhattan in the shadow of powerful financial firms, the occupation of Oakland took place in the heart of a primarily black and Latino city that had been ravaged by budget cuts, unemployment and massive levels of state repression. Protesters in Oakland had named their encampment Oscar Grant Plaza in memory of an unarmed black man who had been shot by police in 2009. While issues of racism, police violence and the gutting of working class and poor neighbourhoods had been taken up by OWS, they took on an increased prominence as the centre of struggle shifted to Oakland.

But it was the response of Occupy Oakland that posed the possibility of taking the movement to a new level. The night after the police attack, protesters retook Oscar Grant Plaza in the largest numbers there yet. By a vote of 1,484 to 46 the general assembly called for a general strike on 2 November. While unions had played a pivotal role in the spread of the movement, this was the first attempt to leverage the organised power of the working class in its defence. Most activists recognised that an all-out general strike would not be organised in less than a week. However, support from several critical labour organisations provided a real basis for the action. While stopping short of endorsing the call for a general strike, both the local labour council and the dock workers' union expressed support for actions on that day. The Oakland teachers' union issued a clear endorsement. On the day of the action more than 20,000 people participated. The highlight of the day was a dramatic march of 6,000, led by union members, to shut down the port of Oakland.

The Oakland general strike call, and the work done by activists to connect with labour and community organisations in preparation for it, raised the prospect of developing more powerful connections between the Occupy movement and organised labour. It also began to point a way towards the kind of social forces that would be necessary to successfully defend and advance the movement. However, in retrospect, it is also clear that activists drew very different conclusions about the relationship between Occupy and the organised working class. These differences would become central to the debates within the movement in its post-eviction phase. Unfortunately, many of the political debates and lessons that were beginning to be discussed were cut short by the mass clearing of the encampments.

Impact of the loss of the encampments

It would be difficult to overstate the importance of the encampments to the movement. It is not simply that they offered a symbol of direct confrontation and reclamation of public space. In a very real sense, they provided the physical arena in which people could come together to discuss strategy and through which new people could enter the struggle. They substituted themselves for the organisational structures that most activists rejected. At the most basic level, they allowed activists to find one another.

The experience of OWS, the largest and most developed of the encampments, is indicative of the general experience nationally. From the very beginning there was something of a divide between the running of the encampment and the associated "operational" groups and the movement working groups. At the height of the encampment close to 600 people were sleeping there nightly. This involved a massive operation that drew in hundreds of activists. But at the same time, there was a proliferation of movement-oriented working groups around almost every issue; these developed their own trajectory. While originally almost all the working groups met on-site at Zuccotti, most ended up splitting off either to a nearby atrium or even to further off-site locations in union halls or other spaces. In theory, these working groups were chartered by and accountable to the general assembly; in practice, they operated almost entirely autonomously with an uneven level of reporting back to the GA. Very quickly the GA took on a role that was much closer to a clearing house than that of a decision making body.

In fact, it's worth noting that all of the biggest actions of OWS (the 5 October community/labour rally; the 15 October global day of action; and the 17 November labour march) were planned outside of the GA—and, in some cases, almost entirely outside of OWS. For example, most of the organising for the first mass rally on 5 October was carried out by people involved in the "Beyond May 12th Coalition"—a coalition of community and labour groups that had organised a march earlier that year. Two out of the three mass actions were driven in large part by the organised NYC labour movement with young labour-oriented radicals forming a bridge between OWS and the unions.

All of this meant that the movement was very diffuse and that there were no clear centres of decision making. However, as long as the encampment existed there was a practical centre that provided a space for different activities to overlap, for people to enter into the movement and for some level of cohesion to be sustained. There were also particular working groups that helped to provide this cohesion. For example, the facilitation committee met daily before the GAs and planned their agenda; additionally, every major action passed through the direct action committee (even if the centre of organising was frequently elsewhere). Even as what could be described as multiple occupy movements developed, there was a very clear identification with OWS that united everyone.

The reason this history is important is because it underscores how much was lost when the camps were evicted and the centrifugal pulls got exacerbated in the wake of that eviction. The movement was simply not developed enough to withstand the impact. In NYC this was exemplified by the response to the eviction itself. Despite a growing awareness that Mayor Bloomberg was planning to clear Zuccotti, the only real plan for defence involved activists locking themselves down and a text-alert system. On the night of the eviction the police were able to sweep through the park in under an hour and arrest anyone staying. By the time hundreds of people responded to the text-alert system, the area had been cordoned off and police divided and attacked scattered groups of protesters. There was no plan for an emergency response demonstration the next day or for a general assembly to plan the next actions. Most of the key organisers were in jail. Activists made several attempts to gather the next day, but there was no real coordination and so people were left responding to contradictory calls as best they could.

In the first month following the eviction of Zuccotti, the movement was still in a state of flux and it was not clear how much of a loss had been suffered. Just days after the eviction, on 17 November, there was a demonstration of tens of thousands that continued to bring new people into the movement. However, the feel of the demonstration was markedly different from earlier ones. Rather than decentralised "people's mic" speak-outs, there was a large sound system provided and run by the unions and an incredibly heavy security team making sure that people marched away from Zuccotti. The police and city had regained the initiative. By early January it was clear that the movement had become isolated and was in retreat. In this context, the contradictory political currents that had been held together by a growing mass movement began to separate and polarise.

The movement splinters

The most hardened and politically defined current to emerge was that of the ultra-left, hard anarchists. This current is most concentrated on the West Coast and politically articulated through blogs/groupings such as Bay of Rage, the Oakland Commune, and the Black Orchid Collective.[4] However, it also exerts a national influence and is politically connected to the insurrectionary anarchist current that emerged several years ago and was most closely identified with the occupation of the New School in NYC.

Occupy activists had always prided themselves on taking bold, militant action and saw themselves as standing in contrast to the "boring", permitted marches traditionally called by unions and the left. However, at the height of the movement there was a mass character to the struggle that allowed it to constantly connect with broader layers of the working class. And most activists, even if they expressed concerns about co-optation, saw the importance of developing collaborative relationships with unions and other social organisations. However, as soon as the movement lost its mass character, politics that substituted individual confrontation for collective action began to dominate. While many movement activists gravitated towards these politics out of frustration and impatience, the hard anarchists offered up a theoretical justification and consciously attempted to lead the movement in this direction.

The call for a general strike in Oakland on 2 November had represented a high point of collaboration between unions and the Occupy movement. However, rather than seeing this as an opportunity on which to build, the hard anarchists drew the conclusion that activists could substitute their own militant action for that of workers at the point of production. In this conception, the flow of capital could be disrupted without the active participation of workers in a particular workplace. This could happen either in the process of circulation or through an attack on production from the outside. One collective of writers known as the Oakland Commune expressed the typical logic of this argument: "The subject of

---

4:    For examples of their writing, see their websites at www.bayofrage.com, http://theoaklandcommune.wordpress.com and http://blackorchidcollective.wordpress.com

the 'strike' is no longer the working class as such, though workers are always involved. The strike no longer appears only as the voluntary with drawal of labour from a workplace by those employed there, but as the blockade, suppression (or even sabotage or destruction) of that workplace by proletarians who are alien to it".[5]

This argument frequently extended to an active hostility to the organised working class. Activists with the Black Orchid Collective in Seattle began in December to formulate a conception of Occupy as representing the 89 percent of workers not organised in unions. While rejecting claims that this slogan expresses hostility towards unions, they portray union members as a privileged caste:

> In the deepening of the economic crisis, it is hard to tell poor, unemployed, undocumented, immigrants, people of colour, that we too have a stake in the struggles of union workers, especially relatively privileged workers... When revolutionaries act as if legitimate class struggle only happens through NLRB [National Labour Relations Board]-recognised unions, they ignore the very real and material divisions between union and non-union workers, many of whom see unionised workers as remote and unrelated to their lives at best and as privileged workers who do not understand the realities of the proletariat at worst.[6]

There are a number of problems inherent in this line of argument. First, it paints a picture of unions as primarily the preserve of white men. In fact, women and people of colour are disproportionately represented in unions as a result of the civil rights and women's liberation movements, as well as of the organisation of the public sector. This is at least part of the reason why unions have played an important role in many of the social justice struggles of recent years—from the defence of immigrant rights to fights against the criminal injustice system. Second, it ignores the fact that far from feeling hostility towards unionised workers, most non-unionised workers would like to be able to join a union. And, in fact, when unions have taken action, even those representing relatively well-paid workers, they have received widespread support. Perhaps this is because most workers, organised or unorganised, instinctively recognise a reality that the anarchists of the Black Orchid Collective do not—when unions fight and win, they raise the potential for *all* workers to move forward.

5:    Oakland Commune, 2011.
6:    Black Orchid Collective, 2012.

Dismissing the need to patiently win workers over, whether union-ised or not, also provides the theoretical justification for an insistence on confrontational tactics. Destruction of property and violent confrontation with the authorities are celebrated as part of the insurrectionary process. For this current, an "unmediated assault on our enemies", as the Oakland Commune describes it, represents a step forward for the movement regard-less of the numbers or character of those involved. The hard anarchists measure the strength of the movement by the willingness of people to engage in such assaults. An article posted on Bay of Rage after the recent May Day protests is illustrative. In it the authors point to what they see as the successful aspects of the day:

> No other 24-hour period in recent memory has unleashed such a diverse array of militancy in cities across the country. From the all day street fighting in Oakland, to the shield bloc in LA, to the courageous attempt at a Wildcat March in New York, to the surprise attack on the Mission police station in San Francisco, to the anti-capitalist march in New Orleans, to the spectacular trashing of Seattle banks and corporate chains by black flag wielding comrades, the large crowds which took to the streets on 1 May were no longer afraid of militant confrontations with police and seemed relatively comfortable with property destruction. This is an important turning point which suggests that the tone and tactics of the next sequence will be quite different from those of last fall.[7]

They fail to mention the fact that each of these actions involved, at best, hundreds of activists. Perhaps more tellingly, they ignore some of the more impressive mass actions that took place on that day. The high point took place in NYC where as many as 30,000 immigrants, union members, students and other activists marched from Union Square back to Zuccotti in a protest that was reminiscent of the early days of OWS. Smaller, but nonethe-less significant, marches ranging from 3,000 to 7,000 took place in cities like LA, San Francisco, Oakland and Chicago. But because most of these actions were legally permitted marches, they were not seen as a step forward or a potential basis for revitalisation of the movement, despite bringing the largest numbers of people onto the streets since November. In fact, at an assess-ment meeting in NYC the anarchists who had organised the Wildcat March (which drew a few hundred people) argued that the mass march was respon-sible for larger numbers not engaging in militant actions throughout the day.

7:    Oakland Commune, 2012.

In reality, this insistent emphasis on confrontational tactics focuses the movement on a terrain with which the police and authorities have become quite comfortable. There has developed an all too predictable rhythm to these confrontations: the police wait for the numbers to dwindle and scatter, then attack and divide protesters from one another and use overwhelming force to quickly quell any resistance. In the early days of the movement police violence served to radicalise and bring larger numbers into it as people were horrified by unprovoked assaults on peaceful protesters. Today this dynamic has shifted. The movement is increasingly isolated and has become identified with its most adventurist wing. Activists are trapped in an exhausting and demoralising cycle of confrontation followed by the need for jailhouse solidarity and medical and legal support.

At the same time that the ultra-left, hard anarchist current advanced, many of the most important social forces that helped give support to Occupy, most notably the unions, began to retreat. A critique of the anarchist dismissal of the organised working class should not obscure the reality that there are inherent tensions in the relationship between the Occupy movement and the unions. The union leadership saw in Occupy an opportunity to infuse new energy into the labour movement. But they will also seek to contain that struggle within acceptable bounds and, in particular, would like to harness that energy into their support for President Obama's re-election campaign. This was glaringly apparent when the president of SEIU, one of the country's largest unions, issued an endorsement for Obama the day before the 17 November demonstration in NYC. The next day the full weight of the union's bureaucratic apparatus was on display as it attempted to control and marshal the demonstration. There was clearly a conscious decision on the part of SEIU and its allies to make sure that the 30,000 people on the demonstration did not attempt to march to, let alone retake, Zuccotti, but instead were directed to an outer borough.

While the decentralised nature of the Occupy movement makes it difficult for the unions or Democratic Party to simply co-opt it, there is no doubt that both forces would like to steer activist energies into the 2012 elections. The splintering of the movement makes it much easier for anyone to take the language of "Occupy" and use it to their advantage. Most recently the liberal Democrat non-profit group MoveOn.org, in alliance with the major unions, conducted a series of non-violent trainings that they called the "99 percent spring". More than 100,000 people—constituting much of the base of the movement's early phase—participated in the trainings. While organisers insist that these trainings are not about getting the vote out for Obama, they do provide a very tangible and organised potential base of support for such an effort. Moreover, they are an indication of where some of the largest and most well-funded organisations intend to put their efforts.

Where next?

Today the Occupy movement is at a crossroads. If it is to move forward, it must connect with the broad layers of the working class that gave the movement its initial mass character. This would entail a series of more modest struggles around concrete issues such as police brutality, housing, public education and more. This work is being done, and sincerely so, with an increased corps of dedicated activists. But it does not find a political expression in the movement as a whole. Instead the public face of Occupy remains focused on attempts at renewed occupations, unpermitted marches and direct confrontation.

There are two critical obstacles that need to be overcome. First, most activists within the movement look to recreating the tactics that led to the explosion of the movement in the fall. This frequently means an insistence on direct confrontation with the police through unpermitted actions. There is an underlying assumption that police repression will, like it did in the autumn, ignite mass sympathy. Instead it tends to exhaust movement forces as activists deal with repeated rounds of repression and the resulting need for jailhouse solidarity, medical support and legal defence. It also raises the bar for passive sympathy to be translated into active participation. Finally, it can form a real barrier to genuine collaboration with emerging movements, such as those around criminal injustice, where participants instinctively understand the need for a more serious approach.

Secondly, the movement has not managed to replace the critical functions played by the encampments. There are hundreds of activists who are wrestling with the question of how to take the movement forward. But there is no political space in which they can come together and have these discussions. And, even more critically, there is no organisational mechanism for translating any agreed-upon strategy into action. Thus the most destructive actions taken by sections of the movement undermine any of the positive attempts to link up with working class forces. The widely shared political commitment to horizontalism and a "leaderless" movement acts as a block to the development of such structures.

The myopic focus on confrontational tactics and insistence on structurelessness both stem from a widely held belief that OWS was successful precisely because it broke new ground. Most commentary on the movement, as well as the self-assessment of movement activists, focused on the tactic of occupation and the fact that OWS emerged independent of trade union, liberal or left forces. There is no doubt that the occupation—both its existence and its imagery—played a key role in catapulting the movement to national attention. But it is equally true that there were a whole series of conjunctural factors that facilitated this. Some of these factors were truly unpredictable—such as the unwarranted, highly televised brutality against protesters and the resulting mass sympathy. Others were the result of the conscious efforts of longstanding activists, such as early links forged to labour and anti-racist activists.

Regardless of the initial reasons for the explosion of the movement, it tells us little about how to move it forward now. OWS tapped into a deep vein of accumulated bitterness and discontent in the US. But as a movement, it far exceeded the existing organisational and political capacity of the working class. That class has been in retreat for 35 years and suffers the scars of defeat and demoralisation. The monumental events of 2011, from the Egyptian Revolution to the occupation of the Capitol in Madison to OWS, all began a process of reversing that tide. But it is precisely that—a process, which will advance spectacularly at times, suffer defeats at others and need to consolidate its forces.

It is unclear in what way the Occupy movement will revive or even whether, in its current form, it can. But it has fundamentally altered the landscape of American politics and exposed the fault lines of class anger. In that sense, it has made a contribution to the rebuilding of working class confidence, organisation and militancy. There is no shortage of issues around which to organise. And certainly the continuing assault of the ruling class in this country guarantees new upheavals. Recently the struggle for justice for Trayvon Martin—an unarmed black teenager murdered by a racist vigilante—has played a role in galvanising an emerging anti-racist movement. In May as many as 10,000 protesters marched against the NATO summit in Chicago. And as of this writing, the 32,000 members of the Chicago Teachers' Union are preparing for a potential strike in the autumn. These struggles may not flow through the structures of the Occupy movement. But they are part of the same dynamic that gave rise to it. The most important contribution that those on the existing left and those inspired by the movement can make is to draw the lessons of the most recent wave of struggle and help extend the organisation of this resistance in all directions possible.

References

Black Orchid Collective, 2012, "Longview, Occupy and Beyond: Rank and File and the 89% Unite", Black Orchid Collective blog (30 January), http://blackorchidcollective. wordpress.com/2012/01/30/longview-occupy-and-beyond-rank-and-file-and-the-89-unite-2/

Durgan, Andy, and Joel Sans, 2011, "'No One Represents Us': The 15 May Movement in the Spanish State", *International Socialism 132* (autumn), www.isj.org.uk/?id=757

Jones, Jonny, 2012, "The Shock of the New: Anti-capitalism and the Crisis", *International Socialism 134* (spring), www.isj.org.uk/?id=796

Oakland Commune, 2011, "Blockading the Ports is Only the First of Many Last Resorts", Bay of Rage website (7 December), www.bayofrage.com/from-the-bay/blockading-the-port-is-only-the-first-of-many-last-resorts/

Oakland Commune, 2012, "Occupy Oakland is dead. Long live the Oakland Commune", Bay of Rage website (16 May), www.bayofrage.com/featured-articles/occupy-oakland-is-dead/

Singsen, Doug, 2012, "A Balance Sheet of Occupy Wall Street", *International Socialist Review,* 81 (January-February), www.isreview.org/issues/81/feat-occupywallstreet.shtml

Trudell, Megan, 2012, "The Occupy Movement and Class Politics in the US", *International Socialism 133* (winter), www.isj.org.uk/?id=775

Rochdale: an anatomy of the sexual abuse scandal

Judith Orr

The case of nine men convicted of appalling sexual exploitation of young women in Rochdale in north west England has unleashed a renewed tide of racism and Islamophobia.[1] The media coverage of the case asserted that the most shocking aspect of the story was not the abuse itself, but the fact that the male abusers were Pakistani Muslims and the women they abused were white. Fascists and racists have used the case to mobilise, supported by the tabloids whose front pages were an invitation to see all Muslim men as dangerous paedophiles. At the same time the mainstream right used the comment columns to pour out their barely concealed racist filth about Muslims and Pakistanis. Even the judge in the Rochdale case, Gerald Clifton, joined in, saying, "I believe one of the factors which led to that is that they [the young women victims] were not of your community or religion."

His words are now used on British National Party leaflets headlined "Racist Muslim Paedophilia". Throughout the hearing the British National Party (BNP), the English Defence League (EDL), and other racist and fascist organisations picketed the court. It was revealed at the end of the case that on the opening day two barristers on the defence legal team, both Asian, were attacked outside the court. They pulled out of the case in fear for their safety

1:    I would like to thank Bea Kay, Tony Staunton, Andy Brammer, Sam O'Brien and Michael Lavalette for their helpful advice.

and that of their families. The hearing was delayed by two weeks, the jury was discharged and new barristers were found to represent the defendants.[2]

At the end of the trial an investigation into whether jury confidentiality had been compromised had to be set up. This was after BNP leader Nick Griffin tweeted that seven of the men had been found guilty while the jury was still deliberating. The investigation concluded that there was no evidence that the jury had communicated with Griffin.

But the Nazis and the tabloids are not the only ones using the issue of sexual exploitation to stoke up racism. When children's minister Tim Loughton was asked about the Rochdale case he said, "Political correctness and racial sensitivities have in the past been an issue." He added that the authorities still "have to be aware of certain characteristics of various ethnic communities".

As Hassan Mahamdallie pointed out in *Socialist Worker* about his experience living in Rochdale in the 1980s, "Rochdale police are not known for operating in 'politically correct' or 'racially sensitive' ways".[3] But the implication that there is something specific among Muslims or Pakistanis that makes them more likely to commit these crimes has become the common theme on the right. The first Muslim woman to serve in the cabinet, Baroness Warsi, joined the chorus in an interview in the *London Evening Standard* newspaper, saying:

> There is a small minority of Pakistani men who believe that white girls are fair game. And we have to be prepared to say that. You can only start solving a problem if you acknowledge it first... This small minority who see women as second-class citizens, and white women probably as third-class citizens, are to be spoken out against... Communities have a responsibility to stand up and say: "This is wrong; this will not be tolerated... Cultural sensitivity should never be a bar to applying the law".[4]

Columnist Melanie Phillips ranted in the *Daily Mail*, "The police maintain doggedly that this has nothing to do with race. What a red herring. Of course it doesn't! This is about religion and culture—an unwesternised Islamic culture which holds that non-Muslims are trash and women are worthless. And so white girls are worthless trash".[5]

2: Carter, 2012.
3: Mahamdallie, 2012.
4: Murphy, 2012.
5: Phillips, 2012.

TV historian David Starkey spoke at a conference of school heads shortly after the trial ended and proclaimed, "If you want to look at what happens when you have no sense of common identity, look at Rochdale and events in Rochdale… Those men were acting within their own cultural norms. Nobody ever explained to them that the history of women in Britain was once rather similar to that in Pakistan and it had changed".[6] This is the same David Starkey who showed his commitment to women's equality when he denounced the "feminising" of history by women historians who turned it into "soap opera" for their "mainly female audience".[7]

There has not been the same denouncing of the "cultural norms" of how women are treated when it comes to non-Muslim sex attackers. Look no further than the number of footballers in cases of alleged rape. The gross custom of footballers or their representatives cruising the shops of Manchester picking up women to have sex with even has its own term, "harvesting". These women are brought to clubs and hotels where they are then assumed to be willing to have sex with numbers of footballers—coined "roasting", often while being filmed.

In a recent case Ched Evans, Welsh international and Sheffield United player, was jailed for five years for rape. The teenager he raped after he and other male friends picked her up drunk in the street had her name revealed on social media and was abused for taking the case out against him. His sister and a group of fans even tried to organise a public tribute to him as a show of support at a match after he was imprisoned.[8] We do not see front pages devoted to denouncing the misogynist culture of football, or calls for footballers as a collective to examine why a number of their colleagues have been accused of sex crimes.

Yet all the time Muslim representatives are called upon to denounce the crimes as if in some way by nature of a shared religion they are collectively responsible. On a Unite Against Fascism protest against the EDL I met Mohammed Shafiq who represents an organisation called the Ramadhan Foundation. He has been widely quoted in the media for saying that Pakistani men do have a specific problem in terms of sexual grooming. He spoke out against the racist backlash from the platform. Afterwards he was arguing with his friends that the "whole Pakistani community" had to take responsibility for what the convicted men had done.

6:    Shepherd, 2012.
7:    Allen, 2009.
8:    Gaskell, 2012.

His position shows the contradictions and the real pressure many Muslims feel under the onslaught of Islamophobia.

Rape and sexual abuse are horrendous crimes whoever the perpetrator. Women often feel unable or unwilling to report assaults for fear they will not be believed, their sexual history will be on trial or they will be judged culpable because of what they wore or how they behaved.

The reaction to the Rochdale case was seen through the prism of race. But this will not bring us any nearer to understanding or stopping the problem of sexual abuse. In fact, if grooming and sexual exploitation are seen as solely a crime carried out by Pakistani men, many victims will not get the help and justice they deserve.

Racist stereotypes and women's oppression

Whatever the spin, it is not concern for women's rights but race that is driving the agenda in these debates and it is not for the first time. In January 2011, after a case in which two Asian men were convicted of rape and sexual abuse in Nottingham Crown Court, Labour MP Jack Straw declared that young Muslim men were "fizzing and popping with testosterone" and saw young white women as "easy meat".[9]

These views reflect centuries-old racist stereotypes of black men as sexual predators, which deemed even consensual sexual relationships between a black man and a white woman an aberration. From the days of slavery through to the 20th century black men have been brutally punished for having sexual relations with white women. White slave-owners on the other hand saw raping their black slaves as perfectly normal.

With the rise of Islamophobia overt racism has been veiled in talk of "culture". This approach has been used by both fascists and mainstream politicians alike in recent years. In the Rochdale case it has served the purpose of allowing naked prejudice to be dressed up as concerned commentary. Below the screaming headlines some tried to cite academic research to legitimise the racialisation of this crime.

One study in particular was regularly quoted. The research, by the Jill Dando Institute of Crime Science at University College London (UCL), supposedly showed that Pakistani men are the main perpetrators of grooming and abusing young women. In fact, this study, done over a year ago, does no such thing. Eleanor Cockbain and Helen Brayley, the academics who did the research, are concerned at how their work is being used. Cockbain said, "The citations are correct but they have been taken

9:    *Socialist Worker*, 2011.

out of context. Nor do they acknowledge the small sample size of the original research, which focused on just two large cases".[10]

The study's purpose was precisely to look at the nature of social networks of the perpetrators and victims in two cases that involved groups of Pakistani men. It explains that gangs and paedophile rings are rare and goes on to say, "Contrary to stereotypes of sinister paedophile rings, most child sex offenders act alone," and quotes research on child sex offenders showing that "only 4 percent were involved in an organised network and 92 percent had no contact with other offenders prior to arrest".

The researchers were worried that "limited data had been extended to characterise an entire crime type, in particular of race and gender". They said of the cases they studied that there was no evidence that white girls were targeted by offenders, saying, "Though the majority were white, so too were the majority of local inhabitants."

Referring to the Rochdale case Assistant Chief Constable Steve Heywood of Greater Manchester Police was careful to point out that it was not about race, but "adults preying on vulnerable young children". "It just happens that in this particular area and time, the demographics were that these were Asian men," he said. "However, in large parts of the country we are seeing on-street grooming, child sexual exploitation happening in each of our towns and it isn't about a race issue".[11] The police themselves have confirmed that 95 percent of those on the Greater Manchester sex offenders register are white.

Those who claim that statistics prove that "street grooming" is predominantly committed by Pakistani men have difficulty in explaining how they have come to this conclusion as "street grooming" is not a specific criminal offence. It is a term that serves to racialise the crime of sexual exploitation in the same way as the term "mugging" became used to denote a crime committed by mainly young black men.

What about the women?

Amid the obsession about the race and religion of the male perpetrators less attention has been spent on their victims. The real question of Rochdale is how could the system have let down these young women. They were vulnerable, in or around the care system, and their abuse took place over a number of years. Race was not the issue that made getting justice difficult for these women. It was deep-seated prejudice that deemed their lives less

---

10: Vallely, 2012.
11: http://www.bbc.co.uk/news/uk-england-manchester-17996245

worthy as young women from poor working class backgrounds who had already had troubled lives.

The police comment said it all: they described the young women as coming from "chaotic" or "council house backgrounds". Being a council house tenant is obviously seen as being a problem in itself. In other words they were not from stable middle class families.

Even when one young woman alerted the police to the abuse she was suffering as far back as 2008 the case did not get to court. At 15 she was arrested for causing a nuisance outside a kebab shop and during questioning explained that she had been having sex with a number of men based there in return for gifts of food, phone cards and vodka. She even gave the police an item of her underwear that had traces of DNA evidence of a 59 year old man who was eventually one of the nine convicted.

After almost a year's investigation the Crown Prosecution Service (CPS) did not take the case to court because they decided the young woman would be an "unreliable witness" and would not be believed by a jury. These assumptions about the credibility of the young woman condemned her to yet more abuse until the case was taken up again.[12]

This is the common experience of children and young people who report cases of sexual abuse. The CPS calculates that of the 17,000 reported cases of sexual offences involving children under 16, just under a quarter went on trial this year. Even adult women reporting rape find the legal system often judges them rather than helps them. In February of this year a report by inspectorates of police and crown prosecutors found evidence that rape cases were "no-crimed", that is, recorded as if no crime had taken place, more often than other crimes.

According to figures from different police forces around the country in 2010/11 the volume of rape offences "no-crimed" was 2,131, nearly 12 percent of the total number of recorded rape crimes. Offences of rape are "no-crimed" four times more often than, for example, the offence of causing grievous bodily harm with intent.[13] This massages statistics that can help fulfil targets for conviction rates while burying clues that could lead to serial rapists being tracked down.

The Metropolitan Police's specialist sex crime unit Sapphire underwent an overhaul in 2010 after two serial rapists were allowed to continue to commit crimes even after women's reports of rape. The women were simply not believed. In June 2012 the unit is once again under investigation and

12: Martinson, 2012.
13: HMCPSI, 2012, p20.

two officers are accused of perverting the course of justice. It has emerged that officers were closing cases and informing women that no charges were going to be brought in their case even though this had not been decided.[14]

All this shows that while a woman's experience of rape or abuse is judged by the preconceptions of a society in which women's oppression is entrenched they will not get justice.

Grooming

The horror of such cases as the Rochdale abuse is that the life experience of these young women had been so difficult that they could be "groomed" into believing that serial abuse and rape were something they had to live with. The whole purpose of grooming is to lead a vulnerable young person into believing they are in a loving relationship. Some of the women in this case refused to give evidence to the police against men they continued to perceive as their "boyfriends". In some cases it took many hours of interviews and counselling for them to come to terms with the reality of the situation they were in. Such was the paucity of love and respect in their life that the experience of being groomed was perceived as being positive.

Helen Brayley, one of the researchers at UCL, wrote an advisory note on grooming for police saying, "Many of the victims in our data set were either too scared or too extensively groomed to go to the police. They either believed they were in a relationship with one of the offenders and therefore did not want to get them into trouble, or they somehow felt complicit in their abuse".[15]

Bea Kay is a GMB union steward in children's social care in Sheffield, training those who work with young people on issues of grooming and sexual exploitation. She told *Socialist Worker*, "The support for young people today is pitiful. Vulnerable young people often feel worthless. An older man or group of men who pay attention to them and give them 'gifts', however trivial, can make them feel valued".[16] This means that overt physical violence is not necessarily a component of these abusive relationships. And certainly at the beginning the abuser concentrates on building up the victims to feel important, desirable and valued and to separate her or him from any networks of family or friendship that might offer an alternative.

Women of all ages in our society are encouraged to see themselves as sex objects, to see being attractive as a measure of their value. Whether it's

---

14: Laville, 2012.
15: Gilbert, 2011.
16: Orr, 2012.

in the numerous women's magazines with top tips for makeup, cosmetic surgery or clothes it is assumed we are all aspiring to be sexually attractive. With the rise of raunch culture over the last decade or so we are witnessing an increasing tolerance of women's sexuality being used as a commodity in ever more crude ways.

Sex has become a valuable currency in our society—and for some women it may be their only currency. Sexual exploitation is one of the most extreme and distorted expressions of women's oppression and the alienation of human relationships. Of course, young men can also become victims, although they are the minority.

Abuse and the family

The reality is that the form of sexual abuse exposed in Rochdale is not the most common, although it receives a disproportionate amount of media coverage. The charity Barnardo's found that "child sexual exploitation is much more likely to happen in private than in public, and this year's survey showed that street-based grooming and exploitation remains rare".[17]

Despite all the media frenzy children and young people are more at risk of abuse, physical and sexual, within the family unit rather than on the street—most adult abusers are known to the victim. "The majority of perpetrators sexually assault children known to them, with about 80 percent of offences taking place in the home of either the offender or the victim".[18]

The roots of women's oppression lie in the institution of the family, which Frederick Engels identified as becoming established with the rise of class society and private property. The role the family plays in people's lives and in wider society has gone through many profound changes. Yet it still plays an important function in modern capitalism. It is still the place where majority of the next generation are brought up. Although marriage rates have been declining, and in 2010 nearly half of all babies were born outside marriage or civil partnerships (46.8 percent) compared with 39.5 percent in 2000, the number of births registered with only one parent has been declining.[19]

Politicians, both Labour and Tory, extol the virtues of the traditional family. The Tories use it overtly to impose the idea that any problems people suffer are their individual responsibility and not rooted in the structured inequality of society. This ideological offensive is designed to make people feel it is their responsibility to carry an extra burden when

---

17: Barnardo's, 2012, p6.
18: Grubin, 1998.
19: Office for National Statistics, 2011, p6.

cuts mean there are fewer affordable residential homes for the elderly, or less respite care for those looking after a relative or child with disabilities. This is the strategy behind Tory communities minister Eric Pickles's latest assault on "troubled families".[20]

Now, a troubled family according to the Tories is one that fulfils five out of seven criteria: "having a low income, no one in the family who is working, poor housing, parents who have no qualifications, where the mother has a mental health problem, one parent has a longstanding illness or disability, and where the family is unable to afford basics, including food and clothes".[21] Pickles is not identifying people with any of these very real material problems for support; instead he is going for policies that show "a little less understanding".

The role of the family and how children are brought up goes right to the heart of the debate over child sex abuse and sexual exploitation. The young women who were preyed on by the men in Rochdale were on the streets and vulnerable because they had no effective network of support from a family or from the state. Social services had had contact with all the young women in the case. At least one was sent to a care home in Rochdale to escape problems experienced at home.

What happened to those young women cannot be separated from the contradictions in the nature of the family in society, contradictions that mean that families can act as a bulwark against the harshness of life under capitalism and when they break down can leave people more vulnerable. But at the same time they can be the place where all the rotten experience of alienation and inequality is distilled and distorts relationships in the most brutal fashion.

Solutions under capitalism

If the family is a frightening and dangerous place for some, what is offered by the system as an alternative can be equally problematic. Institutions for children without a family, orphanages, children's homes, poor houses, whatever the good intentions of many of those who worked in them, have historically been seen as the option of last resort.

Some, like the Christian Brothers' "industrial" schools in Ireland, have become notorious for the brutality meted out to their young charges. Such institutions should be a refuge from suffering; instead they can be places where already damaged children and young people are vulnerable

---

20: Pickles revealed his true feelings when on a ministerial visit to Plymouth in 2011 he mistakenly referred to "troublesome" rather "troubled" families.
21: Chorley, 2012.

to abuse. In some cases they have enabled networks of abusers to coalesce to mutually cover up and perpetuate the crimes. The scale of child abuse that is still being revealed by victims, now adult, in the Catholic church is a good example of this. Many of those who carried out the abuse did so in the sure and certain knowledge that they would be protected because even if their victims spoke out the church would never allow itself to be exposed to the scandal.[22]

Today such institutions are no longer seen as the best way to look after children in the care of the state. But social workers are constantly under the spotlight, particularly those dealing with child protection cases. They are denounced for taking children from families without enough evidence, but when something goes wrong then they are criticised for not removing a child sooner. This is against a background of ever shrinking budgets and cutbacks which means increasing workloads on fewer staff.

Many of the young people in the up to 47 private care homes in Rochdale are not from the area and so are not the responsibility of local social services. Young people are sometimes sent there from hundreds of miles away. Their local social services may have moved them to a new area to help them break from a cycle of abuse in their family or in their home-town. Sometimes their local council will have chosen to move them there due to the cheaper cost of care in the area. The high number of private homes in Rochdale is partly due to cheap housing. But if a young person has been taken into care because of abuse, moving them into a new town may not help if nothing else is done to support the individual. Instead they can fall into a new cycle of abuse if they are left exposed.

Rochdale has its own problems; a town of just over 200,000 people, it is the tenth most deprived district in England, measuring factors such as employment, income, health and housing.[23] It has a life expectancy below the national average and such is the inequality within the town between some wards there is a difference in life expectancy of ten years.

The main shopping high street is crowded with charity shops, pawnbrokers and cash converters. The burger chain McDonald's has recently shut down its branch. Alongside the "To Let" notice is a poster thanking people for their custom over 28 years. All around are reminders of the town's past as an industrial powerhouse: the imposing gothic town hall is now a grade 1 listed building. As one local youth worker told me, "We are now a manufacturing town without any manufacturing."

22: Devine, 2010.

23: www.communities.gov.uk/communities/research/indicesdeprivation/deprivation10/

Such deprivation can become a breeding ground for deep-seated social problems and the government's policies will only make the situation worse—the council budget faces cuts of £125 million.

There's profit in misery

Up to 75 percent of children's services in Britain are privatised. There are millions to be made from looking after the most vulnerable young people in society. The search for profit can result in low pay for workers and slackening of standards for skills and supervision.

Green Corns was the private company that ran the care home responsible for the care of the 15 year old young woman who was one of the victims of years of sexual abuse. The company was providing "solo care". Solo care means that a number of staff on round the clock shifts are dedicated to looking after one young person. For this care of a single young person a council can be charged over £250,000 a year. The company had received repeated warnings from Ofsted about care standards and advice that its staff needed training in sexual exploitation issues.

Green Corns was bought up by private equity group 3i for £26 million in 2004 and became part of the Continuum Care and Education Group. Annual operating profits reached £2.7 million. In turn Continuum was bought up by Advanced Childcare Limited (ACL) which itself had been bought by another private equity company, GI Partners, in April last year. Then managing director Alfred Foglio boasted, "Advanced Childcare has pioneered the trend of managing children's care services on behalf of budget constrained local authorities".[24]

ACL is now the largest provider of specialist children's care and education services in Britain. It reported an annual turnover of £15 million in 2010, up from £11 million a year earlier. Pre-tax profit increased to £2.6 million during that period, up from £700,000 in 2009. Most of this income is from local authority contracts for residential care. The combined company now runs 143 children's homes with 416 placements, 15 special schools and over 100 fostering placements. The company's founder, Riz Khan, expressed his high hopes for future profits: "We would be disappointed if we cannot at least double the size of the business in the next three to five years".[25] This is what privatisation of the welfare state means. Profit-driven multinationals owned by venture capitalists are put in charge of providing comfort and succour to young people damaged by the system.

24: GI Partners, 2011.
25: GI Partners, 2011.

Conclusion

The reaction to the Rochdale case has generated a moral panic—the perception of the danger of Pakistani men and street grooming is totally disproportionate to the reality. This is because it has not happened in a vacuum. Instead it has happened when the level of Islamophobia in British society is intensifying.

The racists' and the fascists' attempts to exploit the issue have so far been not been a great success for them. The first demonstration by the EDL in Rochdale after the conviction of the nine men, on 9 June, was billed by their members as going to be the biggest of the year and yet they mustered only around 300, mostly from outside the town. But this doesn't mean they won't continue to try to whip up racism and fear around the issue in the months to come. This can break out in unpredictable ways. In Luton in May several hundred local Sikhs demonstrated outside a police station after an alleged sexual assault on a Sikh woman by a Muslim man. Leading EDL member Tommy Robinson and other EDL members joined the demonstration.[26]

The question of child abuse and sexual exploitation is not straightforward. Sexual exploitation of children and young people is evidence of just how distorted humans and their relationships with each other can become under capitalism. Socialists have to avoid the danger of simplistic explanations: there are multiple factors involved in such cases and when Islamophobia is added it becomes a toxic mix. But it is vital that we challenge the dominant "common sense" about the issue and expose the bigotry that is being whipped up to distract people from the real scandal: how the system fails people, especially the most vulnerable.

26: Hough, 2012.

References

Allen, Vanessa, 2009, "Women turn history into a bizarre soap opera, says Starkey", *Daily Mail* (31 March), www.dailymail.co.uk/news/article-1166125/Women-turn-history-bizarre-soap-opera-says-Starkey.html

Barnardo's, 2012, "Cutting them free", www.barnardos.org.uk/cuttingthemfree.pdf

Carter, Helen, 2012, "Rochdale gang of guilty exploiting girls", *Guardian*, (8 May), www.guardian.co.uk/uk/2012/may/08/rochdale-gang-guilty-exploiting-girls

Chorley, Matt, 2012, "Problem families told—'Stop blaming others'", *Independent on Sunday* (10 June), www.independent.co.uk/news/uk/politics/ios-exclusive-problem-families-told--stop-blaming-others-7834235.html

Cockbain, Eleanor, Helen Brayley and Gloria Laycock, 2011, "Exploring Internal Child Sex Trafficking Networks Using Social Network Analysis", *Policing*, volume 5, issue 2, http://policing.oxfordjournals.org/content/5/2/144.full

Devine, Kevin, 2010, "Turmoil in the Catholic Church", *Socialist Review* (May), www.socialistreview.org.uk/article.php?articlenumber=11257

Gaskell, Simon, 2012, "Bid for public show of support for Ched Evans at Sheffield United falls flat", Wales Online (28 April), www.walesonline.co.uk/news/wales-news/2012/04/28/bid-for-public-show-of-support-for-ched-evans-at-sheffield-united-falls-flat-91466-30861200/

GI Partners, 2011, "GI Partners Expands Specialist Care and Education Portfolio with the Acquisition of Advanced Childcare" (18 March), www.gipartners.com/news/gi-partners-expands-specialist-care-and-education-portfolio-with-the-acquisition-of-advanced-ch

Gilbert, Helen, 2011, "Tackling Trafficking", *Police Magazine* (February), www.polfed.org/09_Tackling_Trafficking_Feb11.pdf

Grubin, Don, 1998, "Sex offending against children: understanding the risk" (Home Office).

HMCPSI, 2012, "Forging the links: Rape investigation and prosecution" (Her Majesty's Inspectorates of Constabulary and the Crown Prosecution Service), www.hmcpsi.gov.uk/documents/reports/CJJI_THM/BOTJ/forging_the_links_rape_investigation_and_prosecution_20120228.pdf

Hough, Andrew, 2012, "Hundreds of members of the local Sikh community protesting outside a Luton police station", *Daily Telegraph* (30 May), www.telegraph.co.uk/news/uknews/crime/9299139/Luton-local-Sikh-community-protesting-over-sex-attack-police-failures.html

Lavile, Sandra, 2012, "Met police urge rape victims to come forward as new detective arrested", *Guardian* (8 June).

Mahamdallie, Hassan, 2012, "Rochdale: Media distortion will put women in danger and will only benefit racists", *Socialist Worker* (19 May), www.socialistworker.co.uk/art.php?id=28457

Martinson, Jane, 2012, "Why the Rochdale 'grooming trial' wasn't about race", *Guardian* (9 May), www.guardian.co.uk/society/2012/may/09/rochdale-grooming-trial-race

Murphy, Joe, 2012, "Baroness Warsi: Some Pakistani men think young white girls are 'fair game' for sex abuse", *London Evening Standard* (18 May), www.thisislondon.co.uk/news/politics/baroness-warsi-some-pakistani-men-think-young-white-girls-are-fair-game-for-sex-abuse-7766319.html

Office for National Statistics, 2011, "Births and Deaths in England and Wales", Statistical Bulletin.

Orr, Judith, 2012, "Rochdale sex abuse is nothing to do with race", *Socialist Worker* (19 May), www.socialistworker.co.uk/art.php?id=28456

Phillips, Melanie, 2012, "The Rochdale sex ring shows the horrific consequences of Britain's 'Islamophobia' witch-hunt", *Daily Mail* (9 May), www.dailymail.co.uk/debate/article-2141930/The-Rochdale-sex-ring-shows-horrific-consequences-Britains-Islamophobia-witch-hunt.html

Shepherd, Jessica, 2012, "Starkey makes 'cultural' link to gang jailed for sexually exploiting girls", *Guardian* (10 May), www.guardian.co.uk/culture/2012/may/10/starkey-comment-gang-sexually-exploiting-girls

Socialist Worker, 2011, "Jack Straw opens door to racism again" (15 January), www.socialistworker.co.uk/art.php?id=23571

Vallely, Paul, 2012, "Child sex grooming: the Asian question", *Independent* (10 May), www.independent.co.uk/news/uk/crime/child-sex-grooming-the-asian-question-7729068.html

Resistance: the best Olympic spirit

Dave Zirin is one of the most celebrated Marxists writing about sport today. He spoke to Gareth Edwards about the contradictory nature of the Olympic Games

With the Olympics rapidly approaching, what does history tell us London can expect over the coming months?
You will get displacement, you will get an incredible police crackdown and you will get one hell of a bill when the party is over—which then has to be paid for. Wherever the Olympics go they act as a neoliberal Trojan horse showing up festooned in a kind of celebratory bunting, and there is an effort to marshal the nation behind it. Some people have dubbed it "celebration capitalism" insofar as you are meant to celebrate the excess and greed. Yet when all is said and done you are in some financial trouble. The explosion of debt after the 2004 Athens Games is one of the least discussed aspects of the current crisis in Greece. These Olympics were roughly 1,000 percent over budget! The budget for the 2012 Games has already increased from £2.4 billion to £11 billion and I have no doubt that the eventual figure will be far greater.

And what is particularly interesting and frightening about the London Olympics is the level of security on show and its capacity to operate. The security costs have already doubled to more than £550 million. If it were really about terrorism you wouldn't have missile launchers on residential buildings. Do they really expect an aerial assault from Al Qaeda? These are visual representations of state power intended more to send a message to the local population than it has to do with any kind of external threat. It is about intimidation, increasing surveillance on ordinary people's lives, and it is about a message from the International Olympic Committee (IOC) and the Cameron government that the enemy is internal. The Olympics are a huge stage-managed television spectacle and they have to make sure that it runs without a hitch, and we are the hitch.

Obviously there has been repression at previous Games. In particular I am thinking of Mexico City in 1968 where the state police killed hundreds of students and workers who were protesting. You could also look at the example of Atlanta in 1996 where, in crude fashion, the police filled out over 9,000 arrest citations with the wording "black male" in advance of the event. Compare that to London where you will have the latest security technology, with drones flying overhead, setting surface to air missiles on the tops of buildings, a warship in the Thames. It will be very interesting to see how people respond in the face of that kind of overt technological capacity to crush dissent.

I also think these are going to be the last Olympics in quite some time to be staged in a standard Western democracy. The IOC is looking more and more to extend its reach into the BRIC countries, like Russia and Brazil who will host the Summer Games in 2016. There is little doubt that we will see the Olympics taking place in India in the near future.

It says a lot about the Olympics that there was no mention of sport in the answer to that question!
Don't get me wrong, I love sport. And I love Olympic sport specifically for two reasons. Firstly because it is one of the few times that you actually get a diversity of sporting events on display. In the US especially we are fed a steady diet of American football, baseball and basketball—and it is almost entirely dominated by male sports stars. And this is the second reason—that the Olympic Games are one of the few times when women athletes get to have the highest possible stage. But in the hands of the IOC the Olympics have about as much to do with sports as the war in Iraq had to do with democracy.

This is not about a celebration of sport, games or play; it is absolutely for the 1 percent. If this were really about sport and nothing else, the Olympics would be held in the same location every four years so as to avoid the massive disruption to successive host cities. And if they are to be held in various cities then at the very least tickets should be available to all people at a decent price, but that is simply not what takes place. Once you get past the 1 percent, the five-star hotels, the special access in the stadiums, it's not that at all. As John Carlos says, "The reason they have the Olympics every four years is that it takes them that long to count all the money!" People may deny the reality of what role the Games are playing and what effect they are having on a given country when they go there—just as people can wrap themselves in the notion of democracy with the war in Iraq—but this is about profit for the corporations and the IOC.

It seems that in an effort to sell the idea of hosting the Olympics politicians have developed a narrative of "legacy". They argue that staging the event will create jobs, prompt investment and urban regeneration, and get more children playing sport. How much truth is there in these claims?

Every Olympics has a legacy narrative. It is the only way that they can justify the vast government spending on a one-off event. People simply would not tolerate this so they are forced into dressing it up as urban regeneration and renewal. There is this big mythology about the Olympics transforming a host city into a world leader. They sell it by saying that they are turning your home into a kind of international Mecca. They say that the Olympics are good for tourism but I can point to studies that say people stay away from host cities *because* of the Olympics.

I remember Tony Blair being asked if he would still have bid for the Games if he had know in advance what kind of disruption they would cause, and he was shocked they even asked the question. He said, "This is London. Of course we can do this. It isn't some Third World country." His contempt was astounding. The problem is that there is so much history, so much evidence, which says the opposite. If you go to Montreal you can still see facilities built for the Olympics in 1976 that are abandoned. In Greece there are news reports of people sleeping in old, disused Olympic venues because of the effects of austerity. A lot of these sports facilities are so specific to the event that once the Games are over they simply have no use value.

The Olympics have their origin in the late 19th century, a creation of a French aristocrat, Pierre de Coubertin. Were these Games any different from those we see today, and how have they developed over the years?

There are a lot of points that you can look at. Certainly a lot of people put the original sin of the Games at their founding in 1896 and on Pierre de Coubertin. It is no coincidence that the Olympics start at the same time as modern empire. These things go hand in hand, this idea of the celebration of the nation-states which puts itself above sport. At that time there is a collection of various dukes and princes—people freaked out by the thought of global revolution and who celebrated the dominance of one nation over another while dividing up the world. Another point in history when you can really notice a shift is, of course, in 1936 when the Games were staged in Hitler's Germany. Before this point the Olympics really were a kind of stripped down affair, where people would get together and play sports. But it was Hitler and his department for propaganda that took it to a whole new level. For instance, the running of the Olympics torch was the brainchild of Joseph Goebbels. The idea of having marching armies, having athletes themselves march as though they are in an army— all of these things are part of the glorification of Nazism, which you can see as nationalism on steroids. So Nazism and the Olympics went together hand in glove. What is so fascinating is that this all happens in 1936, but when the Olympics return in 1948, after Second World War, you still have all the trappings of those Nazi Games.

Another watershed moment comes in 1984 with the Los Angeles Games. The LA Olympics *were* the US Olympics. Ronald Reagan opened the Games and the boycott by the Soviet Union and its satellites meant that it was a gold medal glut for the host nation. The head of the LA Games organising committee was Peter Ueberroth, a man who was one step ahead of corporate America before they caught up with a vengeance. Almost out of nowhere he came up with the idea that corporations would underwrite everything, put their branding everywhere, see everything as a marketing opportunity. Not a dollar of taxpayers' money was spent on the Olympics in that year, and it is estimated that they made in excess of $230 million—the first Games to turn a profit since 1932. This was important because it meant that staging the Olympics then appeared to be a viable and profitable venture for potential host cities, and this at a time when even some IOC members were beginning to doubt the future of the Games.

What you have seen develop since then, in a similar fashion to areas like the banking sector, is a situation where the debt of the Games becomes collectivised and the profit becomes privatised. In 1984 corporate America hadn't got the idea of being the sponsors of the event while at the same time having public money foot the bill, although there was a history of host cities being left crippled with mountainous debt. Montreal hosted the Olympics in 1976 and did not manage to pay off its debt until 2006. It took 30 years to pay off their Olympic debt, which I think is going to seem modest compared to Athens and possibly London as well. That model is now the dominant model and you now have official corporate partners such as Dow Chemicals, McDonald's and BP. It's bizarre that you should now have this private-public partnership where the corporations are only paying for 2 percent of the cost and yet making enormous profits.

You mention the importance of the Berlin Games. They are remembered primarily for the outstanding athletic feats of Jesse Owens, the African-American track and field star who won four gold medals and made a mockery of Hitler's claims of Aryan superiority in the process. Yet very few people are aware that there was a mass campaign in the US to boycott the 1936 Games.

I have a very different view on this to a lot of sports writers, many of whom view Owens as an example of terrific heroism. It is often described in terms of Owens spitting in Hitler's eye by winning four gold medals, and then Hitler refusing to shake his hand. This is a myth. Hitler was not even at the event, precisely because he didn't want to be put in the position of having to congratulate a black athlete. In 1940 Owens campaigned for the Republicans, saying, "Hitler didn't snub me: Franklin D Roosevelt snubbed me." At this time it was not uncommon for prominent African-Americans to be Republicans, because until the civil rights movement the Democrats were still seen as the party of slavery while the Republicans were the party of Abraham Lincoln. It's a history that both parties like to keep silent about, though obviously for different reasons.

But when Owens comes home he is still subjected to racism, and ends his career racing horses in exhibition events. Indeed, Owens does not have a role in the US Olympic movement until the 1960s when they employ him as an elder statesman in an attempt to dissuade the younger generation of black athletes from using the Olympics as a platform from which to air their grievances. It shows that even the greatest athletes in the history of the Games were subjected to racism.

The interesting and little-known fact is that there was a boycott movement in the US, even though there was very little knowledge as to who the Nazis were, what their plans were, what their agenda was. You didn't have to be Leon Trotsky to know the threat that Hitler represented, although it helped. People had an idea: if you politically understood their class composition and where they were coming from, there were things you could foresee. It's not as though you had an international human rights campaign around the regime in the 1930s, but you did have a lot of concern. The Amateur Athletic Union, which included all of the athletes in the US, collected over half a million signatures in favour of a boycott, and a majority of their members wanted to boycott. And you had the head of the National Association for the Advancement of Colored People, Walter White, openly calling for a boycott, saying that the Nazis were white supremacists and asking why anyone would want to legitimise what they are doing.

It is at this point that Avery Brundage steps onto the scene of history. He was the head of the US Olympics Committee, a former Olympian himself, having competed in the 1912 Games, and the future head of the IOC. He was also a Nazi sympathiser, an anti-Semite and a white supremacist. This was somebody who was kicked out of the America First Committee—an anti-Semitic, right wing, anti-war organisation—for being too anti-Semitic. In the run-up to the 1936 Games he meets with Hitler and other Olympic officials for the press, before giving a glowing report about the preparations in Berlin. Brundage claimed to have also met with Jewish sportspeople and leaders—although there is no proof that he actually did—and goes on to imply that criticism of the Nazi regime is nothing more than communist propaganda.

People have compared Brundage to J Edgar Hoover. These were two men who were absolutely despised but somehow proved incredibly durable, especially skilled in the art of keeping power. Brundage, like Hoover, knew everybody's weak points, what scandals they were involved in, and was never shy about pushing buttons if it meant keeping his own grip on power. His assurances about the participation of Jewish athletes in Germany certainly played a part in ensuring the vote in favour of boycotting the games was (very narrowly) defeated.

Not only was there a mass campaign to boycott the 1936 Games but an alternative Workers' Olympics was scheduled to take place in Barcelona. The 1920s and 1930s saw many such events organised by the Workers' Sport movement. Can you tell us a little bit about that?

Barcelona had lost the vote to host the 1936 Olympics four years previously. Worker athletes arranged a Workers' Olympics in protest at the Games in Berlin but they were halted before they began by Franco's fascist uprising. The fact that the Barcelona Games were explicitly anti-fascist is important because it pulls away the fiction that nobody knew what Hitler was about at that time, and that Avery Brundage cannot really be blamed for delivering the Olympics to Nazi Germany. The symbolic value of those Games not going ahead and the Olympics taking place in Germany was huge. The credibility of the Olympics and the credibility of fascism were in question and eventually the two walked very comfortably hand in hand.

More broadly there is a history—when the left has been more powerful—of doing things like the Barcelona Games or the Chicago Counter-Olympics in 1932. Unlike the Olympics these were integrated games. Since 1982 you've had the Gay Games—they weren't allowed to use the word "Olympic" and were threatened with lawsuits by the IOC. If you think of some of the AIDS hysteria in the 1980s then you can see how radical the Gay Games were. They had HIV-positive athletes competing at a time when idiot scientists were saying that you could catch AIDS from handshakes and toilet seats. It was hugely powerful. In these examples you can see the potential for sports to operate in a very different way, because I do believe that they can bring people together. Sports are like fire: you can use fire to make a meal or fire can burn down your house. When you realise what the IOC have been doing all these years then you realise that they are real arsonists, city after city after city.

There is a wonderful line in Christopher A Shaw's book, **Five Ring Circus: Myths and Realities of the Olympic Games***, where he lists the people who have run the IOC: "Of nine actual or acting presidents, the IOC has put three barons, two counts, two businessmen, an overt fascist and a fascist sympathiser in its top job." Is that a fair reflection of the IOC?*

The starting point is to understand that the IOC, who a lot of people won't know are a non-voting representative in the United Nations, are a stateless actor, with a huge amount of power. This is an unaccountable and decidedly shady organisation who are sitting on untold amounts of money and don't seem to pay tax anywhere on the planet. They ensure that they—or any of the corporate sponsors of the Olympics—are not liable for any cost overruns associated with staging the Games.

It is interesting to chart the development of the IOC. They started as a collection of royalists and monarchs, then they became a den of fascist organisers, and they have since morphed, over the past 25 years or so, into being a group of staunch corporatists. The corruption scandals—not just the pay-offs and bribes but also the use of prostitutes and the trafficking of women—are something that has been a feature of so many bids to secure the Olympics. The amount of impropriety is simply staggering. I would recommend people read either *Five Ring Circus* or the book *Lords of the Rings* by Andrew Jennings and Vyv Simson, because the story of the IOC is simply unbelievable.

They have an enormous amount of leverage over people who hold state power. This is a very ugly group of people who, judging by their history, represent the worst of the worst. It is remarkable how selective we are. Politicians in America, like Strom Thurmond or Jesse Helms, who were involved with racist organisations in the 1950s, are still stained by it years later but with the IOC it all gets forgotten. Not only was there Avery Brundage but also there was Juan Antonio Samaranch who was a youth fighter for Franco. There were times in the history of the IOC when you would have had to go back to outtakes of the Nuremberg trials to find so many fascists in one location.

Given the history of the Olympics and the IOC, how would you explain the continued popularity of the Games?
The whole concept of the medal count should be anathema to the spirit of the Olympics yet I've heard a lot of people say that they don't find the Olympics as fascinating since the end of Cold War. You need to have a proper enemy! So obviously nationalism plays a large part. But there is also a mystique about the Olympics. To achieve at the Olympics is to achieve under the brightest possible spotlight, with the widest possible audience. There is recognition that in sports, at least sports under capitalism, this really counts for something.

Anyone who has played or watched sport knows that your body reacts differently when you are under pressure. People want to see it because of the stakes, and that only adds to the tension. It's about achievement at the highest possible level. There is a paradox of the Olympics. Women's participation at the Olympics acts as a challenge to male authority. It's about their strength, it's about their endurance and it's about their not positioning themselves to be pleasing to men. Because the IOC are so retrograde on every imaginable front it's hardly surprising that they are an organisation rife with sexism. Women and men—or at least men who aren't in a cage of sexism—want to see women athletes perform, and this is one of the few places available.

Going all the way back to the start of the modern Olympics, when Pierre de Coubertin dismissed women playing sport as "impractical, uninteresting, unaesthetic and incorrect", the IOC have treated female athletes disgracefully.
The IOC only allowed women to be members of their club in 1981. Women were not allowed to run a marathon until 1984, and as recently as the 1950s they were debating the elimination of all the women's track and field events so that the audience would be, as they put it, "spared the spectacle of watching women trying to look and act like men". There were debates in the 1950s about not allowing black women from any nation to participate in track and field events because, as one member of the IOC said, they were hermaphrodites. You still hear the echoes of that kind of sexism and racism today. Just look at the case of Caster Semenya, who won the women's 800 metres title at the World Athletics Championship in 2009. Here is a phenomenal athlete who has had to endure all manner of allegations and innuendo simply because she does not fit the stereotypical body shape of a female runner.

This idea of binary gender norms is something that the Olympics—indeed the whole sports world—are going to have to address whether they like it or not. There will be more and more transgender athletes and this arbitrary dichotomy is going to be challenged. The idea that boys play in one place and girls in another is not something inherent to human nature; it is something that has had to be enforced and codified. Of course there will be different divisions of athletes, but why base this on gender? Why not on strength or speed or body mass? It is arbitrary and yet at the same time not arbitrary—it becomes yet another way to divide us and make us feel different from each other.

The IOC constantly state that the Olympics are a politically neutral event. How would you assess that claim?
The neutrality claim has worked in very interesting ways. People say that you are bringing politics into the Olympics if you try to keep settler Rhodesia and apartheid South Africa out of the Games, as though it is not political to welcome them into this "community of nations". One person's "keep politics out of sport" is another person's "political decision". If you listen to Brundadge's speech after the Israeli athletes were killed at the Munich Olympics in 1972, he equates their death with keeping Rhodesia and South Africa out of the Games. Essentially he is saying that this is what happens when the Olympics become politicised. He doesn't call for a day off from the Games; it was simply: "The Games must go on." A shameless decision.

Historically you have two kinds of boycott: boycotts from above and boycotts from below. Simply put, the former should be rejected; the latter should be embraced. So a prime example of the boycott from above would be the US refusing to go to the Moscow Olympics in 1980, or the Soviet bloc boycotting the 1984 LA Games. This was all just state posturing and Cold War rhetoric. Boycotts from below would include those campaigns to isolate apartheid South Africa where they used the claim of Olympic neutrality to their advantage. When I interviewed Dennis Brutus he told me, "Our goal was to use the Olympic Charter and hang South Africa with it." The IOC's Charter has all kinds of flowery, beautiful and, I would even say, admirable language—about athletics creating a global community, about rejecting any kind of prejudice—but it is all in the abstract. To quote those words and then ask why the IOC were supporting South Africa and Rhodesia was an incredibly powerful statement.

Dennis Brutus did more to leverage sports to make an impact on politics than anybody else in history. His organisational genius and his political sharpness led him to see sports as a place where ideas could find an audience. It is no doubt that this helped to enlighten masses of people as to the plight of black people in apartheid South Africa. Going strictly by the Charter of the Games, equality of opportunity is a prerequisite for being part of international sport. I would argue that the sporting world should be a part of the Boycott, Divestment and Sanctions movement against Israel. For that matter I would quite happily sign a petition saying that the US shouldn't be allowed in the Olympics because of what they have done in Iraq and Afghanistan.

Grassroots protests have become part and parcel of the modern Olympics. Campaigns seem to have sprung up in every host city as people protest at the expense lavished on the Games and the disruption they inevitably cause. How important is it to demonstrate against the Olympics?
People have always protested against the Olympics and in some cases they have met with terrible repercussions. You can find people protesting against the Olympics all the way back in 1936 in Hitler's Germany. That should tell us something about our own responsibility. The most famous protest was in Mexico City in 1968. Students and workers demonstrated in huge numbers over a whole range of issues—and connected that to the Olympics. And that is all the more reason why, when you are in a place like London, where people can assumedly assemble without the worst kinds of repression, that there is a responsibility that the victims of the 2012 Olympiad have a voice.

I was impressed when I was in London with the amount of campaigning groups getting active around issues to do with the Olympics. Whether we are talking about militarisation, the police crackdown on dissent, gentrification, the housing displacement issue, people certainly wanted to do something about it—not just among the people you would expect, those people who are already seasoned campaigners, but among regular working class folk. A lot of people are saying that these Games are a waste of time, a waste of money and a terrible disruption. There is real discontent; it's about organising it. I think a big problem is that often the left in general is so dismissive of sports as an avenue of struggle that the effort isn't made to try and articulate what these sporting events actually represent—an opportunity for corporations and governments to carry out their neoliberal agendas even more aggressively.

Perhaps most famously the Olympics became an arena of struggle at the Mexico Games in 1968, when the African-American athletes Tommie Smith and John Carlos gave Black Power salutes on the medal rostrum.
A lot of people remember the moment of John Carlos and Tommie Smith raising their fists, but they don't realise that there was a movement called

the Olympic Project for Human Rights (OPHR). They stood on four principles: they wanted South Africa and Rhodesia uninvited from the Olympics, they wanted Muhammad Ali's world heavyweight boxing title to be restored, they wanted Avery Brundage to step down as president of the IOC, and they wanted more African-American assistant coaches hired.

If these demands were not met then they were going to call for a boycott of the Mexico Olympics, not just by black American athletes, but by *all* athletes, black and white, who supported their cause. These demands have been proven right by history and that is one of the reasons why Smith and Carlos have been embraced in recent years. People are concerned not to stand on the wrong side in retrospect. The boycott failed, partly because the IOC did withdraw their invitations to South Africa and Rhodesia, and partly because, as John Carlos says, athletes "followed the carrot". Smith and Carlos were faced with a choice: do we stay at home or do we go and try to represent the movement? They had a plan: should they get to the medal rostrum, they would not only wear their gloves but also go barefoot to protest poverty, wear beads to protest lynchings, and wear buttons that said OPHR.

Carlos says that when they made it to the medal stand and bowed their heads he was thinking of the movement, of the struggle, of the hundreds of Mexican students and workers who had been killed before the Games—people who they had been attempting to make contact with in advance. There were other acts of defiance. The Australian Peter Norman, who finished second in the 200 metres, wore an OPHR button in solidarity. The American rowing eight—all white and Harvard schooled—came out in support of Smith and Carlos. Lee Evans, Larry James and Ron Freeman wore black berets to the 400 metres medal ceremony, but removed them during the national anthem. The Games will be remembered, however, for the action of Smith and Carlos. It is the most iconic image in the history of American protest. For this they paid a terrible price for many, many years. But they regret nothing. The people who do have regrets are the track and field athletes of 1968 who did nothing.

The Syrian crucible

Jonathan Maunder

The Arab revolutions have been a great inspiration for the struggle against capitalism and imperialism across the world. They have inspired and fed into a global mood of alienation and anger against the system as expressed in strikes, occupations and protests.[1]

However, the revolutionary process has developed unevenly across the region. In Tunisia and Egypt quick advances were made, with Ben Ali and Mubarak overthrown in a matter of weeks. In Libya Gaddafi was deposed following a longer struggle which ultimately relied upon NATO military intervention. In Yemen, Saleh was removed following a deal which leaves his regime intact. At the time of writing the situation in Syria appears to be following a different trajectory, with a stalemate emerging between the regime of Bashar al-Assad and the popular uprising.

Some on the left have viewed the uprising fundamentally in geopolitical terms, as a clash between the West and its regional allies, manipulating the uprising to advance their interests, and the Assad regime, which has represented a challenge to Western domination in the region.[2] I argue that while the geopolitical dimension is important, it needs to be integrated with an understanding of developments within Syria since

1:   Thanks to Anne Alexander, Simon Assaf, Alex Callinicos, Joseph Choonara and Sam Southgate for their extremely useful comments and discussions on an earlier draft of this article.
2:   See Amin, 2012; Galloway, 2011; Ibrahim 2012; Ramadani, 2012.

2000, which have seen a breakdown in the historic "social pact" under-pinning Ba'ath Party rule, leading to an intensification of class inequality and state authoritarianism. In this sense the Syrian uprising is motivated by the same issues and concerns as the other Arab revolutions. This context is vital in order to understand the Syrian uprising in its totality. I argue that, like the regimes of Ben Ali and Mubarak, the Assad regime represents a ruling class fundamentally opposed to the interests of Syrian workers and the poor. Furthermore, its position towards both imperialism and the resistance movements in Palestine and Lebanon is deeply contra-dictory, reflecting its geo-strategic interests as a ruling class.

The working class in Syria has not yet exercised its collective power through strikes on the same level as it has in Tunisia and Egypt, where mass strikes were vital to the early successes of the revolutions. I argue that, despite serious challenges, the Syrian working class has the potential power to play such a role, and that this is the only way to fully realise the goals of the uprising for real freedom, equality and democracy. Furthermore, the development of a confident, self-organised workers' movement is the best defence against imperialist intervention and manipulation.

I do not provide here a detailed account of how the uprising began and has developed since February 2011.[3] The aim of this article is to try and under-stand the nature of the Assad regime in Syria, the social and economic roots of the uprising, and assess the prospects for a workers' movement to emerge which can provide an alternative to the regime and imperialist intervention.

The political economy of the Syrian regime

In order to understand the nature of the regime it is necessary to start with the historical context in which it emerged. The period following Syrian independence from France in 1946 was one of social turmoil in which the different class interests of those involved in the national liberation struggle came to the fore. The landowners constituted a conservative force, fighting to maintain a feudal system in the countryside, while peasants and workers fought for a more equal distribution of land and wealth and for meaningful democracy.[4] The small industrial capitalist class, deeply afraid of the move-ments from below, vacillated between cooperation and conflict with the landlords, and failed to push through industrialisation.[5]

3: For a concise and accessible overview of the uprising see Assaf, 2012. For a more detailed account see International Crisis Group (ICG), 2011.
4: Petran, 1972, pp80-106.
5: Heydemann, 1999.

This period saw important struggles from below which helped to make Syria "the political and cultural mecca of the Arab world" at this time.[6] In 1946 strikes forced the passage of advanced labour laws, including the establishment of the right to strike, leading to a tripling of union membership. A national peasant uprising in 1950 was followed by the first peasant congress in the Arab world in Aleppo in 1951.[7] These movements coalesced around nationalist and socialist currents such as the Ba'ath Party, the Arab Socialist Party and the Communist Party.

However, to different degrees these political forces dissipated and then suppressed the popular struggles. The Ba'ath Party had a narrow middle class base and a nationalist ideology which combined opposition to imperialism and the landowning class with hostility to class struggle from below. The Arab Socialist Party had a wider peasant base but surrendered its political independence by merging with the Ba'ath. The Communist Party, following the Stalinist strategy of the time, vacillated between the workers' and peasants' struggles and the "progressive nationalists" of the Ba'ath. In 1955 the three parties formed an electoral alliance under the name of the National Front.[8]

In 1958 a group of army officers, terrified by the movement from below, led Syria into a union with Nasser's Egypt, forming the United Arab Republic (UAR). This was supported by the Ba'ath and not opposed by the Communist Party. The reforms of the UAR period laid the basis for the "social pact" which would become the foundation of Ba'ath Party rule in the following decades. This involved land redistribution, establishing social provision for workers and the poor, and industrialisation, in exchange for complete state control of the popular movements. The right to strike was repealed in 1959 and all independent trade unions and peasant organisations were banned.[9]

The UAR collapsed in 1961 but was followed by a Ba'ath military coup in 1963 which retained the "social pact" model. The Ba'ath used the power of the state to push forward industrialisation which meant challenging the immediate interests of the ruling class through land redistribution and nationalisations as well as blocking independent organisation by workers and peasants.[10]

Syria's entry into the UAR and the 1963 coup can be seen as examples of what Tony Cliff called "deflected permanent revolution", a deviation

---

6:   Petran, 1972, p111.

7:   For the struggles in this period see Petran 1972, pp86-88 and p101.

8:   Petran, 1972, p114.

9:   Petran, 1972.

10:   Heydemann, 1999.

from the process of permanent revolution as outlined by the Russian revolutionary Leon Trotsky. Trotsky described how, in countries emerging from colonialism, the working class would have to take on the task of breaking the dominance of the old feudal ruling class and, in doing so, lead the struggle towards socialism. However, due to the political forces leading it and its relatively small size in comparison to the mass of the peasantry, the Syrian working class did not manage to establish itself as the leading force in society. At the same time, the industrial and agrarian ruling class was too timid and divided to take up the task of economic and political development. Cliff's theory described how in this situation radicalised sections of the middle class connected to the state could drive through national development. The results of this "deflected permanent revolution" were forms of state capitalism, not socialism.[11] Cliff describes the outlook of this social layer:

> They hope for reform from above and would dearly love to hand the new world over to a grateful people, rather than see the liberating struggle of a self-conscious and freely associated people result in a new world for themselves. They care a lot for measures to drag their nation out of stagnation, but very little for democracy. They embody the drive for industrialisation, for capital accumulation, for national resurgence. Their power is in direct relation to the feebleness of other classes, and their political nullity.[12]

Cliff's theory provides important insights into the role played by the Syrian Ba'ath in the 1960s and by Hafez al-Assad following the coup which brought him to power in 1970. It highlights how this process involved the suppression of struggles from below, which is why the 2011 uprising is so significant.

Hafez's "corrective movement" can be seen as the point in the process of "deflected permanent revolution" when state capitalism is fully established and any connections of the state apparatus to the revolutionary struggles of the past are broken. A member of the minority Muslim Alawi sect, Hafez used sectarianism to build a loyal core of Alawi army officers and to purge Sunni Muslim officers, before cementing an alliance with the Sunni bourgeoisie, to whom he offered new opportunities to invest and trade.[13] Sectarianism was therefore used to create "an advance guard of

---

11: For an introduction to the theory of state capitalism see Haynes, 2009. For a recent discussion of the theory of deflected permanent revolution see Choonara, 2011.

12: Cliff, 1963.

13: See Batatu, 1981, and Haddad, 2012a.

an elite or class coalition",[14] part of an attempt to establish a stable ruling class. Hafez's rule did bring stability in comparison to the repeated military coups after independence, but it was a stability built on the basis of smothering popular struggle from below. The Syrian Communist Party were complicit in this process through their alliance with the Ba'ath since the 1950s, who they described as a "basic revolutionary force" which had adopted "scientific socialism", rather than a clear orientation on the mass struggles of peasants and workers.[15] This highlights the danger of the left putting its faith in supposedly "progressive" and "anti-imperialist" nationalist leaders rather than in mass struggles from below, a mistake made by some today who have illusions in the Assad regime.[16]

The years from 1970 to 1982 saw a substantial growth in the size of the Syrian working class. Following land redistribution many peasants ended up with holdings which were too small to support a family, and the reforms made no provision for access to machinery and water to irrigate land. The result was proletarianisation in the countryside.[17] Between 1970 and 1981 the number of full-time peasants decreased from 440,000 to 290,000, forming a pool of wage-labour which was drawn upon by larger landowners who had increased their share of land.[18] These peasants also went to work in the new factories and mines. The industrial labour force increased between 1972 and 1982 from 276,515 to 433,609.[19]

By the early 1980s the number of the population in relative poverty had declined, due to the impact of reforms against the worst inequalities of the post-independence era, the expansion of relatively well-paid jobs in the state apparatus and remittances from Syrian workers in the Gulf states following the 1970s oil boom. However, life for many workers was still tough. The 1981 housing census showed that in Aleppo, Syria's largest city, 62 percent of the population were living in overcrowded and cramped conditions, including 20 percent living with more than four persons per room.[20] Interviews in 1980 with Damascus factory workers revealed similar overcrowding, regular flouting of employment laws by bosses, and workers threatened with fines or imprisonment simply for leaving state companies.[21]

14: Van Dam, 1996, p141.
15: Marshall, 1995.
16: See, for example, West, 2012.
17: Perthes, 1997, p86; Ababsa, 2010.
18: Perthes, 1997, p85.
19: Longuenesse, 1985, p22.
20: Perthes, 1997, p131.
21: Longuenesse, 1985, pp20, 23.

In the mid-1980s the regime responded to poor economic growth and declining foreign investment by slashing wages, benefits and subsidies on everyday goods. The result was a reversal of the gains made in the preceding period so that by the mid-1990s 70 percent of the population were living below the relative poverty line.[22] The passing of Investment Law Number 10 in 1991 opened up new areas of the economy to private capital.[23] By the mid-1990s Volker Perthes could write that "an upper class has emerged both greater in number and wealthier than the bourgeoisie of the pre-Ba'athist era".[24]

This was the situation when Bashar al-Assad came to power in 2000 following his father's death. Bashar went even further in opening up the economy to private capital, cutting back the social functions of the state and relying increasingly on its repressive functions. The historic "social pact" underpinning Ba'athist state capitalist rule since the 1960s was significantly weakened. It is this context which is vital for understanding the roots of the 2011 uprising and why it spread so quickly and has proved so difficult to crush.

The social roots of the 2011 uprising

Bashar's neoliberal reforms occurred at the same time as a number of important events effecting Syrian society. Perhaps the most significant of these was the drought of 2008-10, which caused tens of thousands of peasants to flee to the cities.[25] Around the same time thousands of Syrians working abroad who sent remittances back to their families returned following the Syrian withdrawal from Lebanon in 2005 and the Dubai financial crisis in 2008. Further to this was the arrival of 1.5 million Iraqi refugees following the 2003 invasion by the US and Britain. These groups sought work and housing largely in the impoverished peripheries of the cities.[26] It is these areas that have been the main centres of urban opposition during the 2011 uprising.

The impact of these events was intensified by the neoliberal reforms. The effect of the drought was made worse by the privatisation of state lands in 2000, which led to an increase in peasant evictions and intensive commercial farming which depleted the water table.[27] The state-controlled Agricultural

---

22: Perthes, 1997, p117.
23: Polling, 1994.
24: Perthes, 1997, p109.
25: Ababsa, 2010, p83.
26: ICG, 2011.
27: Ababsa, 2010, p84; ICG, 2011.

Workers Union pointed to subsidy cuts to fuel and the abolition of price controls on pesticides and animal feed as further causes of rural distress.[28] In the cities the abolition of rent controls and an influx of Gulf investment in real estate made it increasingly difficult to obtain affordable housing.[29] Reductions in import tariffs put many small manufacturers out of business, contributing to already high unemployment rates, particularly among the young. Wages declined in relative terms, following subsidy cuts and inflation, with 61 percent of workers earning less than $190 a month in 2010.[30] Other reforms, such as cutting corporation tax, further increased the surge in wealth for the rich.[31] In contrast to Egypt, where there was wholesale privatisation of sections of the economy and opening up to global capital, neoliberal reform in Syria often involved alliances between private capital and the state, an undermining of social provision and workers' conditions *within* the state sector and strengthening ties to regional capital. So in the World Bank's measurement of how open economies are to foreign capital Syria is ranked very low compared to Egypt, but in the measurement for "labour flexibility"—the extent of control bosses have over workers—the two countries are much closer.[32] Across society, forms of social provision which workers had come to expect were undermined. In health and education creeping privatisation and the introduction of charges created a two-tier system with exclusive universities and hospitals for the rich.[33]

The impact of these reforms on Syrian society was profound. By the mid-2000s the World Bank's index of inequality placed Syria lower than Egypt.[34] As the Syrian economist Samar Seifan puts it, "Syria used to have a social pyramid characterised by a wide base, a big middle stratum and a low peak; under economic reform, the middle stratum are shrinking while a rich stratum is emerging at the top, resulting in a social pyramid with a broad base, a narrowing middle stratum and a higher peak".[35]

Similarly Raymond Hinnebusch and Soren Schmidt have described the years preceding the uprising as representing "a decisive turn…in which authoritarian power is put in the service of a new stratum of crony

28: *Syria Report*, 2011.
29: Hinnebusch, 2012, p102.
30: Seifan, 2010, p127.
31: Economist Intelligence Unit (EIU), 2008, p3.
32: Zorob, 2008, p6; Aita, 2009, p31.
33: Aita, 2009, p50; Seifan, 2010, p19.
34: World Bank, 2005.
35: Seifan, 2010, p24.

capitalists".[36] Echoes of this reality could be heard within the regime, with an internal memorandum to Assad from his advisory committee in 2009 warning of popular perceptions that the state was "abandoning the poor for the sake of the rich".[37] One week before the 2011 uprising a peasant from the agricultural district around the southern city of Deraa presciently told a journalist, "You cannot keep pressuring people like this. You simply cannot. All it needs is a spark".[38]

The increasing class polarisation in Syrian society also meant that the relationship between the state and the people became increasingly based on harassment and corruption. Transparency International moved Syria from 69th position in 2003 to 93rd position in 2006 on its international corruption index.[39] Widespread alienation from the authorities fed trends in popular culture, with TV dramas, novels and cartoons satirising corrupt officials.[40]

The unravelling since 2000 of the historic "social pact" forged by the Ba'ath Party in the 1960s and 1970s is therefore key to understanding the roots of the 2011 uprising. As Bassam Haddad puts it:

> Deep economic deterioration, elite capture of public policy, and authoritarian rule…created a pressure cooker effect for many years, leading to a sense of despair across broad sectors of the population… What tilted the calculus of individuals and groups in Syria in terms of going to the streets is the feeling that, after Tunisia and Egypt, they can actually do something about it.[41]

This unravelling has revealed the fundamental division in Syria between a corrupt and authoritarian ruling class and the mass of workers and the poor. It shows clearly why the left should have no illusions in Assad being somehow more worthy of support than Mubarak or Ben Ali. It also highlights the deep social roots from which the uprising has emerged, which will make it difficult for both the regime and foreign governments to contain and shape it in their interests.

The foreign policy of the Syrian regime

Since Hafez came to power, Syria has been seen as the key "rejectionist" state in the Middle East, due to his refusal to sign a peace treaty with Israel,

---

36: Hinnebusch and Schmidt, 2009, p4.
37: Hinnebusch, 2012, p102.
38: *Syria Report*, 2011.
39: Seifan, 2010, p28.
40: Lesch, 2005, p223.
41: Haddad, 2012a, p121.

and Bashar's support for the Hamas and Hezbollah resistance movements in Palestine and Lebanon and alliance with Iran.

But far from representing a principled anti-imperialism Syrian foreign policy since 1970 has involved a series of manoeuvres motivated by the geopolitical and internal economic interests of the Syrian state capitalist ruling class. These manoeuvres have led to repeated changes in relations with international powers, primarily the US and the Soviet Union, regional powers, such as the Gulf States, and the resistance movements in Palestine and Lebanon.

The humiliating defeat of the Arab armies by Israel in the 1967 war was the key event shaping Hafez's foreign policy on coming to power. The war led to Israel's occupation of Syria's Golan Heights, just 50 miles south of Damascus, which continues to this day. Following this Hafez was determined to achieve conventional military parity with Israel in order to negotiate from a position of strength. This involved breaking with the idea of a popular resistance war to liberate Palestine and attempting to control the Palestinian movement in order to use it as a bargaining chip in negotiations with Israel and the US. As one study puts it, "the main issue over which Hafiez came to power was opposition to a guerrilla war against Israel".[42] Early on Hafez launched an attack on the Palestinian guerrilla movement based in Syria, arresting its leaders and closing its offices. When Jordan's King Hussein launched his first assault on Palestinian guerrillas based in Jordan in 1970, Syria intervened on the side of the Palestinians, but a year later Assad seized arms sent for the rebels by Algeria and offered only diplomatic protests when Hussein launched his final assault on the Palestinians.[43]

The build-up of conventional military power allowed Syria to join Egypt in launching a surprise attack on Israel in 1973 and inflict significant military losses on it. Hafez used the authority of this victory to open up politically and economically to the US while refusing to join Egypt and Jordan in "peace talks'"with Israel.[44] US recognition of Syria's importance in the region was summed up at the time by Henry Kissinger: "There can be no war in the Middle East without Egypt and no peace without Syria".[45]

After inflicting a defeat on Israel Hafez now sought to further cement his control over the Palestinian resistance movement through intervention in the Lebanese civil war. In the mid-1970s an alliance of Palestinian guerrillas

---

42: Slater, 2002, p93.
43: Petran, 1972, p253.
44: Rogan, 2011, p467.
45: Traboulsi, 2007, p195.

in the Palestine Liberation Organisation (PLO) and left wing Lebanese groups were engaged in a historic challenge to the ruling class in Lebanon. Israel and the US intervened on the side of the government and the extreme-right Christian Phalangist militias.[46] Syrian troops entered Lebanon in 1976 to prop up the government. They offered protection to Christian areas enabling the Phalangist militias to go on the offensive, leading to the massacre in the Palestinian Tel al–Za'atar refugee camp in 1976.[47] Shortly afterwards Assad routed the PLO from Lebanon by sponsoring a Palestinian faction to mutiny, then assisting it in laying siege to the remaining PLO fighters around the Lebanese city of Tripoli. Robert Fisk described the scene:

> The two Palestinian camps of Badawi and Nahr Al-Bared were besieged by the mutineers, assisted by Lebanese Ba'athists and Syrian artillery batteries which shelled not only Arafat's men but the civilian population of Tripoli… I would drive through the shattered city, run through the shellfire to the hospital and ask for the number of victims. Outside the building there stood a refrigerated meat lorry packed with civilian bodies.[48]

The final betrayal of the Palestinians came in 1983 when Syria backed Elie Hobeika, leader of the infamous massacre of around 2,500 Palestinians in the Sabra and Shatila refugee camps, to be the new leader of the Christian militias. Hobeika argued that Syria had a "major role" to play in Lebanon and later fled to Damascus, receiving help from the regime in setting up his own militia.[49] Syria's intervention in Lebanon reflected Assad's desire to manipulate and control the Palestinian resistance in order to strengthen his own position in the region and possible future negotiations with Israel and the US. As well as smashing the PLO in Lebanon this strategy also involved sponsoring pro-Syrian Palestinian guerrilla groups who could be used to advance Hafez's strategic interests.[50] The same cynical sponsoring of resistance movements to bolster Syria's geopolitical position informs Bashar's strategy towards the movements today.

By the early 1990s the collapse of the Soviet Union and Syria's economic crisis prompted Hafez to make a turn towards the US. He supported the first US-led war on Iraq in 1991, helping to secure major investment from Saudi Arabia and the Gulf States throughout the 1990s. As part of this shift

46: Traboulsi, 2007, pp187-204.
47: Fisk, 2001, p85.
48: Fisk, 2001, pp529-530.
49: Fisk, 2001, p601.
50: Fisk, 2001, p569.

Hafez also sought renewed negotiations with Israel. In 1996 and 2000 a "cold peace" deal was very nearly struck in which Syria would agree to diplomatic normalisation, economic cooperation and security measures in exchange for Israel's withdrawal from the Golan Heights—justice for the Palestinians was off the agenda.[51] An Israeli government adviser later recounted, "I heard senior members of the Israeli delegation saying that an agreement was possible within two or three months. On all the issues—normalisation, security, and water—we got more than we'd gotten before".[52]

By the time Bashar came to power in 2000 following Hafez's death, the outbreak of the second Palestinian intifada, coinciding with the announcement by Israel of plans to build 1,500 new settlements in the Golan Heights, put an end to the possibility of a peace agreement with Israel.

Bashar's strategy in this period is usually seen as one of straightforward opposition to Israel and US foreign policy, in particular the Iraq War. In reality his approach has been more nuanced, reflecting the strategic dilemmas and calculations of the regime. On the one hand, support for the Palestinian and Lebanese resistance movements allowed Bashar to apply pressure on Israel without directly confronting its occupation of the Golan Heights.[53] Alliances with Iran and Iraq under Saddam Hussein had important economic and political benefits. But at the same time Bashar sought to strengthen Syria's ties to pro-Western states such as Egypt and Saudi Arabia, in order to insulate the regime from an aggressive US administration following 9/11. As Raymond Hinnebusch puts it:

> Syria was trying to position itself to manipulate two opposing regional alliance networks, the traditional pro-Western one that tied it to Cairo and Riyadh and what at times looked like a potential new anti-Western one with Iraq [under Saddam Hussein] and Iran.[54]

On an economic level this can be seen in the way that under Bashar the hostile ruling classes in Iran and the Gulf States have exploited Syrian workers and resources. While Iran built a gas pipeline and Syria's first car factory in 2007, billions of dollars of real estate investment have poured in from Saudi Arabia (including from the Bin Laden family), Kuwait, Qatar

---

51: Slater, 2002, pp94-100.
52: Slater, 2002, p100.
53: As a chant of the 2011 uprising put it, "Bashar—butcher of Damascus, coward of the Golan." Thanks to Simon Assaf for this reference.
54: Hinnebusch, 2003, p200.

and the UAE.[55] On a geopolitical level, it can be seen in the way that, as well as backing resistance to Israel and opposing the war on Iraq, Bashar cooperated with the US in sealing the border with Iraq to stop insurgents fighting the US/UK occupation and participated in the torture of "terror suspects" through the CIA's "extraordinary rendition" programme.[56]

Bashar's contradictory role in the region can be seen in the response of Saudi Arabia and Israel to the 2011 uprising. As the *New York Times* commented in May 2011 on the Saudi response:

> An initial statement of support by King Abdullah for President Bashar al-Assad has been followed by silence, along with occasional calls at Friday prayer for god to support the protesters. That silence reflects a deep ambivalence, analysts said. The [Saudi] ruling family personally dislikes Mr Assad—resenting his close ties with Iran and seeing Syria's hand in the assassination of a former Lebanese prime minister, Rafik Hariri, a Saudi ally. But they fear his overthrow will unleash sectarian violence without guaranteeing that Iranian influence will be diminished.[57]

Similarly some Israeli officials expressed concern that the fall of Assad could lead to "the freeing of Palestinian organisations from any restraints and [their belief] that the Syrian regime represents a central authority that regulates behaviour and keeps events from slipping out of control".[58] This "regulating" position was reflected in comments by the chief of Syrian intelligence in 2003 that threats of regime change against Syria from the US "could unleash groups that had hitherto been checked by Syrian intelligence networks, namely Hezbollah, Hamas and Islamic Jihad".[59]

If the position of Bashar's official enemies is not straightforward, neither is that of his supposed allies. Hamas has refused to back the regime during the uprising and has moved its political office out of Damascus, while Hezbollah's leader Hassan Nasrallah has stayed loyal, even though this threatens to undermine Hezbollah's credibility in Syria and the Arab world in general.[60]

Hafez and Bashar al-Assad's opposition to Israel and support for

---

55: Khosrokhavar, 2012, p286; Seifan, 2010, p22.
56: Salloukh, 2009; LaHood, 2005. Arar, 2003, provides a harrowing account by one victim of Syria's participation in extraordinary rendition.
57: Khosrokhavar, 2012, p289.
58: Policy Analysis Unit, 2012.
59: Salloukh, 2009, pp164-165.
60: Sadiki, 2011.

resistance movements has been shaped primarily by their geopolitical interests as representatives of a state capitalist ruling class, concerned above all to maintain their influence and strength in relation to other states. This has involved repeated manoeuvring between support, restraint and repression of these movements. In contrast to such cynical manoeuvring socialists should look to the mass struggles of the Arab revolutions as the greatest hope for challenging imperialism in the region and liberating Palestine.

Beyond stalemate?

At the time of writing the Assad regime remains in power. There is some uncertainty about what will happen if it does fall. Some argue that it will mean a boost for the US and Israel, and a further step along the road to a war with Iran. Another concern is the descent into sectarianism and civil war. All these outcomes are possible and should not be treated lightly.

The key question is whether the working class can use its collective social power in the workplaces through mass strikes to tip the balance against the regime and make it more difficult for outside powers to manipulate the uprising. Beyond the regime's suppression of the uprising, whether this happens depends on the role of other forces within the opposition such as the Free Syrian Army (FSA) and Syrian National Council (SNC), and the influence of sectarianism.

The FSA mostly comprises defecting soldiers and officers, and civilians who have taken up arms to defend themselves from regime attacks. It is no surprise that armed resistance has developed given the ruthless suppression of the uprising and the legacy of the regime's brutal war against the Muslim Brotherhood in the late 1970s and early 1980s, which destroyed the city of Hama and killed around 20,000 of its inhabitants.[61]

The "umbrella" of the FSA includes a number of different groups who maintain a loose connection with the leadership based in Turkey. There has been much discussion about the extent of assistance being provided to the FSA by external powers such as Qatar, Saudi Arabia and NATO. While it is likely that some form of assistance is being provided, and may well increase in future, it is important not to exaggerate such claims. Credible reports in early 2012 suggested that the FSA remained poorly armed and with a significant proportion of its arms coming from defectors, raids on government weapons bases and black market purchases.[62]

Photographs from Aleppo in April 2012 showed predominantly

61: Rogan, 2011, p515.
62: Holliday, 2012; Abouzeid, 2012.

young FSA fighters taking on tanks with small and defective weapons, pipe bombs, improvised body armour and Molotov cocktails.[63] The FSA has real popular roots within the uprising and is simply too diverse for it to be easily turned into a unified proxy force acting in the interests of outside powers.

However, it is likely that outside powers will try to build up loyal units and co-opt leaders within the armed resistance. There is a danger that a protracted military confrontation with the regime will make the FSA increasingly reliant on external support. In such a situation the FSA could also become a barrier to popular participation and the emergence of a workers' movement. As Lee Sustar and Yusuf Khalili have argued:

> the question of non-violent mass protest—and whether and how to conduct an armed struggle—is key to the Syrian Revolution. Organising self-defence of a neighbourhood or city under attack from the armed forces is different from building the FSA as a fighting force—particularly if foreign powers are attempting to dominate the FSA. Meanwhile, the emergence of Iraq-style jihadist attacks on civilian targets would only play into Assad's hands by giving credence to the idea that the revolution is simply the work of foreign agents.[64]

Therefore while socialists should defend the right of armed resistance against the regime, and oppose abstract calls for the resistance to lay down its weapons while the murderous Assad regime remains in power, the dangers of a situation where the FSA becomes a substitute for mass popular action also need to be recognised. Such a development will make it harder for a workers' movement to emerge.

The SNC was formed by exiled leaders, dominated by the Syrian Muslim Brotherhood, in an attempt to persuade the West to carry out a similar military intervention in Syria to that which it carried out in Libya. The leaders of the SNC have thus focused most of their attention on lobbying for military intervention rather than building international support for the uprising. They represent the most pro-Western element within the opposition, and are positioning themselves to become a new ruling elite. However, their role is contested by the opposition in Syria. They have alienated many of the activists based around the Local Coordinating Committees, which are largely opposed to military intervention, as well as Syria's Kurds by refusing to back Kurdish autonomy or independence in a

---

63: Cantlie, 2012.
64: Sustar and Khalili, 2012.

post-Assad state.[65] The SNC's support for the "Libya model" has been discredited both by the fact that it is less certain that the West will intervene in the same fashion against Assad and by the result of the intervention in Libya, which has led to the installing of a secretive and corrupt Transitional National Council and the deaths of tens of thousands of civilians.[66]

The role of sectarianism

Syria is one of the most diverse countries in the Middle East. Around 65 percent of the Syrian population are Sunni Muslims and the rest are Muslim Alawis (14 percent), Christians (12 percent) and smaller Shia Muslim and Druze minorities.[67] Historically the regime, made up of a core of Alawi military officers in alliance with the Sunni bourgeoisie, has played on fears of a Lebanese-style civil war to pose as the keeper of stability.

During the uprising the regime has worked hard to bind the minority groups to it through fear of violent Sunni retribution. On occasions it has been able to hold significant pro-Assad protests based on their support. The statement of responsibility by an Islamist group for the massive car bomb which ripped through Damascus in May 2012 increased fears of sectarianism: "We tell the regime: stop your massacres of Sunni people or you will bear the sins of the Alawis".[68]

But it is important to stress that anti-sectarianism has been a key part of the slogans and chants of the uprising.[69] It is also not the case that the minorities have uniformly backed the regime. As one analysis puts it:

Many an Alawi, especially amongst intellectuals and simple villagers, resents how his community has been taken hostage by the regime. The Druze are split somewhere down the middle. Christians, who are geographically dispersed, adopt remarkably different viewpoints depending on how much they see of the security services' abuse on the ground…Ismailis, based in the town of Salamiyya, were among the first to join the opposition.[70]

This highlights how the regime's talk of sectarianism conceals the reality of class division in Syria. The minority communities are divided by class just as much as the majority Sunni Muslim population. This is

65: Sustar and Khalili, 2012.
66: Milne, 2011.
67: EIU, 2008, p2.
68: Pearse, 2012.
69: See Zenobie, 2011.
70: Harling and Birke, 2012.

yet another reason for the importance of the development of a workers' movement within the uprising. Such a movement would be a powerful means of uniting Sunnis, Alawis, Christians, Druze and others through common class demands. In the absence of such a movement both the regime and the Gulf States will have more chance of stoking sectarian tensions.

The working class

How likely is it that a working class movement will emerge within the uprising? In objective terms, the working class in Syria today is a potentially powerful force. Out of a population of around 22.5 million, around 2.7 million are wage workers.[71] This means that close to 70 percent of the population depend on wage labour directly or indirectly once families and the unemployed are taken into account. Around 75 percent of the population live in the largest six cities: Damascus, Aleppo, Homs, Hama, Latakia and Tartous.[72] Each of these cities contains powerful groups of workers. Syria has a large mining and manufacturing sector and over the past 20 years workers in airports, railways, ports and power stations have all become increasingly important to the economy.[73] Alongside them are public sector workers such as civil servants, teachers and doctors who make up around 25 percent of the workforce and whose wages have declined in relative terms since the 1980s, leading 40 percent of them to take on second jobs.[74]

However, while the Syrian working class exists as a powerful social force in objective terms, there is no inevitability that this will translate into subjective action. This depends on the confidence of workers to fight and the development of independent networks of organisation. In contrast to the working class in Tunisia and Egypt the Syrian working class has a weaker tradition of such organisation. As the Egyptian revolutionary socialist Mostafa Bassoumy has argued:

> The main difference between the Tunisian and Egyptian revolutions and the Syrian uprising is the role played by the labour movements in each country...
>
> The labour movement is simply absent in Syria. This may be because Syrian unions are controlled by the state and have been relatively listless compared to those in Egypt and Tunisia. The existence of semi-

---

71: Seifan, 2010, p42.
72: EIU, 2008, p3.
73: EIU, 2008, pp9, 17.
74: EIU, 2008, p18.

independent Tunisian unions and an increasingly active Egyptian labour movement in the past few years helped catapult the organised workers into the heart of revolution. In both cases, this led to a quick resolution of the uprising in favour of the people.[75]

By contrast the last major strike wave in Syria was in 1980-1, which led to the imprisonment of hundreds of union activists. Beyond low levels of independent workers' organisation, the growth of "informal labour" and the persistence of small workplaces in the economy also pose challenges for the formation of a strong working class movement.[76] Those counted as unemployed in Syria, around 20 percent of the working population (the percentage is much higher among the young), blend in with those in the "informal" economy, who might work on street stalls or as part of an established company on an "unofficial" temporary basis. In terms of small workplaces, one study from 2004 estimates that, out of 600,000 companies in Syria, 500,000 employed fewer than five workers.[77]

However, as analysis has shown in other countries in the Global South, it is likely that there is no clear division between these groups of workers.[78] The same workplace can employ both "formal" and "informal" workers, and individual workers may work "formally" by day and "informally" at night.[79] The dominance of small workplaces also varies. Workplaces of fewer than 14 workers make up around 60 percent of companies in Damascus and Aleppo, whilst in the more industrial cities of Homs and Hama they make up around 20 percent of companies.[80] Therefore the total picture of the working class in Syria is one in which more strategically powerful groups of workers are part of a broader mass of workers and the poor who are either unemployed, informally employed or employed in small workplaces, a situation common across the Global South.[81]

There have been many recent examples of struggles in Latin America, Africa, Asia and the Middle East where strikes by powerful groups

---

75: Bassyouni, 2011.

76: Haddad, 2012b, describes those in the "informal sector" as "functioning, and living, almost completely outside the market"—p119.

77: Seifan, 2010, p54. It is possible for these kinds of figures to be exaggerated. In Bolivia the number of small workplaces has been inflated by bosses artificially dividing up their companies for tax purposes. However, I have no evidence that such practices are occurring in Syria. Thanks to Joseph Choonara for this point.

78: See Harman, 2009, pp337-352.

79: The findings of Fourtuny and al-Husseini, 2010, and Longuenesse, 1985, suggest this.

80: Seifan, 2010.

81: Callinicos, 2007.

of workers have fused with the resistance of the wider mass of poor and unemployed.[82] It was this process which developed in the Egyptian and Tunisian revolutions where after weeks of street protests the spread of strikes provided the crucial pressure which brought Mubarak and Ben Ali down.[83] In Syria forms of organisation have included the formation of the Local Coordinating Committees, strikes by market stall holders and small shopkeepers and the establishment of road blocks and check-points. There have also been some limited strikes at factories, offices and hospitals. But what has been missing so far is sustained and coordinated strike action by those powerful groups of workers—in the oil refineries, ports, factories, offices, mines, railways, airports, schools and hospitals—who potentially have the power to bring the economy to a grinding halt and break the regime.

The collective power workers have in the workplace is unique because it can hit the regime directly by shutting down whole sections of the economy and the state. It is also the most powerful way of breaking down sectarian divisions, which is one of the reasons why the regime has managed to hold on to power so far. It is by no means inevitable that such a workers' movement will emerge, and it is made difficult by the brutality of the regime and the militarisation of the conflict. But unless it emerges, the revolution cannot fully achieve the real and profound change desired by ordinary people.

Conclusion

Socialists should identify clearly with the forces from below which are fighting the Assad regime. There is no contradiction between this and opposition to imperialist intervention. On the contrary, belief in social change and socialism "from below" is the most consistent and solid basis for opposing imperialism. The importance of the Arab revolutions is that they raise the possibility for the mass of ordinary people in the region to challenge the control of both regional ruling classes and the imperialist powers.

Despite significant challenges, and some important contrasts with the struggles in Tunisia and Egypt, the Syrian uprising is part of the same struggle across the region against poverty, inequality and state repression. It has emerged out of the regime's drive to reform the economy in the interests of the ruling class while strengthening its means of internal repression.

82: Harman, 2009, pp343-344.
83: See Naguib, 2011, and Alexander, 2011.

The uprising can be seen as a new phase in an important tradition of popular struggle in Syrian history. As Hanna Batatu wrote of Syria in 1981:

> Connected with these struggles is a phenomenon that repeats itself: rural people, driven by economic distress or lack of security, move into the main cities, settle in the outlying districts, enter before long into relations or forge common links with elements of the urban poor, who are themselves often earlier migrants from the countryside, and together they challenge the old established classes.[84]

A crucial difference this time is the greater objective potential for the Syrian working class to lead the struggle, due to its growth in both absolute and relative terms, and the fact that a majority of Syrians now live in urban areas. The developing strength of this class, using its unique collective power in the workplaces, is the only way the Syrian Revolution can can fully realise its emancipatory potential—not just bringing down the regime, but beginning to address the deep social and economic issues facing workers, the youth and the poor.

The further development of the revolution faces substantial obstacles. The massacre in the town of Houla in May 2012 shows the extreme lengths to which the regime and its militas will go to in order to strike fear into the hearts of the opposition. But at the same time reports suggest the revolution is drawing in increasing numbers of people, with a growing armed insurgency and bigger and more frequent protests and strikes. What is certain is that both the regime and foreign forces ultimately want to crush the movement from below. The success or failure of the Syrian uprising will have an impact on the confidence of revolutionary movements across the region and the rest of the world. For this reason socialists should oppose all attempts by imperialist powers and their allies to intervene in Syria, and stand firmly in solidarity with the workers, peasants, soldiers and students in their struggle against the Assad regime. Their victory will be our victory, just as their defeat will be our defeat.

84: Batatu, 1981, p337.

References

Ababsa, Myriam, 2010, "Agrarian Counter-reform in Syria (2000-2010)", *Agriculture and Reform in Syria* (University of St Andrews Centre for Syrian Studies).

Abouzeid, Rania, 2012, "Undergunned and Overwhelmed", *Foreign Policy* (30 March), www.foreignpolicy.com/articles/2012/03/30/syria_undergunned_and_overwhelmed

Aita, Samir, 2009, *Labour Market Performance and Migration Flows in Syria* (Robert Schuman Centre for Advanced Studies).

Alexander, Anne, 2011, "The Battle of Tunis", *Socialist Review* (February), www.socialistreview.org.uk/article.php?articlenumber=11546

Amin, Samir, 2012, "An Imperialist Springtime? Libya, Syria, and Beyond", *Monthly Review* (April), http://mrzine.monthlyreview.org/2012/amin280412.html

Arar, Maher, 2003, "This is what they did to me", Counterpunch website (5 November), www.counterpunch.org/2003/11/05/this-is-what-they-did-to-me/

Assaf, Simon, 2012, "Syria's Revolution", *Socialist Worker* (18 February), www.socialistworker.co.uk/art.php?id=27513

Bassyouni, Mostafa, 2011, "Labour movement absent in Syrian revolt", *Al Akhbar* (18 October), http://english.al-akhbar.com/content/labor-movement-absent-syrian-revolt

Batatu, Hanna, 1981, "Some Observations on the Social Roots of Syria's Ruling Military Group and the Causes for Its Dominance", *Middle East Journal*, volume 35.

Callinicos, Alex, 2007, "'Dual Power' in our hands", *Socialist Worker* (6 January), www.socialistworker.co.uk/art.php?id=10387

Cantlie, John, 2012, "Free Syrian Army in Aleppo—in Pictures", *Guardian* (11 April), www.guardian.co.uk/world/gallery/2012/apr/11/free-syrian-army-in-pictures

Choonara, Joseph, 2011, "The Relevance of Permanent Revolution: a reply to Neil Davidson", *International Socialism* 131 (summer), www.isj.org.uk/?id=745

Cliff, Tony, 1963, "Deflected Permanent Revolution", www.marxists.org/archive/cliff/works/1963/xx/permrev.htm

Crooke, Alastair, 2011, "Syria and Iran: the Great Game", *Guardian* (4 November), www.guardian.co.uk/commentisfree/2011/nov/04/syria-iran-great-game

Economist Intelligence Unit, 2008, *Country Profile: Syria* (Economist Intelligence Unit).

Fisk, Robert, 2001, *Pity the Nation: Lebanon at War* (OUP).

Fortuny, Mariangels, and Jalal Al Husseini, 2010, *Labour Market Policies and Institutions: a Synthesis: The cases of Algeria, Jordan, Morocco, Syria and Turkey* (International Labour Office), www.ilo.org/wcmsp5/groups/public/---ed_emp/---emp_policy/documents/publication/wcms_161400.pdf

Galloway, George, 2011, "Syria plot is clear as Qatar sky", *Daily Record* (14 November), http://blogs.dailyrecord.co.uk/georgegalloway/2011/11/syria-plot-is-clear-as-qatar-sky.html

Haddad, Bassam, 2012a, "The Syrian Regime's Business Backbone", *Middle East Research and Information Project*, number 262.

Haddad, Bassam, 2012b, "Syria and Authoritarian Resilience", *Interface* (May), www.interfacejournal.net/wordpress/wp-content/uploads/2012/05/Interface-4-1-Full-PDF-no-images.pdf

Harling, Peter, and Sarah Birke, 2012, "Beyond the Fall of the Syrian Regime", *Middle East Research and Information Project* (24 February), www.merip.org/mero/mero022412

Harman, Chris, 2009, *Zombie Capitalism: Global Crisis and the Relevance of Marx* (Bookmarks).

Haynes, Mike, 2009, "S is for State Capitalism", *Socialist Review* (January), www.socialistreview.org.uk/article.php?articlenumber=10673

Heydemann, Steven, 1999, *Authoritarianism in Syria: Institutions and Social Conflict, 1946-70* (Cornell).

Hinnebusch, Raymond, 2003, "Globalization and Generational Change: Syrian Foreign Policy between Regional Conflict and European Partnership", *The Review of International Affairs*, volume 3, number 2.

Hinnebusch, Raymond, 2012, "Syria: From 'Authoritarian Upgrading' to Revolution?", *International Affairs*, volume 88, number 1.

Hinnebusch, Raymond, and Soren Schmidt, 2009, *The State and the Political Economy of Reform in Syria* (University of St Andrews).

Holliday, Joseph, 2012, "Syria's Armed Opposition", Institute for the Study of War (March), www.understandingwar.org/sites/default/files/Syrias_Armed_Opposition.pdf

Ibrahim, Nasser, 2012, "Syria: the Middle East's tipping point", Alternative Information Center (9 February), www.alternativenews.org/english/index.php/component/content/article/34-opinion/4128-syria-the-middle-easts-tipping-point

International Crisis Group, 2011, *Popular Protest in North Africa and the Middle East (VI): The Syrian People's Slow-Motion Revolution* (6 July), www.crisisgroup.org/en/regions/middle-east-north-africa/egypt-syria-lebanon/syria/108-popular-protest-in-north-africa-and-the-middle-east-vi-the-syrian-peoples-slow-motion-revolution.aspx

Khosrokhavar, Farhad, 2012, *The New Arab Revolutions that Shook the World* (Paradigm).

Lesch, David W, 2005, *The New Lion of Damascus: Bashar al-Assad and Modern Syria* (Yale).

Longuenesse, Elisabeth, 1985, "The Syrian Working Class Today", *Middle East Research and Information Project,* number 134 (July-August).

Marshall, Phil, 1995, "The Children of Stalinism", *International Socialism 68* (autumn), http://epress.anu.edu.au/history/etol/newspape/isj2/1995/isj2-068/marshall.htm

Milne, Seumas, 2011, "If the Libyan war was about saving lives, it was a catastrophic failure", *Guardian* (26 October), www.guardian.co.uk/commentisfree/2011/oct/26/libya-war-saving-lives-catastrophic-failure

Naguib, Sameh, 2011, *The Egyptian Revolution: a Political Analysis and Eyewitness Account* (Bookmarks).

Pearse, Damien, 2012, "Islamist group al-Nusra Front claims responsibility for Damascus bombings", *Guardian* (12 May), www.guardian.co.uk/world/2012/may/12/al-nusra-damascus-bombings-video

Perthes, Volker, 1997, *The Political Economy of Syria Under Assad* (IB Tauris).

Petran, Tabitha, 1972, *Syria: Modern Nation of the Modern World* (Ernest Benn).

Policy Analysis Unit, 2012, "The Israeli Position Towards Events in Syria", *Palestine News Network* (9 February), http://english.pnn.ps/index.php/politics/821-the-israeli-position-toward-the-events-in-syria

Polling, Sylvia, 1994, "Investment Law Number 10: Which Future for the Private Sector?", in Eberhard Kienle (ed), *Contemporary Syria: Liberalization Between Cold War and Cold Peace* (IB Tauris).

Ramadani, Sami, 2012, "Should socialists support the revolt in Syria?", *Socialist Worker* (24 March), www.socialistworker.co.uk/art.php?id=27876

Rogan, Eugene, 2011, *The Arabs: A History* (Penguin).

Sadiki, Larbi, 2011, "Hezbollah's Hypocritical Resistance", *New York Times* (13 December), www.nytimes.com/2011/12/13/opinion/hezbollahs-hypocritical-resistance.html

Salloukh, Bassel F, 2009, "Demystifying Syrian Foreign Policy under Bashar al-Asad", *Demystifying Syria* (Saqi).

Seifan, Samar, 2010, *Syria on the Path to Economic Reform* (University of St Andrews Centre for Syrian Studies).

Slater, Jerome, 2002, "Lost Opportunities for Peace in the Arab-Israeli Conflict: Israel and Syria, 1948-2001", *International Security*, volume 27, number 1 (summer).

Sustar, Lee, and Yusuf Khalil, 2012, "A Stalemate in Syria?", *Socialist Worker* (US) (24 April), http://socialistworker.org/2012/04/24/stalemate-in-syria

Syria Report: Syria's Leading Economic and Business Newsletter, 2011, number 50 (2nd quarter).

Traboulsi, Fawwaz, 2007, *A History of Modern Lebanon* (Pluto).

Van Dam, Nikolaos, 1996, *The Struggle for Power in Syria: Politics and Society Under Asad and the Ba'ath Party* (IB Tauris).

West, Jane, 2012, "The imperialist counter-offensive against the Arab Spring: Libya, Syria, Iran", *Socialist Action* (January), www.socialistaction.net/International/Middle-East/Middle-East-Politics/The-imperialist-counter-offensive-against-the-Arab-Spring-%E2%80%93-Libya-Syria-Iran.html

World Bank, 2005, "Gini Index", http://data.worldbank.org/indicator/SI.POV.GINI

Zénobie, 2011, "The Power of the Word in the Syrian Intifada", *Le Monde Diplomatique* (June), http://mondediplo.com/2011/06/06syria

Zorob, Anja, 2008, "The Syrian-European Association Agreement and its Potential Impact on Enhancing the Credibility of Reform", *Meditterranean Politics*, volume 13, number 1, (March).

The rise and fall of the Jewish Labour Bund

Sai Englert

The history of the Bund, or *Algemeyner Yiddisher Arbeter Bund in Rusland un Poyln* (General Jewish Labour Union in Russia and Poland), is one riven with contradictions. It brought together tens of thousands of Jewish workers during its 52 years of existence in struggle against oppression and exploitation. It emerged out of the Russian-speaking Jewish intelligentsia and found itself at the heart of the most important Yiddish[1] revival in poetry, theatre and literature. It rejected Bolshevism and was central to major polemics against Lenin, while at the same time laying the foundation for many of the organisational structures that we would call "Leninist" today. It professed its support for socialism and revolution, yet it joined the reformist Second International in the 1930s. It defended internationalism and saw its struggle as that of the toilers of the world, yet it organised solely Jewish workers and put specific Jewish national demands at the heart of its programme. It rejected Zionism as a "bourgeois reactionary" ideology, yet up to this day has a branch in Israel.

This article will attempt to shed light on some of these contradictions as well as to unearth a too often forgotten past of struggle, which goes to the roots of our revolutionary tradition as well as offering an alternative history of the Jews in Eastern and Central Europe to that of the Zionist mainstream:

1:    The Eastern European Jewish language.

Jews resisting, fighting back and changing their lives, not the caricatured victims of history, longing to "return" from a so-called exile.

Through exploitation and oppression

At the end of the 19th century, Eastern European Jews made up the majority of the world's Jewish population. They did so until the Nazi genocide. They resided mainly in a region called "the Pale of Settlement". Successive waves of Tsarist decrees, pogroms, wars and forced migrations in the 18th and 19th centuries, concentrated around 4 million Jews in this area, "which stretched from Lithuania in the North to the Black Sea in the South, and from Poland in the West to 'White Russia' and the Ukraine, in the East".[2] It was in the 1880s and 1890s, mainly in the Pale of Settlement, that events took place which forced the Jewish community to seek collective organisation.

On 1 March 1881 the small terrorist group Narodnaya Volia (the People's Will) assassinated Tsar Alexander II. Alexander II was, of course, the representative of a long tradition of violent tyrannical Tsarist rule. But he had also softened anti-Semitic laws in the Russian Empire, allowed Jewish students in universities and authorised Jewish emigration out of the Pale.[3]

After his murder, and with the crowning of his successor Alexander III, the era of reform came to an end and the Jewish people were once again the target of Tsarist decrees. Indeed, in order to deflect the rising tide of discontent against his rule, Alexander III launched a scapegoating campaign against the Jews of the Russian Empire: "Under Alexander III...224 pogroms took place between 1881 and 1883. Other sources indicate 215 pogroms in 1881 alone, most of which took place in the Ukraine".[4] At the same time, Jews were forbidden to work the land and between 700,000 and 800,000 Jews were forced to emigrate into the cities of the Pale. Jews could no longer work in the Tsarist administration, and in universities a maximum of 10 percent of the student intake could be Jewish.[5]

These policies pushed Jews into the expanding urban centres of the Pale to look for work in its workshops that were emerging. It also forced Jewish communities to organise collectively to defend themselves from anti-Semitic attacks. This process of proletarianisation of the Jewish masses

---

2:   Rose, 2004, p98.
3:   Minszeles, 2010.
4:   Minszeles, 2010, p28.
5:   Minszeles, 2010, pp30-32.

was such that by 1897 "the number of Jewish workers [was] estimated at 105,000, which represents one Jewish worker for every three active Jews".[6]

In this rapid process of forced proletarianisation lie the origins of the Jewish workers' movement, as well as the explanation for the over-representation of Jews in the organisation and theoretical life of different political movements in the Russian Empire, from anarchism to Marxism in all its shades. As Kopel Pinson puts it:

> The last decade of the 19th century witnessed the beginnings of active political agitation among workers. In part, this was due to the rapid spurt of industrialisation which set throughout Russia during that time. It was further inspired, however, by the growing policy of repression initiated by the Tsarist government against the Jews. In Lithuania and White Russia, in particular, economic and political activities began on a large scale. Here in the crowded urban centres of the "Pale", among the Jewish workers in paint factories, the Jewish bristle makers, textile and tobacco operatives of Vilna, Byalistok, Smargon, Grodno and Minsk, as also among Jewish girls employed in tobacco and envelope factories, there emerged a group of class-conscious Socialist workers and intellectuals.[7]

Jewish activists were part of the early Narodnaya Volia, or Narodniks, groups of students and left wing intellectuals who organised acts of terrorism against the officials of the Tsarist regime, and hoped to spark large-scale revolt in the peasantry. Jewish participation in the Narodniks seems to have been short lived due to the unwillingness of the Narodniks to challenge anti-Semitism in the peasant masses or in their own circles.[8]

Later, as the Marxist movement in Russia developed into reading circles, which brought workers and intellectuals together in underground social democratic study groups, Jewish activists were once again heavily involved, particularly in the Pale. At that time the majority of Jewish intellectuals wanted circle activity to be exclusively in Russian, and thought that workers who only knew Yiddish should be taught the language of the empire. Russian was considered superior, and Yiddish, they argued, broke the unity between workers of the empire.

Finally, when the most advanced of those circles started to turn to agitation in workplaces and focused on organising workers in struggle,

---

6:   Minszeles, 2010, p43.
7:   Pinson, 1945, p236.
8:   Minszeles, 2010, p58.

Jewish revolutionaries were once again at the forefront of the movement. Arkady Kremer, who would become a key organiser of the Bund and a leading member of its Central Committee (CC), wrote a pamphlet in 1893, *On Agitation*, in which he argued that the main task for social democrats was to turn their attention towards the masses of workers. The pamphlet was introduced by Pavel Axelrod, another Jewish revolutionary, who would later collaborate with Lenin on the newspaper *Iskra*, before becoming a leading Menshevik.

It was in the process of turning to agitation that the question of Yiddish emerged. At first the choice by the forerunners of the Bund to adopt Yiddish in their publications and agitational material was a practical necessity rather than an ideological statement about the Jewish nation.

The turn to agitation led to the organisation of the first workers' groups. Although this took place in several Russian centres, it seems to have been particularly effective in the Jewish working class of the Pale.[9] Jewish workers were often hired last because they were considered to be too quick to organise, strike or revolt. A Jewish factory owner in Vilnius explained: "I prefer to hire Christians. The Jews are good workers, but they are capable of organising revolts against the boss, the regime and the Tsar himself".[10]

This is not to say that only Jewish revolutionaries were leading and waging arguments for turns in the movement. But it does suggest that the consequence of the dual experience of rampant anti-Semitism and rapid proletarianisation of the Jewish masses was a particular openness from Jewish radicals to the arguments about the need to do away with oppression and exploitation. It is in this context that the emergence of the Bund has to be considered.

Revolutionaries with a Yiddish twang

The Bund was officially established at a congress held in the attic of a farm near Vilnius, in today's Lithuania. It was held in September, at the same time as the Jewish festivals of Rosh Hashanah and Yom Kippur, in order to limit the suspicion of the Russian secret police, which was closely monitoring the 13 labour activists who met that day. The conference brought together "11 men and two women, five intellectuals and eight workers, who represented some 3,500 members".[11] They were all between 20 and 35 years old and the editors of two Yiddish agitational newspapers were

9:   Minszeles, 2010, pp64-66; Brossat and Klingberg, 2009, pp49-57.
10:   Minszeles, 2010, p43.
11:   Minszeles, 2010, p147.

present as well: *Der Arbeiter Shtime* (the Workers' Voice) and *Der Yiddishe Arbeiter* (the Jewish Worker). The formation of the Bund was thus a process of bringing together several existing components of workers' struggle. Vladimir Medem, one of its leading theoreticians, wrote:

> The Bund! Founded? That is the wrong expression. It was not founded, but it was born, it developed, grew like every living organism develops and grows... A movement of instinctive attraction of the worker for the worker provoked the agglomeration of grains of sand, of little human dust in a block of granite.[12]

The experience of the rising wave of struggle forced Jewish workers to strengthen their collective organisational structures. The professional revolutionary, an activist paid by the members of an organisation to facilitate and support the struggles it is involved in; the agitational paper, which can spread political debates and news of struggles around the country while putting forward a political line to guide workers in struggle; a workers' party to bring together the agitational and educational work of revolutionaries, were first thought of and tried out by the Bund. It is only later, after coming into contact with the Bund, that Lenin, among others, argued for the generalisation of these forms of organisation.

The high level of organisation of the Bund, as well as its organic emergence out of existing working class networks, explains the central role played by the party in the formation of the Russian Social Democratic Labour Party (RSDLP). At the RSDLP's founding congress in 1898, three of the nine delegates were Bundists and one of them was elected to the three-man CC. The balance of forces also illustrates how politically developed the Jewish workers' movement in the Pale was in comparison with its allies in the rest of the Russian Empire.

Only a month after the founding conference of the Bund another Jewish group made its first organisational steps, although in a very different direction. The Zionist movement, rejected by the Bund from the onset as a "bourgeois reactionary" ideology, held its conference in Austria in October 1897. The Zionists believed that the solution to anti-Semitism lay in emigration to Palestine and the creation of a Jewish state that had the backing of imperial powers. The conference "was a dazzling affair: over 200 men wearing frock coats and white ties and about 20 elegantly attired women observers gathered at Basel's ornate Stadt Casino; the

---

12: Medem, in Minszeles, 2010, p152.

galleries were crowded with distinguished visitors, Jews and Christians, alike; and correspondents from all over Europe filed long reports about the proceedings".[13]

It is no chance of history that both conferences took place almost simultaneously. Indeed, if they brought together different crowds on the basis of different politics, they had nonetheless two important similarities: they were responses to the rise of anti-Semitism across Europe—from Eastern European pogroms to the French Dreyfus affair—and saw Jewish self-organisation as the way to defeat it.

The difference was class. The Jewish workers of the Pale saw their liberation linked directly with their struggle against exploitation. They wanted to do away with the pogromist and the boss at the same time. The Zionist movement on the other hand was an association of assimilated middle class Jews, frustrated by the barriers of anti-Semitism to their social ascent. They saw the solution in the creation of a state through colonisation.

The national question

The Bund rejected the claims made by anti-Semites and Zionists alike, that there was such a thing as a world Jewry with a common culture or plight. It also opposed what it called "emigrationism", the idea, supported by the Zionists, that the problems of the Jews could only be solved in a Jewish state in Palestine. The Bund argued that the Jewish state would be yet another class-ridden society in which Jewish workers would have to fight their Jewish bosses. The Bundists defended the right of Palestinians to organise against Jewish colonisation. In 1929, for example, the Bund defended the Palestinians riots, which were depicted by the Zionists as anti-Semitic rather than anti-colonial.[14]

For the Bund, the world in its entirety had to be changed, class society had to be overthrown completely and everywhere, and this was a struggle that began at home. The Bund called this *doykayt* (literally "here-ness"). However, the Bund disagreed on two fundamental questions with the wider revolutionary movement: nationality and organisation.

The Bund's decision to organise Jewish workers grew out of material conditions: anti-Semitism and the enforced geographical separation of Jewish and gentile workers. The Bund itself was conscious of that fact. In its report to the International Socialist Congress in 1900 it explained:

13: Brumberg, 1999, p197.
14: Cohen, 2001, p120.

The first Jewish intellectuals who started to carry on propaganda among Jewish workers had no idea of creating a specifically Jewish labour movement. Confined to the Pale and not having the possibilities to dedicate their energies to the Russian labour movement, they were forced willy-nilly to start working among the Jews, and thus at least quench to some degree their thirst for revolutionary activity.[15]

It is also worth saying that segregation was not the same everywhere. For example:

in such industrial centres as Bialystok and Lodz, where large contingents of Jewish and non Jewish workers resided, in close proximity. In such cases, relations between Jewish and gentile workers often held the key to the success or failure of a given strike.[16]

Yet the Bund took it for granted from its very inception that the task of fighting anti-Semitism was that of the Jewish workers, rather than the working class as a whole. The implication was that Jewish workers needed to organise themselves into a separate Jewish workers' organisation. For example, Kremer declared at the founding congress of the Bund: "We will also have the special task of defending the particular interests of Jewish workers, conducting a struggle for their civil rights, and above all, waging a campaign against anti-Jewish legislation".[17]

The Bund considered the Russian Jews a nationality, in the sense that the Yiddish speaking Jews of the empire formed a nation, and that the revolution would deliver national autonomy for all oppressed nationalities.

At its fourth Congress in April 1901 in Bialystok it passed a motion to the effect that "Russia, which is made up of many different nations, will in the future be transformed into a federation of nationalities, and that each will have full autonomy independent of the territory in which it resides".[18]

This position came from the Austrian Marxists, who called for a similar federalist solution to the "national question" in the Austro-Hungarian Empire. As Rick Kuhn points out:

15: Bund, in Pinson, 1945, p238.
16: Mendelsohn, 1968, p245.
17: Zimmerman, in Jacobs, 2001, p30.
18: Zimmerman, in Jacobs, 2001, p34.

National cultural autonomy was a means by which the German-Austrian leadership [of the Social Democratic Workers' Party of Austria—SDAPÖ] reconciled social democracy to its own identification with the German-dominated Austrian imperial state and its unpreparedness to support the break-up of the empire. The SDAPÖ's own federal structure represented a capitulation to nationalism within the workers' movement.[19]

The Bund saw the revolution as opening the possibility for legislation that would combat anti-Semitism and offer a degree of cultural freedom and protection to the Jews, through the creation of autonomous cultural entities across the empire. It disputed the idea that what it considered to be Jewish problems could be solved or addressed by non-Jewish organisations.[20]

The Bolsheviks, on the other hand, argued "to integrate the Jewish workers' movement into the wider workers' movement and to make the fight for Jewish equal rights, and unequivocal hostility to all forms of anti-Semitism, an integral part of the revolutionary programme".[21] They rejected the idea that workers could change the world without simultaneously fighting oppression—whatever their creed.

The tensions between the Bund and the RSDLP ran high on this matter. At the 1903 conference of the RSDLP in Brussels the Bund demanded "recognition as the sole representative of the Jewish proletariat and that no territorial limitations be placed on its activities";[22] in other words all Jewish members of the RSDLP would become members of the Bund. The so-called "Jewish question" and its organisational consequences fed the wider debates over organisation inside the RSDLP. It is in the light of this wider debate that the split with the Bund needs to be understood.

Lenin is often accused of having engineered the split in the RSDLP. The truth is more complicated. Lenin was not prepared to accept the Bund as the sole representative of all Jewish workers, but neither did he want to expel them from the RSDLP.[23] In the course of the conference unexpected divisions appeared on the question of organisation between the previously united board of the *Iskra* newspaper. These divisions would prove to be the breaking point of a united party.

During the debates both Martov and Lenin were formulating and clarifying their respective understanding of the party—as a vanguardist body

---

19: Kuhn, in Jacobs, 2001, p148.
20: Brossat and Klingberg, 2009, pp42-43.
21: Rose, 2004, p110.
22: Tobias, in Jacobs, 2001, p356.
23: Lenin, 1903.

for Lenin and an open mass party for Martov. It is worth noting that this interpretation is disputed by Lars Lih who argues that Lenin's conception of the party was not yet fully formulated and that therefore the debate was mainly focused on tactics.[24] He describes the issues at the conference as "dense and tangled, combining personal animosities, organisational jockeying for position and genuine difference in revolutionary tactics".[25] Nonetheless, the further development of the different positions led to fundamentally incompatible organisational structures and political positions.

Whatever the reason may have been, the conference turned into complete disunity. In this context it was impossible to compromise on the Bund's demands, and the Bund left the RSDLP.[26] The RSDLP split further into the majority and the minority—the Bolsheviks and Mensheviks.

Tried in the fire of the dress rehearsal

In 1905 Russia was losing the war with Japan. The hardships put on soldiers and the poor ignited revolt, then revolution. The unrest had started in 1904 with a strike in the Putilov works in St Petersburg. It was rapidly followed by solidarity strikes, with up to 80.000 workers walking out. In early 1905 the Orthodox priest and police informant Father Gapon led a march to the Tsar's Winter Palace. Demonstrators were peaceful, sang religious hymns glorifying the Tsar, and wanted to deliver him a petition. The army opened fire on them, sparking mass outrage and protest. In the Black Sea the starved and demoralised sailors of the now famous *Battleship Potemkin* revolted against their officers, killing seven and arresting 11. The revolt quickly spread across the Tsarist empire and demonstrations and strikes developed in most of its towns and cities.

The Pale was engulfed in the revolutionary wave. Workers of all nationalities (mainly Russians, Poles, Lithuanians, Ukrainians, Germans and Jews in the Pale) revolted against the Tsar, for better pay and against oppression. The Bund "fought with devotion, played a key role in most events of the revolution, and suffered the largest casualties during the clashes with the Russian army and police".[27] Indeed, the Bund threw its entire apparatus into the building of the revolution. Its press celebrated the strikes and demonstrations and argued for more action against the Tsar. In workplaces its members agitated and built Jewish trade unions (illegal in Tsarist Russia) across the

---

24: Lih 2008, pp489-553.
25: Lih, 2011, p81.
26: The Bund rejoined the RSDLP in 1906 at the fourth unity conference.
27: Wrobel, in Jacobs, 2001, p158.

Pale. At the same time the Bund organised against those who tried to derail the revolution by dividing the movement through anti-Semitic propaganda and pogroms. It organised Jewish workers' self-defence squads.

It is difficult to judge the precise effectiveness of the Bund's action. It is, however, safe to say that it put itself at the centre of the revolution and was largely recognised for it. Between January 1905 and October 1906 its membership exploded to between 33,000 and 40,000. In the city of Lodz for example, an industrial centre of the Pale where 29.4 percent of the population was Jewish, it rocketed from 100 to 1,600 members. It organised student groups in the gymnasiums and universities, and built nine trade unions, which organised about 3,500 workers. The Bund's self-defence squads broke up three attempts at organising pogroms between 1905 and 1906.[28]

But the revolution was defeated. It went down in history, in Lenin's words, as the "dress rehearsal" for the 1917 Revolution. The regime survived and defeated the revolutionary outburst through a mixture of heavy state repression, economic decay and nominal reform, for example the creation of a parliament, the Duma. If the Bund dealt well with the outbreak of the revolution, defeat almost dragged it into oblivion. By the end of the year 1907 the Bund was virtually decimated.[29] In Lodz its membership fell back approximately to where it was before the revolution by 1908, and in 1910 it only had two trade unions, which organised 144 workers.[30]

As a consequence of the loss of the majority of its members and the demoralisation that hit the working class, the Bund's activity turned from organising illegal trade unions and agitating in workplaces to the creation of a network of cultural organisations (mainly Yiddish schools) and participation in local Jewish elections.[31]

It was, of course, necessary to re-evaluate the possibilities of agitation after a revolutionary defeat, but the Bund's turn led it down a different political path. Indeed, when the Bund re-emerged from near collapse in 1911 it was a close ally of the Mensheviks, having moved to the right of the Russian revolutionary movement.

This tendency of the Bund to be a victim of the ebbs and flows of the class, rather than fighting for a clear strategy and adapting it to the circumstances, stayed with it throughout its history. Partly this was due to the workerist tendency that had developed in the organisation after the

28: Samus, in Jacobs, 2001, pp98-100.
29: Kuhn, in Jacobs, 2001, p143.
30: Samus, in Jacobs, 2001, p101.
31: Pinson, 1945, p254.

turn to agitation that led it to explain the behaviour of the working class rather than attempting to lead it. Partly, its focus on a particular and isolated section of the working class (both a voluntary and involuntary isolation) limited its ability to judge the workers' movement as a whole.

As a matter of fact, all of the revolutionary tendencies in the Russian Empire entered a period of crisis and isolation. The Bolsheviks did not escape this tendency, but their "organised retreat", as Lenin called it, allowed them to protect an active and disciplined core while weathering the storm of repression and crisis. The Bolshevik approach rested on two pillars: firstly, the recognition of a need to change their tactics to fit the new period and, secondly, the expulsion of those ultra-leftist elements who refused to accept the need to adapt. Lenin explained that political survival was possible only because the Bolsheviks "ruthlessly exposed and expelled the revolutionary phrasemongers, those who did not wish to understand that one had to retreat, that one had to know how to retreat", and because they understood that it was necessary "to work in the most reactionary of parliaments, in the most reactionary of trade unions, co-operatives and insurance societies and similar organisations".[32]

From one to two Bunds

The outbreak of the First World War and the invasion of Poland by the German army had two consequences for the Bund: to divide the Pale and therefore the Bund geographically, and create different conditions for the Russian and Polish Bund.

As the war deepened and it became clear that Poland would not return under Russian control any time soon, it was no longer possible to organise in a unified Bund. The CC of the Bund appointed a new committee in Warsaw, which in practice became the new leadership of the Polish Bund as soon as it was appointed in 1914.[33] The split was made official in December 1917.

The second, and perhaps more surprising, consequence of the German invasion was that the political field became much more open to the Jews in German-occupied Poland. Indeed, the anti-Semitic laws and institutions of the Tsarist empire disappeared and German standards applied. This meant that "Jewish educational, cultural, political, social, and economic institutions mushroomed".[34] The result was greater

---

32: Lenin, in Cliff, 1986, p248.
33: Wrobel, in Jacobs, 2001, pp158-160.
34: Wrobel, in Jacobs, 2001, p159.

political freedom for the Polish Bund. For example, Medem received a permit from the German occupying forces to print the paper of the Polish Bund: *Lebensfragn*.[35]

The Polish Bund intensified what had been its organisational focus since the revolutionary defeat and would become the backbone of its organisation in Poland: Yiddish education. Nathan Cohen explains:

> The changes in government, and the enormous numbers of refugees, gave greater freedom of action to organisations and institutions that were willing to lend assistance and thus, under the pretext of private volunteer activities, two early childhood teachers opened the first children's home, named in memory of Bronslav Groser.[36]

The education network of the Bund in Poland would keep expanding and is considered today as one of the greatest achievements of the Polish Bund. It is worth noting that this liberalisation under German rule was part of the German war propaganda at the time. The Germans claimed they were invading Poland in order to save its Jewish population, which led it to be the main attention of Zionist hope for an imperial sponsor in Palestine, alongside France and Britain.

The Russian Bund kept fighting as part of the Russian workers' movement against Tsarist anti-Semitism and exploitation, while the Polish Bund, now in a separate Polish territory, had to relate to its new circumstance. It did not use the political relaxation to throw itself into agitation, but to develop a network of Jewish culture, education and sports.

It is with these split structures that the Bund responded to the outbreak of the 1917 Russian Revolution.

The universalising pull of the revolution

The effect of the war in Russia was to usher in a second, successful, revolution. It is impossible to do justice to the Russian Revolution in this article, but it is important to mention the impact it had on Jewish workers across the Russian Empire. Indeed, while sweeping away Tsarist rule and opening up the possibility for workers' power in Russia, the revolution also started to erode what Frederick Engels called "the muck of ages". Oppression, under all its guises, was challenged both by the experience of struggle and the conscious role of the Bolsheviks.

35: Cohen, in Jacobs, 2001, p118.
36: Cohen, in Jacobs, 2001, p114.

Of course, the attraction of the Russian Revolution for the Jewish workers has to be understood as part of the general effect it had on workers across Russia. The creation of workers' councils, direct involvement in the running of workplaces and communities, and the promises of a better tomorrow without exploitation or oppression rallied hundreds of thousands to the communist cause. But two other factors are significant for the Jewish communities in the Russian Empire. The first one is the immediate withdrawal by the Soviet government of the Tsarist anti-Semitic laws:

> The revolution decreed the abolition of all forms of national discrimination; the soviet government engaged an effective struggle against anti-Semitism; the abolition of the zone of residence allowed Jews to circulate and disperse freely on the entire territory of the country, the proclamation of the equality of all citizens opened the doors [to Jews] of the new administration.[37]

The October Revolution showed the possibility of making true the promises of the French Revolution and challenged the idea that anti-Semitism is inevitable or that Jewish and gentile workers do not share common needs and goals. The Bund suffered from this universalising tendency, as its base was pulled into the whirlwind of revolution.

The second point of attraction of the Bolsheviks appeared during the civil war. The White armies, organised by the old rulers of the empire and supported economically and militarily by European and American powers, attempted to crush the revolution. One of the ways in which they attempted to do so was by mobilising the old reactionary ideas of the Russian peasantry by organising pogroms up and down the country.[38] The Bolsheviks equated anti-Semitic pogroms with counter-revolutionary activity and applied martial law to pogromists. This stance earned the Bolsheviks great respect in the Jewish masses of the empire: "Numerous are the [Jews] who, during the civil war or at its end, joined the Communist Party, swelled the ranks of its new administration, or enrolled in the Red Army".[39]

The role of the Bolsheviks in the protection of Jewish communities during the Civil War also explains the splits in all the Jewish organisations of the empire, and clarifies the Bolsheviks' position on liberation being

---

37: Brossat and Klingberg, 2009, p181.
38: Brossat and Klingberg, 2009, p180.
39: Brossat and Klingberg, 2009, p182.

a central part of a successful revolution. Not only did numerous Jewish workers join the ranks of the Bolsheviks but they were also deeply integrated in its structures and leadership. At the end of the civil war, "at the tenth congress of the Bolshevik Party, in March 1921, out of 694 delegates, 94 were Jewish... In the Central Committee of the Bolshevik party elected in March 1918, five members out of 15 were Jewish".[40]

In the immediate aftermath of the revolution, in addition to a struggle against anti-Semitism led at all levels of the new state, a new cultural and social front was opened by the revolution. At the state level this can be seen in the creation of the Yesvetika, a centre for the promotion of Jewish revolutionary culture.

This revolutionary renewal was mainly based around Yiddish, although Russian texts and influences can be found in its publications too.[41] In the myriad of local sections that sprang up around the Soviet territory a new life was brought into Yiddish culture theatre, literature and poetry, and new education centres saw the day.[42] Alain Brossat and Sylvia Klingberg, who are both otherwise critical of the Bolsheviks for "playing down Jewish political specificities", cannot but describe the early 1920s Jewish cultural revival in laudatory terms:

> It is nonetheless difficult to negate the reality of the Jewish cultural rebirth in the USSR in the 1920s, rebirth attested to by the remarkable development of Jewish theatre in this period, by the intensive and non-uniform Yiddish literary production, by the establishment of Jewish schools, etc. What characterises this cultural boom, this mutation, is that it is a direct consequence of real political factors.[43]

The expression of political liberation and cultural renewal of Jewish life in the early 1920s are the symptoms of a revolution in which the liberation of oppressed communities was becoming a reality.

Since the war had split the Bund in half, across two national entities, the experience of revolution hit the Russian Bund with full force, while its Polish counterpart only experienced the ripples of revolution. It is true that the revolutionary wind unleashed in Russia swept over the entire surface of the globe, but not always in straightforward ways.

40: Brossat and Klingberg, 2009, p183.
41: Brossat and Klingberg, 2009, pp175-191.
42: Brossat and Klingberg, 2009, p190.
43: Brossat and Klingberg, 2009, p189.

Russia

As during the 1905 Revolution, the Bund immediately threw everything into the revolution. The impact of its militants can be seen, for example, with Henryk Ehrlich, a leading member of the Bund, being elected to the executive committee of the Petrograd Soviet, possibly the most powerful body of the revolution. But as the revolution deepened from a political to a social revolution in October, the organisation broke in half.

The leadership of the Bund condemned the deepening of the revolution as a "Bolshevik coup".[44] At the same time, the mass of the Russian Bundist membership identified with the Bolsheviks and understood that they were the only organisation leading the revolution forward. A majority of the Russian Bund voted to accept the 21 points, the condition of membership of the Communist International (Comintern), launched by the Bolsheviks in 1918.[45] The Russian Bund then integrated into the Communist Party, first in the Ukraine in 1919. Then, across the former Russian empire, the local branches of the Communist Party and the Bund merged.[46] In 1921, after heated debates both with the Bolsheviks and inside the organisation, the Russian Bund dissolved itself completely.[47]

The Bund was not the only Jewish organisation that found itself pulled apart in the midst of revolution. The Poalei Zion, a so-called Marxist-Zionist organisation, itself had minority splits, which joined the Comintern.[48]

Many critics of the Bolsheviks and historians of the Bund (and indeed the leadership of both Russian and Polish Bunds at the time) describe the dissolution of the Russian Bund as a loss for the Jewish movement and a consequence of Bolshevik tyranny. What they fail to account for is the democratic nature of the dissolution of the Bund. The revolution opened up the door to a million new possibilities, to a new society built by and for the many. Despite its theory that anti-Semitism had to be addressed by Jewish workers, the Bund was thrown into a revolutionary struggle in which Jewish and gentile workers fought side by side against oppression and exploitation. The Bolsheviks fought against anti-Semitism with the same determination as the hardest cadres of the Bund. The idea that only Jews could and would oppose anti-Semitism gave way to joint struggle with gentile workers. In the struggle against exploitation and the system as a whole, anti-Semitism no longer looked

---

44: Wrobel, in Jacobs, 2001, p160.
45: Brumberg, in Jacobs, 2001, p81.
46: Brossat and Klingberg, 2009, pp36, 176-177.
47: Brumberg, in Jacobs, 2001, p81.
48: Kessler, in Jacobs, 2001, p187.

like a Jewish problem inflicted by all gentiles, but a problem for all workers, enshrined in exploitative structures.

Poland

In Poland, however, where the experience of the revolution was less direct, its consequences were more contradictory. This was also reinforced by the fact that the old leadership of the Bund, until then in Russia, emigrated to Poland as the Bund and the Bolsheviks merged. For example, Ehrlich and Victor Alter, who was a leading Bundist in Moscow and the Ukraine, left Russia and assumed a leadership role in the Polish Bund. They represented the more anti-Bolshevik elements of the Bund, and carried real political weight in the organisation.

The Polish Bund was riven with debates around the 21 points, which came to a head in 1921 at the second conference of the Polish Bund, now the only remaining Bund, in Danzig. The organisation was divided into three camps: those who were prepared to accept only 16 of the 21 points, those who could accept 19 and those who agreed with all of them. The two questions that were the most unacceptable to the large majority of the Bund were "the demand that every new group support the Comintern unanimously, and the demand that every group rid itself once and for all of those members who did not wholly agree with the Third International".[49] Although these can seem like minor disagreements, the objective of the 21 points was to create unity that crossed national borders and could bring together all the revolutionary forces that wanted to generalise the experiences of the revolution. The Bolsheviks wanted to avoid allying themselves with parties that would turn against the revolution when it deepened, as many Russian "revolutionaries" did.

The pro-Communist minority in the Bund split after the conference. First, it became the Kombund, or Communist Bund, and in 1922 it fused with the Polish Communist Party (KPP).[50] This was a minority split, but in some areas carried real strength: in Lodz the Bund lost half its membership to the Kombund.[51] The other two factions remained inside the Bund, but it would continue to exist highly divided for at least a decade.

The influence of the liberatory wind of the revolution had been lessened by distance and lack of direct experience. The Polish Bundists

---

49: Brumberg, in Jacobs, 2001, p81.
50: Wrobel, in Jacobs, 2001, p160.
51: Samus, in Jacobs, 2001, p104.

were unable to abandon Jewish particularism, and remained organised separately to communists in Poland.

From defeat to reform, and back again

The 1920s in Poland were hard for the Bund. Limited to the new Polish state, riven with divisions, and caught between revolutionary ideals and reformist organisation, the Bund was isolated.

The Bund built an ever increasing network of different cultural organisations and shifted away from direct struggle. It created sports groups, theatre companies and academies, a youth organisation and a children's organisation, and, perhaps most importantly, increased its network of Yiddish working class education across Poland.

The second tier of its organisational focus was electoral. The Bund threw itself into the local Jewish elections and workers' delegates elections for the Polish parliament. Its gains were modest to nonexistent throughout the 1920s.

The Bund did not officially take a reformist position in the 1920s. After rejecting membership of the Comintern, the Bund joined the Vienna International Working Union of Socialist Parties, or Second and a Half International. This was an international grouping of centrist organisations, trapped between revolutionary convictions and a lack of confidence in the working class's ability to deliver liberation. Lenin understood that these groups could be pulled towards revolution or reform, depending on the general state of the revolutionary movement internationally. The fate of the Bund, as with many other of the centrist organisations, was to fall into the arms of the reconstituted Second International, although not without fierce internal debate.

This generalised decline took place as the revolutionary wave of the early 1920s was beaten back everywhere, including inside the Soviet Union, with the rise of Stalinism. The possibility of mass workers' action changing the world from below seemed increasingly unlikely.

Between Stalin and Hitler: Fight!

In the 1930s the political situation in Poland and internationally changed dramatically and forced the Bund into renewed action, this time on the defensive.

In the Soviet Union, Stalin consolidated his power through forced collectivisation, the Five Year Plans and the beginning of the purges of the old guard of Bolsheviks. Those who led the revolution and carried its tradition were exiled or killed. From the other border the noises of anti-Jewish marches and pogroms in Germany intensified with the rise to power of Hitler and the Nazi Party. At home the political spectrum was pulled sharply to the right after the death of the "benevolent dictator" Pilsudski, and the possibility of Polish fascism became increasingly credible.[52]

The Bund remobilised. It reorganised self-defence squads—based on its Morgnstern sports groups—and called general strikes. The socialist PPS, as well as the Zionists, threw their weight behind it.

The next year the PPS and the Bund organised joint campaigns against attacks on Jewish students in universities, marched together at May Day demonstrations, formed joint self-defence groups in Warsaw, published a joint newspaper and held joint trade union conferences.[53] For the second time in its history the Bund was forced out of its Jewish particularism by the events around it.

Its membership doubled and grew until the Second World War, staying the biggest Jewish organisation in Poland. It boasted 20,000 members in 1939.[54] It also boosted its electoral success: it came to control "several of the largest Jewish municipal elective bodies and with decisive majorities in several city councils, including Warsaw".[55]

Ironically, it is as the Bund returned to militant trade unionism and anti-fascism that its electoral results improved. It gave confidence to Jewish workers across Poland that it was possible to organise and fight, while the world seemed to crumble around their ears. This is a political message they kept alive, even in the darkest hours of Nazi occupation.

Defeat and extermination

Unfortunately, the resurgence of activity in both the Bund and the PPS was to be crushed by greater forces. In 1939, following the Hitler-Stalin Pact, both the Red Army and the Wehrmacht invaded Poland. On both sides of occupied Poland, the leaderships of most political organisations were arrested, and so too that of the Bund. On the Russian side, Victor Alter and Henryk Ehrlich were arrested, first for being "British agents, then released and re-arrested for being German agents. Ehrlich was executed in 1942. Alter committed suicide".[56]

On the German side, the crimes are better known: the Jews were

---

52: Wrobel, in Jacobs, 2001, p135.
53: Wrobel, in Jacobs, 2001, p207.
54: Wrobel, in Jacobs, 2001, p166.
55: Brumberg, 1999, p206.
56: Wrobel, in Jacobs, 2001, p207.

rounded up in ghettos, where they were starved before being massacred in concentration camps. A less well known history is that of the resistance in the ghettos. The Bund organised an underground press, education system and theatre groups in most ghettos across Poland. It collaborated with the PPS and the Polish Underground in terrorist attacks on the occupying forces. Finally, and perhaps most impressively, it organised, with others, uprisings in several ghettos, of which the Warsaw one is the best known.

After around 300,000 Jews had been deported to the death camps, the remaining members of Zionist groups, Communists and Bundists came together and launched the Jewish Fighting Organisation. Together, and with the few arms they could get from an under-armed and doubtful Polish resistance movement, they launched an uprising in 1943 as the Germans attempted to clear out the ghetto completely. They resisted for a month, against a well fed, trained and heavily armed army. The uprising was finally crushed through the complete destruction of the ghetto.[57]

The ghetto uprising was a last glimmer of hope, a flame of resistance, in the long night of the extermination of nearly the entirety of the Jewish population of the Pale and with it that of the Bund, and those Jewish workers who fought to change the world.

After the war the Bund and all other revolutionary organisations were forced into the ruling Stalinist Polish United Workers' Party.[58] Only a few thousand Bundists survived, many emigrated, and others disappeared. In 1948 in Brussels the Bund called a world Bundist Conference, thereby abandoning the rejection of a united world Jewry, and the necessity to organise where one was, in the particular circumstances one was facing. In the end it even recognised the state of Israel and the Bundist branch in the Zionist state. The Bund suffered the same demoralisation as did a majority of Jews. Its militants looked for peace and refuge, even at the price of dispossession of another people's land.

Conclusion

The history of the Bund is important, first as a corrective to the rewriting of Jewish history by Zionist historians. The history of the Jews in Europe is not one of victims or casualties of history. On the contrary, it is the history of a population in struggle, organising and fighting for a different and better world, one without exploitation and oppression. The Bund

---

57: Edelman, 1994.
58: Wrobel, in Jacobs, 2001, p167.

played an important role in that struggle and took part in the greatest moments of liberation and revolution, as well as the darkest hours of oppression and extermination.

The history of the Bund also shows what many exclusivist revolutionary movements have shown since: the self-organisation of an oppressed working class is in itself a step forward, but a limited one on the road to complete liberation. Indeed, the creation of the Bund created a space where Jewish workers could organise and resist against both the exploitation and racism they faced. It was also a step forward for the revolutionary movement as a whole. The Bund created many of the pillars of revolutionary organisation, from agitational newspapers to full-time revolutionaries. The Bund organised trade unions and fought for better wages and conditions.

At the same time, it found itself limited geographically and structurally by its exclusive base. It is important to understand that its exclusivity, or particularism, was rooted in the oppression faced by the Bund. It was at first not a conscious decision, but a fact of life under an oppressive system, which drove the Bund to become a Jewish workers' organisation: the workers it was in contact with were almost exclusively Jewish.

Nonetheless, it became clear at the highest moments of struggle—in victory and in defeat—that without the alliance and the unity of all workers, victory against oppression and exploitation is impossible. Ultimately, oppression is inextricably linked to exploitation, and it is only through the overthrow of the system as a whole, by all workers, that all forms of oppression can be overcome. Despite the fact that the Bund understood this theoretically, in practice it never accepted the full conclusions. The answer to ending anti-Semitism could never be separate organisations fighting for a federal nationality structure. It could only be unity in action, unity in organisation, unity in objectives, by one class against another.

The Bund's membership came to that conclusion at the height of the revolutionary wave in Russia. Not only was the promise of socialism and a different world opening in front of their eyes a fantastic universalising pull, but the Bolsheviks proved in practice that they were the group that would fight the hardest for workers' power and against anti-Semitism. It was therefore not only the objective situation that created the conditions for the Bundists to join the Bolsheviks, but also the conscious effort of the Bolsheviks to defeat anti-Semitism, that won the Jewish revolutionaries over.

In the defeat of the revolutionary movement from the 1920s onwards the Bund was defeated too. Its defeat was accelerated by its original inability to relate to the revolutionary wave, and its turn to community organising and electioneering. It was disarmed by Stalinism and murdered in the Nazi extermination.

In a sense the history of the Bund is the history of the workers' movement in Eastern Europe, and represents many of its aspects, in both victory and defeat.

Today it reminds us of those who fought for a different world. It reminds us that Eastern European Jews escaped to Zionism amid demoralisation and defeat. It reminds us of the dignified heroism of the condemned at the darkest hour of the century, and crucially it still teaches us lessons in the fight against oppression and exploitation a century later.

References

Edelman, Marek, 1994, *The Ghetto Fights* (Bookmarks).

Brossat, Alain, and Sylvia Klingberg, 2009, *Le Yiddishland Révolutionnaire* (Syllepse).

Brumberg, Abraham, 1999, "Anniversaries in Conflict: on the Centenary of the Jewish Socialist Labour Bund", *Jewish Social Studies*, new series, volume 5, number 3 (spring-summer), http://muse.jhu.edu/journals/jewish_social_studies/v005/5.3brumberg.html

Brumberg, Abraham, 2001, "The Bund: History of a Schism", in Jacobs, 2001.

Cliff, Tony, 1986 [1975], *Lenin: Building the Party 1893-1914* (Bookmarks).

Cohen, Nathan, 2001, "The Bund's Contribution to Yiddish Culture in Poland Between the Two World Wars", in Jacobs, 2001.

Jacobs, Jack (ed), 2001, *Jewish Politics in Eastern Europe: The Bund at 100* (Palgrave).

Kessler, Mario, 2001, "The Bund and the Labour Socialist International", in Jacobs, 2001.

Kuhn, Rick, 2001, "The Jewish Social Democratic Party of Galicia and the Bund", in Jacobs, 2001.

Lenin, VI, 1903, "Letter to the Organising Committees", www.marxists.org/archive/lenin/works/1903/mar/31oc.htm

Lih, Lars, 2008, *Lenin Rediscovered: What Is to Be Done? in Context* (Haymarket).

Lih, Lars, 2011, *Lenin* (Reaktion).

Mendelsohn, Ezra, 1968, "Jewish and Christian Workers in the Russian Pale of Settlement", *Jewish Social Studies*, volume 30, number 4 (October).

Minszeles, Henri, 2010, *Le Movement Ouvrier Juif: Récit des Origines* (Syllepse).

Pickhan, Gertrud, Vladimir Kossovsky, Yekusiel Portnoy and others, 2001, "The Role of Members of the Bund's Founding Generation in the Interwar Polish Bund", in Jacobs, 2001.

Pinson, Koppel, 1945, "Arkady Kremer, Vladimir Medem, and the Ideology of the Jewish 'Bund'", *Jewish Social Studies*, volume 7, number 3 (July).

Rose, John, 2004, *The Myths of Zionism* (Bookmarks).

Samus, Pawel, 2001, "The Bund Organisation in Lodz, 1898–1936", in Jacobs, 2001.

Tobias, Henry, 1968, "The Bund and Lenin until 1903", *Russian Review*, volume 20, number 4 (October).

Wrobel, Piotr, 2001, "From Conflict to Cooperation: the Bund and the Polish Socialist Party, 1897-1939", in Jacobs, 2001.

Zimmerman, Joshua, 2001, "The influence of the "Polish Question" on the Bund's National Programme, 1897–1905", in Jacobs, 2001.

Characterising the period
Nigel Harris

*Nigel Harris, who succeeded Michael Kidron as editor of **International Socialism** during the 1960s, made a welcome return to our pages in issue 132. Then he was reviewing Ian Birchall's biography of Tony Cliff. Here he seeks to sum up the world conjuncture. His basic thesis—that the fundamental contradiction today is that between global capitalism and the system of nation-states—was a matter of much debate in **International Socialism** during the 1980s and 1990s. In this brief but sharp overview Nigel updates his analysis by bringing it to bear on the global economic crisis and the political reactions it is provoking. Readers may disagree with some of what he says (they may doubt, for example, that global capitalism can achieve "the end of world poverty"), but they will also find plentiful food for thought—AC*

It used to be that identifying the central contradiction of a historical period was seen by Marxists as the linchpin of all subsidiary analyses and strategies.[1] But the general decay of theoretical concerns has made this unfashionable.

Nonetheless, much of the left falls back on the threadbare term "imperialism" as a substitute for rethinking the period. The concept now, however, lacks the original theoretical underpinnings (Hobson-Hilferding) which anchored imperial expansion in a change in the core of capitalism, and seems to imply that "freeing nations" (usually from

1:    I am grateful to Ian Birchall and David Renton for critical appraisal of an earlier version of this—neither is in any way complicit in this outcome.

Washington domination[2]) would achieve universal liberation.[3] This article tries to suggest an alternative approach in order to open discussion.

Since about 1980 the constituent national parts of the world economy have been dominated by the transition to a single world economy: "economic globalisation". This increasingly imposes on the world a new changing pattern of territorial specialisation, organised by global markets, not as hitherto believed (rightly or wrongly), by national states. The integration of the separate political territories ("national economies") into a single economic system has been achieved in stages through the state agreeing to relinquish control of trade, of capital, and finally—albeit partially—of labour.[4] The free flow of the factors of production has created a single world economy,[5] outside the control of any one national authority.[6] The destruction of the old Soviet Union, of apartheid in South Africa as well as the coming final transformation of others (Cuba, Myanmar, North Korea, etc) can be seen as only the more extreme casualties of this inexorable economic globalisation.

The first phase of the current transition has been characterised both by extraordinary levels of prosperity in the heartlands of the system (the Atlantic economy and Japan), and an unprecedented geographical spread of economic growth (most dramatically to China and South East Asia, to Latin America and, latterly, to India). In turn, this process may now be drawing in sub-Saharan Africa. In the first phase, opinion rejoiced that the world had apparently mastered the secret of sustained and spreading growth; in the second, marred at the end by severe economic crisis in the heartlands, there were growing fears that globalisation had disastrously undermined the authority of the state, and imposed on the world a territorial division of

2:   Failing to note that, despite being overwhelmingly dominant in military/political terms, Washington remains mired in an insoluble crisis with world capital.

3:   With hindsight, we can see that "national liberation" in practice liberated only a new ruling class (and the security forces to protect it) and licensed entry to the "international community".

4:   Indeed, by now it is doubtful—at least in the developed countries—whether "national economies"—discrete autonomous areas of economic activity, defined by political boundaries—any longer exist as objects of effective state policy. At best, states manage global flows that begin and end beyond their authority or even their knowledge.

5:   As occurred earlier in the creation of national economies (territories governed by the free flow of the factors of production within one politically defined territory), in this case, sacrificing economic linkages beyond the territory of the state to those within it.

6:   The theme is difficult to discuss because data—and policy discussion—are defined by the current distribution of political power, national states and their interests (and international statistics are assembled from national sources). Thus the distribution of political authority defines our perception of the global economy. Indeed, some tell the story of global capitalism, not with reference to global markets, but as the jousting of competing states and their relative share of activity.

labour which made redundant the mass of the labour force in the heartlands, implying long-term mass unemployment. It seemed an existential political crisis of the state coincided with an economic crisis of material survival for the population.[7]

The current transition is, historically, the second great surge towards economic globalisation.[8] The first,[9] between, say, 1870 and 1914, ended with two world wars and the Great Slump, in which states not only clawed back the powers they had conceded to global markets, but immensely enhanced and centralised national political power over their respective national economies to an unprecedented degree, epitomised in the extraordinary concentration of power in the state in Nazi Germany and the Soviet Union.[10] It took nearly 50 years after the end of the Second World War to resume the drive to globalisation, now with much enhanced vigour and comprehensiveness, and encompassing the whole world, not just the Atlantic economy.

Indeed, never before in the history of capitalism has the ethic of competitive markets—neoliberalism[11]—penetrated so deeply into the domestic operations of the state, into virtually every cell of the social order. We are now within sight of the reversal of many of the major historical efforts to tame the destructive power of markets—from the New Deal and

---

7:   In an overheated political climate, the fears were exaggerated. The concentration of high skills, research facilities and infrastructure would give the heartlands of the system an indispensable role far into the future (without this ruling out radical changes in the pecking order of states). This is, of course, no comfort to workers laid off in the here and now. On the other hand, a world social structure is emerging with the rich spatially concentrated for the moment in cities in the West (London, Paris, New York). The "periphery" becomes the site for looting by the local rulers before running to live in the secure environment of Paris, London, New York, etc (witness the Russian oligarchs).

8:   An earlier "surge" might be seen, following Kautsky, in the creation of global markets through the spread of colonial empires. See also Roy, 2012.

9:   Summed up most presciently in 1914 by Leon Trotsky: "The natural tendency of our economic system is to seek to break through the state boundaries. The whole globe, the land and the sea, the surface as well as the interior, has become one economic workshop, the different parts of which are inseparably connected with each other... The present [First World] war is at bottom a revolt of the forces of production against the political form of nation and state. It means the collapse of the national state as an independent economic unit"—Trotsky, 1971, pvii.

10:   The period established an extraordinary faith in the potential of state planning and dominant public sectors; governments everywhere mimicked the imperatives of the war economy, even in peacetime.

11:   "Neoliberalism" is the ideological expression of global capital, not the product of a sudden surge of greed (that was always there) or an intellectual error by economists. The neoliberals are the product of the emerging economic system, not its source. They, like everyone else, are not in control of the system. Government reform arises from practical calculations, not ideological commitments.

Great Society legislation in the US (even the right to collective bargaining) to the welfare state and the provision of social and educational services in Europe. Indeed, in the period from the 1950s to the present there has been an almost complete reversal of the dominant statist narrative throughout the world, especially visible in Europe, but most dramatically in what used to be called the developing countries (and the Eastern Bloc).[12]

In striking contrast to the past, national economic growth (for social prosperity and to fund state coercive power) is now seen as exclusively provided by opening the national economy to global economic integration—allowing domestic economic activity to be determined by global markets rather than state priorities. Such arrangements necessitate domestic reform to open the economy to global capital, to establish transparency and accountability (so all competitors, domestic and foreign, receive the same message). By implication, the state relinquishes any ambition to shape the domestic economy in any particular direction, restricting itself to managing efficiently the accommodation of global forces.

However, the emergence of a national "global state" (that is, a state whose function is to manage the local economy and society in conformity with global, not local, imperatives) profoundly weakens the state compared to the past. It is obliged to relinquish much of what used to be a national agenda, including important instruments of economic policy concerning the management of external trade, capital movements and, in principle, labour. More importantly, politically, it relinquishes powers to bribe the electorate to be loyal and to reward patrons. To put it over-simplistically, the state faces a set of contradictory options—economic growth (through integration with the world economy) but weakened state power (especially relative to economic crisis); or enhanced state power with economic stagnation (which in turn undermines state power). Of course, depending on the specific circumstances of a particular state (including the history of past policies), opening up to the world may not lead to economic growth, in which case, the state has no recourse except to rule by violence. In an existential crisis (such as, for example, faces Assad's regime in Syria today), the state will not hesitate to sacrifice present and future economic growth—as indeed, the population of the country—to hold on to power.

The threat to state power is also political in a different way— through undermining the domestic social solidarity which has hitherto

---

12: In the developing countries of the 1950s and 1960s accelerated economic growth was seen as exclusively attainable through national economic isolation (even if modified in "import substitution"), excluding foreign capital, etc.

been identified as the precondition of a stable state. No population is likely to remain loyal indefinitely to a state seen as working exclusively for foreigners (the "world system"). Nowhere is this more painfully apparent than in the field of immigration, since the mobility of labour is also a precondition of economic growth. No advanced economy is any longer self-sufficient in labour (that includes the changing diversity of skills in the labour force as local economies restructure). The solidarity underpinning the old state required levels of xenophobia and sometimes racism which are incompatible with continual immigration, the "churning" of the labour force required for economic growth. Yet everywhere today, certainly in the heartlands of the system, there are increased restrictions on immigration, despite the damage done to economic growth (not to speak of the welfare of the native-born). States are again caught in a contradictory position—the conditions for growth undermine the elements of national closure (zero net migration) supposedly required to make secure state power (and seen most vividly in North Korea and the old Stalinist states).

It is this contradictory position which inhibits states today from copying the reactions to the inter-war Great Depression, ending the first surge of globalisation—economic closure and domestic authoritarianism. The reaction now is fragmentary and contradictory—some moves to authoritarianism,[13] a ballooning prison population,[14] attempts to block immigration and demonise "illegals" (and Muslims), along with the continued spread of neoliberal reform, but without systematic protectionism. Of course, since the present crisis might be seen as an existential one for states. The longer the crisis lasts, especially if marked by popular revolts against austerity, the greater the danger states will seek to recover their lost powers—and reverse economic globalisation, sacrificing the welfare of their own and the world's population to their own survival. The issue of world slump was only settled last time round by resort to world war and a terrible orgy of self-destruction. At the moment world war seems unlikely but one should not underestimate the potential for auto-destruct when one or other state's existence is threatened—the common ruin of the contending nations/classes.

These trends—if "trends" they are—go with other attempts to disenfranchise citizens, to isolate government from "politics", to protect

---

13: In the US the moves to end habeas corpus, institutionalise torture, etc, are well known—but see the 2011 National Defense Authorization Act to allow indefinite detention without charge or trial (and in Britain steps to allow indefinite detention without charge).

14: For the US, put recently at over 6 million, proportionately the largest number in the world (the number for China is not published but may be larger).

the global system (and states) from popular demands, and install technical or expert administration—through independent central banks and national statistical agencies to reassure "global investors" that mere governments—or "politics"—cannot interfere either with monetary policy or basic data; and in Europe, to institutionalise binding (constitutional) conditions of expert state management. The language betrays the change of emphasis—"citizens" become "clients" or customers for state services, where the criterion of judgement is supposedly the efficiency and cost of service provision, not the right of citizens to exercise popular sovereignty. But the weakening or removal of representation further undermines the state: it is popular democratic self-government that supposedly legitimises the exercise of sovereignty.

The strict limits imposed on national sovereignty by the new order are becoming clear—that is, on the economic front, the global economic nexus, global markets severely discipline national policy and those constraints are reinforced by the political order of states, the so-called "international community". The state now appears to become an agent for an economic and political world order, enforcing global imperatives on the domestic population rather than representing it to the world at large (let alone defending it against external threats). If there is no longer the possibility of state sovereignty, will the world's fascination for two centuries with "national liberation" become undermined? Not while aspirant ruling classes are willing to fight for a place at the top table, and there are no alternative options for popular self-emancipation.

This conjuncture exposes the separation of what we might call two ruling classes—a territorial national ruling class, a class whose very existence depends on holding a national territory (composed of the state administration itself, armed forces and security services, crony capitalism, owners of land and infrastructure, etc), and a global ruling class which directs the companies and corporations that constitute the global economy, the mobile global rich, along with the staff of international agencies, NGOs, etc—that is, a global social stratum for whom nationality is a mere contingency, not a matter of overriding loyalty. The two classes are in practice not at all clearly distinguishable and members pass freely between the two. What is distinguishable is interest (for example, between neoliberalism and economic nationalism) and role (national versus international).[15]

15: It could be argued that a global ruling class cannot be said to exist as a "class for itself" without identifiable institutions of self-realisation, world governance. To pursue this theme here would take us too far from the central thread of the argument.

Thus we may be entering a period which combines both the extraordinary potential for the end of world poverty,[16] and a possible existential crisis of the fractured political order of the world. The danger is that the territorial ruling class may use its overwhelming control of the powers of physical coercion to reassert national dominance over the global economy—producing domestic authoritarianism with economic stagnation (with possible perpetual warfare on the borderlands to enforce social discipline (a combination so brilliantly described in Orwell's *Nineteen Eighty-Four*). In fact, hopefully, global economic integration is by now already so advanced, it cannot be comprehensively reversed even if components can be qualified (eg immigration), and states will continue to cheat and chisel on the rules. States have an interest in inflating the popular fear that the new international division of labour will render redundant large sections of the labour force to support populist authoritarianism and that will damage economic globalisation—and hence the welfare of the people of the world. Elements of a partial restoration of national capitalisms already exist in the nexus between the national military and crony capital which dominate some important states (Russia, China, Pakistan, Iran, Israel, etc).

Many states are already adjusting their domestic orders to accommodate the new circumstances. Some have initiated national debates on what it is to be a native, the supposed values shared by the natives, often under the spurious pretext of the need to secure the "integration" of non-natives (immigrants, refugees, etc). Of course, what united, say, the British was never "shared values", but common subordination to one state, so the debate is both risible and vacuous. As so often, Israel in its peculiar circumstances is a pioneer in this adjustment, combining militarised ethno-nationalism, a return to religious orthodoxy with authoritarianism, employing the Israeli Arabs as the anvil to forge unity out of an immigrant diversity and pursuing a perpetual war in the Occupied Territories to sustain popular fear. However, this combination could be suicidal for an economy as globalised as Israel. Hungary in Europe is also distinguished by its innovations (ending an independent central bank and judiciary, and controlling freedom of the press). This last highlights the role of the technical revolution in communication, breaking—at least for the moment—the state's monopoly of information (many states are seeking means to restore the *status quo ante* through censoring the internet, mobile phones, etc).

16: The reduction in world poverty since 1980 is a staggering record and has persisted through the world economic crisis—partial estimates for 2010 suggest global poverty has been halved since 1990 and has been replicated in all regions of the world—*Economist*, 2012.

Left to itself, the global system seems unable to resist self-destruction: markets—and the competitive drive to profit—seem incapable of the self-discipline to escape crash. The global capitalist class shows little potential for political self-government. For that they are for the moment dependent on the existing political order (international and national). Yet the fragmented political order—where real coercive power is vested—appears incapable of overcoming its ferocious rivalries to achieve unified action to avoid self-destruction.

The core problem is, then, in sum, an integrated world economy, driven by global markets, the outcome of which cannot be predicted or determined, and a fractured political order of competing states that is incapable of unified action. The forces of revolt against this order—national liberation in the Arab world to overthrow the local mafia states; the Occupy movements in different countries (from Wall Street and Oakland to Tel Aviv); the mass worker struggles against austerity (Greece, Spain, Portugal); the widespread rash of peasant rebellions and strikes in China—all assume, insofar as they are political, the decisive role of the national state in securing reform or change. After decades of drilling populations to accept the state as the sole saviour of threatened populations, it is hardly surprising. Indeed, many of the rebels start from a demand to be taken as authentic natives and therefore worthy of being treated with dignity, not as if they were foreigners who deserve nothing from "our" state. The creativity of these movements is not in doubt, but intellectually, we cannot even begin to visualise a realistic road map to one world, a world without war, with a unified drive to end world poverty, secure a livelihood for all with security, and render the environment safe and sustainable. Revolutions in one national state can no longer achieve even "national liberation" (that requires breaking the global order), and though revolutions may spread, as we have seen in the Arab Spring (although not now united by an international proletarian class alliance), this merely reiterates the same order of competing states which is itself at the core of the problem.

Conclusion

These notes began with an implied criticism of the left that identifying the contemporary world as "imperialist" was theoretically inadequate. The charge put Washington at the centre of the world system, implying that achieving national self-determination by overthrowing Washington's domination would achieve the liberation of the world. However, Washington's power is purely military/political, and does not deliver the power to manage global markets, the underlying reality of contemporary capitalism. Indeed, we could identify Washington's attempts to control the world's political order, not as pursuit of empire, but as a misguided attempt to fill the vacuum created by the lack of world government in a global economy—but not in the interests of the world's people so much as what it sees as its own interests. Meanwhile that global capitalist system has severely damaged, perhaps irreversibly, that conjuncture in global flows that is still called the "US economy". Globalisation is not the imperialistic instrument of Washington and a clearly identifiable bloc of "US capital",[17] but a phenomenon that also undermines the US state, allowing the corporations that have their home or origin there to be free-floating in world markets with little or no reference to Washington.

In sum then, the period is dominated by the struggle of national political states to recover what was seen as their former power, the absolute and overriding powers of sovereignty, to resolidify the social foundations of political power while simultaneously securing economic growth, and do so while a global economy is constantly eroding their position. For a very long period capital was able to hide behind the state, but now—in the final phases of the completion of the bourgeois revolution (now on a world scale)—it is obliged to step into the limelight, unprotected by political power. It is perhaps the most dangerous conjuncture ever witnessed in the history of world capitalism, and the final outcome is far from clear.

References

Economist, 2012, "A fall to cheer" (3 March).
Roy, Trthhankar, 2012, "Empire, Law and Economic Growth", Economic and Political Weekly (25 February).
Trotsky, Leon, 1971 (1915), The War and the International (Young Socialist Publications).

17:   The old agenda that assumed each state had its own bloc of capital loyally working to further the ends of the state was never true, and is now increasingly untrue—for global corporations it is no longer possible to identify a nationality.

Twenty five years of revolution
Colin Barker

Twenty-five years ago Bookmarks published a collection of essays under the title **Revolutionary Rehearsals**. *The book has since been republished by Haymarket Press of Chicago. In its pages Ian Birchall wrote about France in May 1968, Mike Gonzalez about the struggle in Chile in the last year before Pinochet's bloody coup, Peter Robinson about popular power during the Portuguese Revolution of 1974-5, and Maryam Poya about the Iranian Revolution, while I produced a chapter about the Solidarity experience in Poland during 1980-1, along with a general chapter attempting to draw some lessons from these brilliant and also tragic experiences. Last year the Chaekgalpi Press in Seoul published a Korean translation of the whole book, kindly inviting me to produce a new preface. What follows is an English version of that text.*

It is almost a quarter of a century since *Revolutionary Rehearsals* was first published in 1987. The book focused on a number of important cases over the previous 20 years, in which a very particular possibility seemed to open up: namely that mass workers' movements might challenge for state power. The exploration of that possibility guided the selection of chapters.

The period since 1987 has been, in one sense, extraordinary in the sheer number of revolutions that have occurred. If one thing seems certain, it is that revolution is alive and well across the globe, and is indeed a very "normal" part of the political process in the modern capitalist world.

There has been a whole series of vitally important and dramatic transformations in political regimes. A wave of "democratisation" has swept away a variety of political dictatorships. If the wave perhaps began in Greece, Portugal and Spain in the 1970s, in the 1980s it brought down dictatorships across Latin America, and in the Philippines and South Korea, followed by the "communist" (actually state capitalist) regimes of Eastern Europe. The 1990s witnessed the end of the apartheid regime of South Africa and the fall of Suharto's dictatorship in Indonesia, along with moves towards democracy in numbers of countries in sub-Saharan Africa, a trend that continued into the new millennium. At the time of writing, in the spring of 2011, a new wave of revolutionary struggles is challenging many autocratic regimes across North Africa and the Middle East.

There is a paradox, however. On the one hand, "liberal democracy" has extended its sway across the world, and its expansion has been aided by extensive popular protests, including strike waves and mass demonstrations, on a previously unimagined scale. Yet, at the same time, social inequality has been growing in rich and poor countries alike, as "neoliberalism" has strengthened its grip on national and international economic policy-making. Neoliberalism is a policy whose intentions and effects are to shift the balance of power and wealth away from working people and towards the capitalist class. Indeed, the past few decades have seen the rich massively increasing their share of income and wealth, and not only in good times.

When the capitalist banking system ran into crisis, the major capitalist states raised *trillions* of dollars to save the banks—and went on to insist that the bill for the subsequent deficits must be paid by working people, and that public services should continue to be privatised, ie converted into new sources of profit for the capitalist class.

All of this is now widely understood across large parts of the working classes of the world. But it has taken time and bitter experience for that to be learned, and the learning has shaped the form of revolutions.

After the Polish military smashed the workers' movement Solidarity in December 1981, the continuing underground opposition to the regime shifted its ideological ground. In the autumn of 1981 Solidarity's first congress had called for a "self-governing republic" that would extend democracy into the workplace and the economy. But now, after its defeat, the movement's leaders and advisers began to look to "the market" as the solution to the ills of their economy and society. Illusions in Western capitalism spread. Instead of looking to the organised power of working people to remake society, they came to identify freedom with the free market. But they were not the only ones to be so convinced: the increasing paralysis of the state capitalist economy also persuaded wide layers among the Polish ruling class that there was no alternative to the market and private property.

The fruits of this parallel development were harvested in the spring of 1989, when Solidarity's leaders sat down at a "Round Table" with representatives of the regime and came to an agreement for a "negotiated transition" in Poland: to parliamentary democracy and the reinstallation of private capitalism.[1] As in neighbouring Hungary, the transition from one regime to another was accomplished with little by way of strikes and demonstrations. Elsewhere in Eastern Europe—notably in East Germany, Czechoslovakia and Romania—it took popular uprisings and mass demonstrations to dislodge the old regimes. Large numbers of workers participated, but there was little sign of the development of new popular institutions from below, and only sporadic challenges to managerial power in workplaces. After 1989 the privatisation of profitable resources proceeded apace, and unemployment and inequality grew.

In South Africa mass strikes and township protests finally compelled the apartheid regime to come to the negotiating table. The outcome was the profoundly popular election of an African National Congress (ANC) government in 1994. However, within two years the ANC leadership followed advice from the IMF and the World Bank, abandoning its previous economic policies in favour of a neoliberal strategy. Working people lost out in a big way. South Africa remains near the top of the list of the world's most unequal societies, with the African share of national income actually falling. Although the level of everyday popular protest in post-apartheid South Africa is also among the world's highest, successive ANC governments have worked to contain and deflect popular resistance.

Thus the years following the first appearance of our book did not prove favourable to the perspectives we discussed. Rather, revolutionary challenges were contained and deflected by what some political commentators called "negotiated transitions"—or what Czechoslovak wits called "velvet revolutions"—a form perhaps first seen in Spain in 1976, but then followed in Latin America, Eastern Europe and South Africa.

These kinds of political transformation seem to have some preconditions. On the ruling class side, sections of the "old regime" must see the writing on the wall, and be prepared to abandon their previous power monopoly. More important, on the side of the opposition, "moderate" leaders must be found who will work to contain the activity of their own

---

1: There were tragic paradoxes. The first minister of labour in the new government was Jacek Kuron, co-author with Karol Modzelewski of the 1964 "Open Letter to the Party". In 1964 Kuron had called openly for a workers' revolution; in 1990 he was giving fireside chats on television to explain the necessity of rising unemployment...

supporters within "safe limits" and to guarantee the safety, and often the continued wealth and security, of at least most of the old regime's cadres. In this way, the "risks" of popular revolution may be reduced, and openings can be created for at least the more far-seeing of the old regime to achieve satisfactory "safe landings" when regime change occurs. The machinery by which "negotiated transitions" are achieved may include "Pacts", "Round Tables", "Amnesties", "Truth and Reconciliation Commissions" and the like. The crimes of former murderers, torturers and thieves may be forgiven. A "negotiated transition" requires both a "reforming" wing within the ruling class and a dominant "reformist wing" within the opposition. The reformist opposition leaders must work to *contain* popular demands and organisations, by a mixture of co-optation and demagogy, and by excluding dissenting voices. There is also a more general condition: politics and economics must be treated as separate and distinct spheres, so that contradictions between political equality at the ballot box and rapidly widening economic inequalities are not too obvious. Such an ideological separation underlay the East European "dream of the market", that everyone would be free—and equal.

The ongoing march of neoliberalism, however, has reduced its ideological appeals. Its social and economic effects have become more prominently apparent, as political and economic power have become more concentrated and more closely interwoven. Across continents there has been a widespread growth of popular suspicion and hostility towards the privatisation of public services, towards the granting of private property rights to wealthy corporations at the expense of the poor, towards the increasing dependence of the poor on food and fuel whose prices are governed by commodity speculators. Increasingly neoliberalism smells, not of "freedom", but of the *corruption* of public offices by the lure of wealth. Major environmental, economic and social crises have offered speculators and those with privileged access to decision-makers new opportunities—to profit at the direct expense of their shattered neighbours' lives.

Many of neoliberalism's advances rested on major working class defeats. Too often commentators have read these defeats as meaning the end of the working class as a focus of resistance. What they missed was that defeats were, as in past history, often the occasion for new beginnings, and for the remaking of workers' movements. Older industries and occupations might crumble, but new sectors were being driven into the proletariat, and bringing impulses to revived insurgency. "White collar" workers have come to play a far more central role in popular resistance, from Mexican teachers in Oaxaca to militant Egyptian tax workers in

Cairo. The gap has continued to narrow between workers and students, who played an unexpectedly prominent role in the May 1968 movement in France, now that "higher education" has become a mass industry run on bureaucratic and capitalist lines. Millions of former peasants have been driven into the hugely expanded cities of the "Third World", where they have developed new capacities for organisation and struggle. Some movement transformations have been dramatic and rapid: the core of Bolivia's labour movement, the organised miners, suffered appalling defeats in the mid-1980s, yet a decade and a half later a recomposed popular movement proved able to achieve an astonishing victory against water privatisation in Cochabamba, initiating a five-year period of revolutionary upheaval.

Thus, if it took a while for the realities of neoliberalism to din themselves into the brains of those subjected to its processes, by the end of the old millennium the evidence of that popular recognition was widespread. The period when popular revolution could be smoothly substituted by "negotiated transitions" as a mechanism of political change was ending. Issues of "economic justice", interweaving economic and political struggles were again becoming more prominent in insurgent agendas. The poetic cries of the rebellion of Chiapas in 1994, which coincided with the official beginning of the North American Free Trade Agreement (a key development in neoliberalism's programme), would be picked up and amplified by a host of different voices and movements over the subsequent period. In the very last month of the 20th century an international demonstration at the World Trade Organisation meeting in Seattle provided slogans that resonated with movements over the next decade and more: "Our world is not for sale" and "Another world is possible".

The idea of freedom was no longer attached to the concept of the market. On the contrary, a new generation now identified the market as a principal cause of injustice and exploitation. The crises and injustices associated with the real workings of capitalist world economy provoked major waves of popular insurgency as the 21st century began. Uprisings in Ecuador in 2000 and in Argentina in 2001, both of them associated with economic crisis, brought down their governments. In Cochabamba the new century began with a successful mass movement against the privatisation of water. In 2002 in Venezuela a right wing coup backed by big business was defeated by a huge popular movement that restored Hugo Chávez to the presidency to which he had been elected four years earlier. In 2003-5, again in Bolivia, popular uprisings drove out successive presidents who failed to respond to their demands. In 2006 a mass movement overthrew the government of Nepal. These struggles were increasingly interwoven with mass strike movements and popular insurgencies that focused directly on economic and social demands. So, too, it has been with the revolutions in Tunisia and Egypt in 2011.

The past 24 years have thus provided many more materials on "revolutionary rehearsals". And the coming years will surely provide many more. The world is still reeling from the largest global crisis since the Second World War, whose aftershocks are being felt both in the heartlands and the peripheries of world imperialism. Everywhere national and transnational governmental institutions are demanding that working people must pay for the banking crisis with cuts in real wages, welfare services and pensions—while those responsible for the crisis are walking away with larger salaries and bonuses. Transnational bodies like the IMF, the World Bank and the WTO, which lock national governments into their neoliberal policy embrace, do not even pretend to be responsive to popular movements and demands.

There is thus every reason to suppose that mass popular movements will again—and in much less than the next quarter century!—pose directly the *possibility* of a socialist transformation of society. Possibility is not, however, inevitability. Reflection on previous experience suggests some of the conditions of success.

What marks the beginnings of a revolutionary era is the entry of large masses of the oppressed and exploited into active engagement with political life. The opening of mass struggles "from below" signals the breakdown of political "normality", a condition nicely described by US historian Lawrence Goodwyn as one where "a relatively small number of citizens possessing high sanction move about in an authoritative manner and a much larger number of people without such sanction move about more softly".[2] Normality is commonly preserved by a mixture of fear and disbelief in the possibility of significant change. Its breakdown is marked by a release of popular energy and imagination.

The question is then, what form does this take? How are popular aspirations formulated and expressed? Is the old distinction between "political" and "economic" demands maintained, or do they begin to dissolve—as famously analysed in Rosa Luxemburg's account of mass strikes?[3] Capitalism's supporters always hope to maintain this separation: recently the *Financial Times*, the leading British capitalist newspaper, summarised its concerns about the ongoing revolutionary situation in Egypt by saying, "The economy

2:    Goodwyn, 1991, pxxxi.
3:    Luxemburg, 1986.

itself must be depoliticised".[4] That "depoliticisation" of economic life was what the capitalist class loved about the 1989 revolutions in Eastern Europe. Socialists take the opposing view, asking whether popular practical hopes are invested only in a change of *government*, or also encompass demands to do with, for example, wages and prices, working conditions, democracy in trade unions, and managerial power in workplaces. Is economic as well as political corruption challenged from below? Are there processes of "*saneamento*" (the Portuguese term from 1974), of "cleaning out" those whose power depended on their connections with the old regime? The expansion of struggles focused on "economic" questions is a vital part of every popular upsurge with the potential to change the very bases of social life.

What's involved is not just a matter of weakening and undermining old patterns, but of beginning to create and spread new kinds of relationships and institutions in all areas of social life. What kind of new regime is possible? If no new regime is more democratic than the movement that creates it, we need to ask whether those engaged in revolutionary upsurge are building new kinds of democratic organisations, not just in the obviously "political" sphere but in neighbourhoods and workplaces, in the organisation of "public order" and justice, and in the institutions of the popular movement themselves, in unions and parties, in people's assemblies and workers' and peasants' councils. Is the *general* demand for democracy and mass participation in every sphere of social life emerging, and being theorised and broadcast across the insurgent movement?

A mass movement from below can generate the conditions for this to occur, as nothing else can. For in such a movement, popular learning and development speed up enormously, once the old barriers of fatalism and fear begin to dissolve and those who "moved about more softly" start to feel their accumulating strength—and to mock and pull down the formerly powerful. The idea that the whole of society can indeed be remade on new foundations takes on a suddenly realistic hue. Issues that once were the debating topics of tiny minorities can become practical questions for millions: what kind of economy do we actually want. Are working people capable of running society themselves?

It is in relation to just such matters that we can measure the deepening of popular revolutions. A merely "political" revolution that overthrows an old government can be accomplished by a determined minority. One estimate is that around 20 percent of the population of Egypt was actively involved in the overthrow of Mubarak—a brilliant popular achievement,

---

4:    *Financial Times*, 2011

but still a minority. A *socialist* revolutionary process, however, will necessarily involve a far larger proportion, for it must reach far deeper into all the forms and aspects of everyday life. To the degree that working people do begin to manage their own productive and organised life activities under their own steam, developing democratic means of decision making, to that degree also their confidence in their own cooperative powers can develop. Their own individual and social transformative growth becomes both a means and an end. The importance of such "cultural" and "psychological" development can hardly be overestimated.

Revolutionary movements make it possible to set aside old assumptions and prejudices, whether about religious, ethnic and national antagonisms, or gender superiority and difference. However, there is nothing automatic about such advances: they have to be fought for openly, and the proponents of old divisive ways pushed back in favour of new, enlarged ideas of solidarity. Popular movements do not only contest power with the old rulers; they involve deep and contentious debate about their own forms, their own procedures, their own meaning and purpose. They develop, for good or for ill, through processes of mass learning, by debating, testing and absorbing the lessons of different engagements with the old forces and forms of authority, through defeats and advances, dramatic turning points and reversals. Leon Trotsky described this experimental method of discovery and learning as one involving "successive approximations" by mass movements, a method involving great leaps of understanding and imagination as well as collapses of mutual trust and fierce internal arguments.

To the extent that, in their development of new forms of organisation and their challenges to old forms of authority, movements burrow away at the institutional and cultural supports of capitalist power, a revolutionary period is marked by a peculiar form of contested government, sometimes termed "dual power" or "multiple sovereignty". The former ruling classes, and their very principles of power, are severely weakened, but they have not yet been decisively replaced. The rising power of the movement of working people has not yet gained full power and confidence in itself. It is a situation of huge instability, but also one, in Trotsky's phrase, of great political "flabbiness". The question of the moment becomes ever more stark: will the popular mass movement march forward to take power for itself, through its own new democratic institutions, or will sections of the old ruling class exploit its uncertainties, divert its energies, and find ways to demobilise the movement and recover their old power in some new form?

In this volume's chapters on Chile and Poland, that ruling class recovery took form as *military dictatorship*, a particularly brutal form of capitalist rule. Barely less brutal was the Islamist dictatorship in Iran, erected on the defeat of left and secularist forces in the 1979 Revolution. But the chapter on Portugal shows that ruling classes have other possibilities, not least a recourse to the politics of *social democracy*. In place of the direct contest of mass movements with capital and the state, let's have an *election*! In just this way, the five years of revolutionary contestation in Bolivia from the great victory of the Cochabamba "water wars" of 2000 ended with the election of the left government of Evo Morales in 2005. Popular energies were displaced onto the electoral path. In one sense, the Morales election registered a huge victory for the people of Bolivia—but also a failure to resolve the crisis of Bolivian society. The capitalist class's property and power remained intact, and poverty for the mass of Bolivians continued.[5]

In conditions of "dual power", the role of revolutionary Marxist parties takes on its maximum significance. Such conditions produce opportunities, not only for socialist advance, but also for reformist politicians to seek to ride to office on the wave of popular discontent and mobilisation. For *their* project to succeed, it is vital that the popular movement demobilise its forces and lower its aspirations, to focus instead on the parliamentary arena. In such circumstances, revolutionary socialists' active involvement in the movement becomes vital, for they can develop an alternative pole of argument and agitation, stressing the need to maintain and further develop the movement's independent activity and organisations—for it is in these, and not in parliament, that the possibility of a real social transformation resides.

In a world locked in crisis, where the flames of revolt are once more rising, these matters will again be posed as practical questions. The republication of this volume seems timely.

5: Jeffery Webber has chronicled the Bolivian experience in two recent books: Webber 2011a and 2011b.

References

Financial Times, 2011, "The economics of the Arab spring" (24 April).

Goodwyn, Lawrence 1991, *Breaking the Barrier: The Rise of Solidarity in Poland* (Oxford University Press).

Luxemburg, Rosa, 1986 [1906], *The Mass Strike* (Bookmarks), www.marxists.org/archive/luxemburg/1906/mass-strike/index.htm

Webber, Jeffery R, 2011a, *From Rebellion to Reform in Bolivia: Class Struggle, Indigenous Liberation, and the Politics of Evo Morales* (Haymarket).

Webber, Jeffery R, 2011b, *Red October: Left-Indigenous Struggles in Modern Bolivia* (Brill).

Daniel Bensaïd and the broken time of politics

Alex Callinicos

I am very conscious of the great honour of being invited to participate in this seminar as someone who did not belong to the same international current as Daniel Bensaïd and only got to know him in the last decade of his life. But as soon as we met, what drew me towards Daniel was not simply his immense personal qualities—his strength of character, warmth and kindness, and a dry sense of humour congenial to an Anglo-Saxon sensibility (although inflected by Daniel's strong southern accent, the product of a clime very different from the damp island I inhabit)—but the presence of an exceptional intellect. Reading the flood of writings Daniel produced in his last 15 years I was strongly attracted to a highly original body of work with whose substance I strongly agreed even though it was expressed in a very different philosophical idiom from my own.[1]

One of Bensaïd's many great virtues was that he was a highly unorthodox Marxist. This was reflected in his vast and unusual range of intellectual reference, but also in the diversity of topics about which he wrote. He must, for example, be the only Trotskyist to have written a book about Joan of Arc. Bensaïd was quite untrammelled by the need to make

1:    This article originated as a presentation to the seminar organised by the Fourth International, "Daniel Bensaïd: L'internationaliste", at the International Institute for Research and Education, Amsterdam, 13-15 January 2012. I am grateful to the organisers, Penny Duggan and François Sabado, for inviting me.

obeisance to any orthodoxy. This didn't mean his views were vague or wishy-washy. On contrary, the very strength of his commitment to revolutionary Marxism allowed him great freedom in articulating its content.

Bensaïd was thus an open but very tough-minded Marxist. This was reflected in the fact that he wrote very well about Lenin. I am proud that a key late text of his on Lenin was published in the journal I edit, *International Socialism*.[2] I want here to explore the theoretical roots of his understanding of Lenin.

A preoccupation with Lenin runs through Bensaïd's writing. Thus, in a celebrated article co-written with Alain Naïr in the heat of 1968, he championed Lenin against Rosa Luxemburg in their famous debate over the question of party organisation. Bensaïd came to regard this text as "tainted with juvenile 'ultra-Bolshevism'".[3] Certainly the idea that the revolutionary party is the "political subject" of revolution, and the working class merely the "theoretical subject", is open to a substitutionist drift that arguably was realised during the Ligue Communiste's quasi-Guevarist phase in the early 1970s.[4] Nevertheless, the text's tough polemic against Luxemburg's "spontaneism" must be seen as a contribution to a much broader effort to turn the generation radicalised by May '68 and its counterparts elsewhere, and heavily influenced by libertarian critiques of Leninism, towards the task of building revolutionary parties rooted in the working class. As such, it should be compared with, in the International Socialist tradition, Chris Harman's fundamental essay "Party and Class", written at much the same time, and for very similar reasons, and, within Bensaïd's own current, with Henri Weber's slightly later *Marxisme et Conscience de Classe*, a work whose value should be acknowledged despite the author's later rightward evolution into the ranks of the Socialist Party.[5]

The primacy of politics

But in Bensaïd's late writing on Lenin his focus is no longer on the questions of party organisation and class consciousness. This is not because he became indifferent to these issues. Another of Daniel's many paradoxes

---

2:   Bensaïd, 2002b.

3:   Bensaïd, 2008. I would like to pay tribute to Pierre Rousset's efforts to put as much as possible of Daniel's writing in various languages online at the Europe solidaire sans frontières website: www.europe-solidaire.org.

4:   Compare Bensaïd, 2002a, p270, where he calls into question conceiving either party or class as subjects. A brief account of Daniel's role in the substitutionism of the early 1970s will be found, along with much else, in Sebastian Budgen's tribute—Budgen, 2010.

5:   Harman, 1968-9, and Weber, 1975.

was that he remained a strong "party man" despite his singularity as both a person and a thinker. But it seems to me he followed Michael Löwy in seeing as central to Lenin's thought the primacy of politics. Löwy writes in a text of the mid-1970s:

> From the methodological point of view, Lenin's principal superiority over most of his contemporaries was his capacity to "put politics in command", ie his obstinate, inflexible, constant and unflinching tendency to grasp and highlight the *political* aspect of every problem and every contradiction. This tendency stood out in his polemic against the Economists on the question of the party in 1902–3; in his discussion with the Mensheviks on the question of the democratic revolution in 1905; in the originality of his writings on imperialism in 1916; in the inspired turn which the April Theses represented in 1917; in the whole of his most important work *State and Revolution* and, of course, in his writings on the national question. It is this methodological aspect which explains (among other things) the striking *actuality* of Lenin's ideas in the 20th century, an age of imperialism, which has seen the political level become increasingly *dominant* (even though, in the last analysis, it is of course *determined* by the economic).[6]

Compare this with what Bensaïd writes 30 years later: "Lenin was one of the first to conceive the specificity of the political field as a play of transfigured powers and social antagonisms, translated into a language of its own, full of displacements, of condensations and of revealing slips of the tongue".[7] It is important not to misunderstand what Löwy and Bensaïd are saying here. The idea of the "specificity of the political field" should not be confused with the thesis of the relative autonomy of the political associated particularly with Nicos Poulantzas.[8] Marx in the *Grundrisse* talks about "the concentration of the whole in the state".[9] In *Capital* he calls the state "the concentrated and organised force of society".[10] The state isn't autonomous, but—precisely because it is where all the antagonisms of capitalist society are condensed—it is special. This means that politics works according to a specific logic that cannot be reduced to that of any of these antagonisms, even those of capital accumulation and class struggle. The key to the Marxist theory of the state lies in simultaneously grasping this specificity and recognising that it reflects

6:    Löwy, 1976, p97.
7:    Bensaïd, 2004, p121.
8:    Poulantzas, 1973.
9:    Marx, 1973, p105.
10:   Marx, 1976, p915 (translation modified).

the way in which, under the reign of commodity fetishism, the social whole is fragmented, broken up into distinct, apparently unrelated parts.[11]

Hence politics has to be read critically in the same way that Freud argued the effects of the unconscious had to be scrutinised (condensation and displacement are the two main mechanisms that he identifies at work in producing the apparently meaningless babble of dreams). Bensaïd draws the parallel explicitly:

> Revolutionary theory has something in common with psychoanalysis. Political representation is not the simple manifestation of a social nature. Political class struggle is not the superficial mirroring of an essence. Articulated like a language, it operates by displacements and condensations of social contradictions. It has its dreams, its nightmares and its lapses. In the specific field of the political, class relations acquire a degree of complexity irreducible to the bipolar antagonism [of exploiter and exploited] that nevertheless determines them.[12]

The discordance of historical times

This understanding of politics is related to some of the most abstract dimensions of Bensaïd's thought. Stathis Kouvelakis has highlighted the importance—especially in *Marx for Our Times*—of a certain understanding of historical time.[13] This is summed up by the title of another book: *The Discordance of Times*.[14]

This idea involves three propositions. First, time is plural. Thus Bensaïd argues that Marx in *Capital* articulates together different temporalities at work in capitalist economic processes. Indeed, he sees the three volumes of *Capital* mirroring the three moments of Hegel's *Philosophy of Nature*, so that production corresponds to "Mechanism", reproduction to "Chemism", and the system as a whole to "Life": "The mechanical time of production, the chemical time of circulation, and the organic time of reproduction are thus coiled and slotted inside one another, like circles within circles, determining *the enigmatic patterns of historical time, which is the time of politics*".[15] Whatever we think of this (in my view highly dubious) interpretation of *Capital*, the italicised phrase already points towards the connection that Bensaïd sees between time and politics: I'll return to this shortly.

11: This view of the state is developed further in Callinicos, 2009, chapter 2.

12: Bensaïd, 2002a, p112. See more generally Bensaïd, 2002a, chapter 4.

13: Kouvelakis, 2010.

14: Bensaïd, 1995.

15: Bensaïd, 2002a, p77 (italics added). See also Bensaïd, 2002a, pp213-221.

In any case, others have recognised that *Capital* articulates together different times. Here is a much more orthodox Marxist, Bensaïd's Fourth International comrade Ernest Mandel:

> Time appears there as the measure of production, value and surplus value (labour time); as the nexus connecting production, circulation and reproduction of commodities; as the medium of the laws of motion of capital (trade cycles, cycles of class struggle, long-term historical cycles); and as the very essence of man (leisure time, life time, creative time, time of social intercourse).[16]

Secondly, the different temporalities don't align together harmoniously. As Hamlet puts it in a scene that fascinated both Marx and Derrida, "The time is out of joint." Bensaïd expresses the same thought almost as elliptically as Shakespeare: "Time stretched and torn apart; concentrated, staccato, broken time; the worst of time, the best of times".[17] Thirdly, the different temporalities nevertheless form a contradictory unity—though "unity" may not be the right word: maybe it's better to say that they *collide.*

One can see this conception of historical time as providing a framework that embraces and integrates some well-established specific Marxist themes. There is, for example, Trotsky's conception of uneven and combined development, which has been the subject of much recent discussion among English-speaking Marxists.[18] Gramsci's concept of contradictory consciousness, in which different class-based conceptions of the world uneasily coexist, is another example. What is the following famous passage from the *Prison Notebooks* if not the discordance of different historical times?

> When one's conception of the world is not critical and coherent but disjointed and episodic, one belongs simultaneously to a multiplicity of mass human groups. The personality is strangely composite: it contains Stone Age elements and principles of a more advanced science, prejudices from all past phases of history at the local level and intuitions of a future philosophy which will be that of a human race united the world over.[19]

16: Mandel, 1978, p20.
17: Bensaïd, 2002a, p87.
18: Dunn and Radice, 2006, and Anievas, 2010.
19: Gramsci, 1970, p324.

More broadly, a major function of the idea of the discordance of times is to help articulate a Marxism that rejects determinism. Bensaïd writes, "Determinate historical development remains full of junctions and bifurcations, forks and points".[20] This points to an obvious influence on this conception of historical time—Walter Benjamin. Indeed, like James Connolly in Terry Eagleton's novel *Saints and Scholars*, Bensaïd's Marx often sounds suspiciously like Benjamin. Jacques Derrida's treatment of time in *Spectres of Marx* is evidently another reference point (hence the tribute implied by the name of the journal—*Contretemps*—that Bensaïd helped to found): "We no longer realise the wear, we no longer take account of it as of a single age in the progress of history. Neither maturation, nor crisis, nor even agony. Something else... Contretemps. *The time is out of join*t... The age is off its hinges. Everything, beginning with time, seems out of kilter, unjust, dis-adjusted".[21]

But within the Marxist tradition one can also point to Louis Althusser's account of differential temporality in *Reading Capital*:

> The model of a continuous and h*omogeneous time*...can no longer be regarded as the time of history... We can argue from the specific structure of the Marxist whole that it is no longer possible to think the process of development of the different levels of the whole *in the same historical time*. Each of these different "levels" does not have the same type of historical existence. On the contrary, we have to assign to each level a *peculiar time*, time relatively autonomous and hence relatively independent, even in its dependence, of the "times" of the other levels.[22]

But these times in Althusser seem simply to coexist—he tends to reduce contradiction to unevenness.[23] Whereas in Bensaïd they *intersect*: "Non-contemporaneity is not reducible to the material unevenness of its moments. It is also their combined development in a novel historical space-time".[24] Interestingly, we find a very similar conception of historical

---

20: Bensaïd, 2002a, p23. More or less simultaneously I tried to develop a very similar conception of historical materialism as a theory of determinate historical possibilities, and invoked Jorge Luis Borges's wonderful short story "The Garden of the Forking Paths", where all possible worlds actually coexist (but which surprisingly Daniel seems never to have mentioned)—Callinicos, 1995, pp151-165.

21: Derrida, 1994, pp77-78. See the discussion of *Spectres of Marx* in Bensaïd, 1995, chapter 11.

22: Althusser and Balibar, 1970, p99.

23: Althusser, 1975, pp219-223.

24: Bensaïd, 2002a, p24.

time as the intersection of temporalities in a recent essay by the American Marxist Fredric Jameson:

Yet the appearance of Time or History as such depends not on the multiplicity and variety of these trajectories, but rather on their interference with each other, with their intersection now understood as dissonance and as incommensurability rather than as conjuncture which augments them all, in the fashion of a synthesis, by the central space of some harmonious meeting and combination.

We must therefore retain this violence and negativity in any concept of intersection, in order for this dissonant conjunction to count as an Event, and in particular as that Event which is this ephemeral rising up and coming to appearance of Time and History as such. Nor is this a purely textual or philosophical matter: for it is the same discordant conjuncture that constitutes the emergence of time and of history in the real world, the world of real time and of real history.[25]

Jameson criticises "the absence of negativity in the Althusserian concepts", which:

seem now to suggest a kind of pluralism and relativism more appropriate for liberal and bourgeois views of history than for any Marxism... The central mechanism of the dialectic—contradiction itself—is still somehow here lacking or at least is hardly underscored and foregrounded by the concept itself.

It is this negativity which the notion of intersection is meant to restore.[26]

Jameson's idea of a "dissonant conjunction", a "discordant conjuncture" informed by negativity, seems very close to Bensaïd's conception of historical time. Yet there is a crucial difference: in Jameson's highly Hegelian version of Marxism, which views history from an almost cosmic perspective, politics plays no role. For example, in a text first read at a conference on Lenin (in which Bensaïd and I also participated), he declares: "The very force and originality of Marxism was always that it did not have a political dimension." Interestingly, Jameson is also quite dismissive of

25: Jameson, 2009, pp543-544.
26: Jameson, 2009, p545.

Lenin as a political thinker (the title of his text), condemning "Lenin's divisive, aggressive, sectarian recommendations for tactics".[27]

Bensaïd's approach is very different: it is precisely politics where the different temporalities intersect. Hence his stress on the present: "The present is the central temporal category of an open-ended history".[28] Why? Because the present is what matters from the perspective of an interventionist political practice. "In struggle, the present permanently commands the past and the future".[29] Or again, in a crucial passage that merits quotation at length:

> The present is no longer a mere link in the chain of time but a moment for selecting among possibilities. The acceleration of history is not that of a time intoxicated by speed, but the effect of the furious turnover of capital. Revolutionary action is not the imperative of a proven capacity to make history, but engagement in a conflict whose outcome is uncertain. Hypothetical and conditional, bristling with discontinuities, the impossible totalisation of historical development opens out into a multiplicity of pasts and futures. For every epoch the historic present represents the result of a history that has been made and the inaugural force of an advent that is beginning anew. At issue is a specifically political present, strategically identified with the notion of the "given and inherited *circumstances*" by which "men make their own history". [30]

The activist orientation of this conception of "a specifically political present" is explicit in the phrase "a moment for *selecting* among possibilities". The openness of history—the forking paths that define its potential courses—requires a politics that actively intervenes by taking one path rather than another. Thus: "This historical present is not a link in some mechanical sequence of causes and effects but a contemporaneity full of possibilities, *where politics takes precedence over history in deciphering tendencies that do not possess the force of law*".[31] There is an element of voluntarism—in a good way—that seems implied here. Politics seems to act as the forcible conjunction of discordant temporalities that might not otherwise have collided.

In any case, this conception of politics helps to provide a principled foundation for Daniel's Leninism. As a very different writer on Lenin, Tony Cliff, stressed, central to Lenin's practice of politics was his conception of

27: Jameson 2009, pp297, 300.
28: Bensaïd, 2002a, p55.
29: Bensaïd, 2003.
30: Bensaïd, 2002a, pp71-72.
31: Bensaïd, 2002a, pp103-104 (italics added).

strategy and tactics, where tactics are the various political methods that, responding to ever-changing circumstances, are selected to achieve the goal of socialist revolution.[32] Daniel stresses on numerous occasions that strategy is a necessity imposed by a history whose contradictions are mobile and uncertain in outcome. Strategy is a means of navigating these contradictions while not losing sight of the ultimate objective. Hence the intrinsic unity of "the broken time of politics and strategy".[33] In other words, Bensaïd's distinctive reading of Lenin and the understanding of politics that flows from it only make sense in the context of his conception of historical time. And the politics makes this conception more than just another philosophy of history. It is here, I believe, that we find Daniel's great originality as a Marxist.

32: Cliff, 1975, chapter 14.
33: Bensaïd, 2002a, p23.

References

Althusser, Louis, and Étienne Balibar, 1970, *Reading Capital* (New Left Books).

Althusser, Louis, 1975, "Is it Simple to be a Marxist in Philosophy?", in Louis Althusser, 1990, *Philosophy and the Spontaneous Philosophy of the Scientists* (Verso).

Anievas, Alex (ed), 2010, *Marxism and World Politics* (Routledge).

Bensaïd, Daniel, 1995, *La Discordance des Temps* (Les Éditions de la Passion).

Bensaïd, Daniel, 2002a (1995), *A Marx for Our Times: Adventures and Misadventures of a Critique* (Verso).

Bensaïd, Daniel, 2002b, "Leaps! Leaps! Leaps!", *International Socialism* 95 (summer), http://pubs.socialistreviewindex.org.uk/isj95/bensaid.htm

Bensaïd, Daniel, 2003, "Fragments pour une politique de l'opprimé: événement et historicité", www.europe-solidaire.org/spip.php?article1415

Bensaïd, Daniel, 2004, *Une Lente Impatience* (Stock).

Bensaïd, Daniel, 2008, "Quarante ans après", introduction to Bensaïd, Daniel, and Alain Naïr, "A propos de la question de l'organisation: Lénine et Rosa Luxemburg", *Partisans*, number 45, December 1968/January 1969, both available at www.europe-solidaire.org/spip.php?article10230

Budgen, Sebastian, 2010, "The Red Hussar: Daniel Bensaïd, 1946-2010", *International Socialism* 127 (summer), www.isj.org.uk/index.php4?id=661&issue=127

Callinicos, Alex, 1995, *Theories and Narratives* (Polity).

Callinicos, Alex, 2009, *Imperialism and Global Political Economy* (Polity).

Cliff, Tony, 1975, *Lenin, volume 1: Building the Party* (Pluto).

Derrida, Jacques, 1994, *Spectres of Marx* (Routledge).

Dunn, Bill, and Hugo Radice (eds), 2006, *100 Years of Permanent Revolution: Results and Prospects* (Pluto).

Gramsci, Antonio, 1971, *Selections from the Prison Notebooks* (Lawrence & Wishart).

Harman, Chris, 1968-9, "Party and Class", *International Socialism* 35 (first series, winter), www.marxists.de/party/harman/partyclass.htm

Jameson, Fredric, 2009, *Valences of the Dialectic* (Verso).

Kouvelakis, Stathis, 2010, "Daniel Bensaïd: la Dialectique du temps et de la lutte", *Lignes* 32.

Löwy, Michael, 1976, "Marxists and the National Question", *New Left Review*, I/96.

Mandel, Ernest, 1978, "Introduction" to Karl Marx, *Capital*, volume 2 (Penguin).

Marx, Karl, 1973, *Grundrisse* (Penguin), www.marxists.org/archive/marx/works/1857/grundrisse/

Marx, Karl, 1976 [1867], *Capital*, volume I (Penguin), www.marxists.org/archive/marx/works/1867-c1/index.htm

Poulantzas, Nicos, 1973, *Political Power and Social Class* (New Left Books).

Weber, Henri, 1975, *Marxisme et Conscience de Classe* (Union Générale d'Éditions).

A reply to David McNally

Joseph Choonara

David McNally writes in response to my review of his *Global Slump* that we need "serious, committed debate designed to strengthen the theoretical and practical capacities of the left".[1] I agree. It is therefore unfortunate that he describes my review as making "cheap shots" and generating "heat about statistics". Rather than stoop to discuss whether the evidence supports his case, he prefers to paint me as a latter-day Witchfinder General engaged in "heresy hunting".

The claims I took issue with in McNally's book are hardly heretical. His arguments—the world economy experienced a global "neoliberal" boom from 1982 to 2007; China's expansion has created a powerful new centre of capital accumulation; the growth of financial transactions and instruments such as derivatives flows from the severing of convertibility between the dollar and gold—would be accepted as common sense for much of the radical left. Indeed, they would barely challenge the preconceptions of columnists at the *Economist* or *Financial Times*.

My issue with McNally's book is not that his arguments are heretical; it is that some of them are wrong. Taking issue with his empirical claims was not, therefore, an exercise in nit-picking. My aim in doing so was to support my challenge to the overall thrust of his argument.

One central claim in his book is that the crisis of 2008 "represents the terminus of a quarter century of economic growth—which I shall call the

---

1:    McNally, 2012, p189.

neoliberal expansion—and the transition to a protracted period of slump", a point he repeats in response to my review. Indeed, he devotes a lengthy chapter of his book to "developing this argument [in which] I dissent from the views of many radical theorists…who see the last 40 years as one uninterrupted crisis, or a 'long downturn' ".[2]

I do not agree with McNally's characterisation of my position. As is clear from my review, I do not see the past four decades as being a period of uninterrupted crisis, a 40-year crisis or a permanent crisis. But it does seem to me that McNally's book is in large part directed at those who, like me, see the recent period as one of *relative stagnation* for capitalism.

My reply to McNally will focus on this question because I think it is the most important substantial disagreement between us. As I suggested in my review, I found the closing chapters, dealing with questions of revolutionary strategy, the interrelation between oppression and class, and so on, pretty thin gruel. In some cases our differences seem to revolve around tone, emphasis or language.[3] Perhaps in some other instances—the derailment of the radical movement by "patriotic nationalism" after 11 September 2001, a period that saw some of the largest ever protest movements in various European countries in opposition to war—McNally is reflecting on a specifically North American experience.

Similarly, his emphasis on the extent to which "business unionism…predominates" and his persistent pessimism about male, white members of the working class would have been disastrous in formulating the approach of the left to the substantial one-day strikes in Britain in 2011, which involved a multiracial workforce with disproportionate numbers of women—but also lots of male, white workers who, in my experience, were proud to unite across lines of race or gender. Other contentious issues, such as McNally's favourable estimation of the Syriza coalition in Greece, are being tested by events far more sternly than they could be by words alone. And I am happy to accept our shared

---

2:   McNally, 2011, p9.

3:   I imagine that we would both agree with the necessity of responding to "every manifestation of tyranny and oppression", to use Lenin's phrase. However, I find claims that class relations are "constituted in and through" gender or racial oppression, or talk of a "constellation of relations of domination", too vague to be helpful in formulating concrete conclusions about the struggle against oppression and for socialism. For me, class is a social relationship flowing from a position in the economic structure of society, relative to the means of production and other classes. I don't know what it would mean to say that my class position manifested itself in or through being Asian, for example.

enthusiasm regarding the role of workers in the Arab revolutions or the potential of such struggles to challenge capitalism.[4]

So on to the evidence.

Lies, damned lies and "heat about statistics"

One of McNally's arguments is that there has been an "upward trend in the rate of return" on fixed capital, a measure often used as a proxy for the Marxist rate of profit.[5] The rate of profit matters because it is a measure of the self-expansion of capital, a concept central to Marx's analysis.[6]

Apparently I was getting "worked up" when I pointed out that McNally's "doubling of US non-financial profit rates" was not reflected in the graph he presented (as if it said more about my troubled emotional state than McNally's case). In my review I used Anwar Shaikh's graph from a recent *Socialist Register* to check McNally's figures, not because I believe Shaikh has the best method of calculating profit rates, but because it graphs the thing that McNally wrote had doubled.[7]

Shaikh argues that after the Second World War the rate of profit "drifted downwards for 35 years, but then stabilised".[8] Over the past 25 years the trend was for it to rise a bit, then fall a bit, ending up where it started. I present a version of Shaikh's graph in figure 1. The trend is surely unambiguous. But how does McNally read this graph? We are told, "Shaikh's data show the same persistent rise in profitability across the period in question [1982-2007]".[9] I leave it to the reader to decide who is right.

It may be that McNally now believes "profit of enterprise", the difference between the rate of profit and the rate of interest, is the important thing. He does not explicitly say this in his book or in his reply to me, merely noting in a footnote that according to Shaikh this figure more than doubled from 1982 to 2007. Shaikh calculates "profit of enterprise" by subtracting the rate of three-month US Treasury bonds from his rate of profit. Unsurprisingly, the figure goes up—it was negative in 1982. I am not

---

4:   Though what my "notable silence" on the six paragraphs in his 230-page book detailing the general strikes in Guadeloupe and Martinique proves, I am not quite sure.

5:   McNally, 2011, p183.

6:   "Capital and its self-expansion appear as the starting and the closing point, the motive and the purpose of production...production is only production for capital and not vice versa, the means of production are not mere means for a constant expansion of the living process of the society of producers"—Marx, 1971, p250.

7:   Shaikh, 2011.

8:   Shaikh, 2011, p49.

9:   McNally, 2012, p184.

convinced by this method of calculating profit of enterprise. But even if it is valid, the crucial variable remains the rate of profit, measuring the total production of surplus value relative to investment, prior to its division into profit and interest. It is this measure that the rate of accumulation (the rate at which capitalists reinvest surplus value pumped out of workers) follows most closely.[10] In other words, looking at the profit rate allows us to understand the relative decline of capitalist accumulation over the recent period.

Figure 1: Rate of profit for US non-financial corporations 1947-2010
Source: Shaikh, 2011

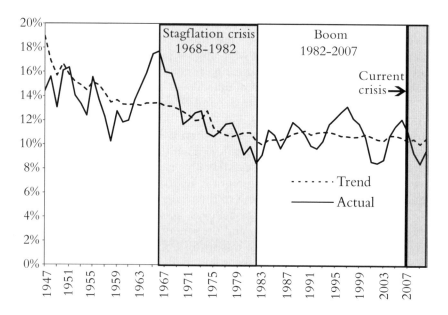

McNally writes, "My concern in this area was not with the methodologies and preferred data sets for tracking movements in the rate of profit, which involve questions that lie far beyond the range of *Global Slump*. My interest was in showing that, notwithstanding the differences in methodology, multiple Marxist studies display a protracted *upward trend* in the rate of profit from the low point of the last crisis until 2006-7".[11]

10: Specifically, the rate of accumulation in the US tended to follow what Andrew Kliman calls the "property income rate of profit"—Kliman, 2012, p91, figure 5.8.
11: McNally, 2012, p184.

In other words, he chooses data that shows what he wants to show. Some of the data, on closer inspection, turns out not to show what he wants to show. When his use of data is criticised he disregards this as "heresy hunting" because it poses questions that lie outside the scope of his argument. By these criteria no argument can be refuted by evidence.

Since writing *Global Slump* McNally has acquainted himself with the work of Michael Roberts, who uses the historic costs of fixed capital to measure the rate of profit, rather than current costs.[12] I too am convinced that historic costs should be used to calculate the rate of return. The problem with using the current cost of fixed capital, or the "replacement cost" as it is also known, is that it does not measure profit against the sums actually invested by the capitalist but the amount that would be required to replace the investment today.[13] In other words, current cost calculations treat capitalism as if profits are generated at the same point at which investments are made—it treats capitalism as if time did not exist. This is obviously a nonsensical way to explore capitalism if we believe it to be a dynamic system, rather than a system in a state of static equilibrium. It turns out that the differences between current cost and historic cost calculations are also significant, and in particular the restoration of profitability in the recent period is, at least in large part, a result of this erroneous method of calculation.

The author who has most effectively argued this point in recent years is Andrew Kliman, whose latest work, *The Failure of Capitalist Production*, is an important analysis of the crisis. Unlike McNally, Kliman does see it as within his remit to explain why different authors arrive at a different picture when assessing trends in profitability, setting out the issues at stake in a commendably accessible manner. Kliman presents several legitimate methods of calculating profit rates, each suitable for particular purposes, using historic rather than current costs. Here I present one of Kliman's measures, the inflation-adjusted before-tax profit rate for the US corporate sector, in which the dotted line shows McNally's method for obtaining a rise in profitability.[14]

12:   Roberts runs an excellent blog: http://thenextrecession.wordpress.com
13:   This is a question of the actual value advanced to make the investment at a certain point in history, not whether the data is adjusted for inflation. Historic costs can obviously be "inflation-adjusted" as in the graph I have used below.
14:   Kliman, 2012, p84, figure 5.5. I have selected the measure that I hope will be least contentious. Kliman's book came out after *Global Slump*, but his data have been in wide circulation for some time—see for example http://akliman.squarespace.com/persistent-fall

Figure 2: Inflation-adjusted US corporate sector before-tax profit rate
Source: Kliman, 2012

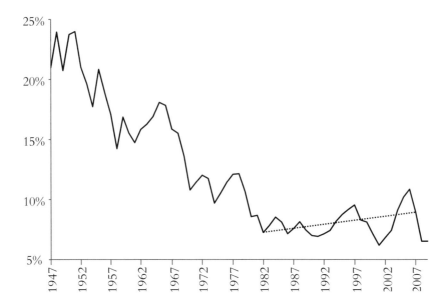

I have added the dotted line showing how one could detect an increase in the rate of return between 1982 and 2007. There is a similar rise between 1982 and 1997. However, as I pointed out in my review of McNally's book, both 2007 and 1997 lie near peaks in profitability; 1982 is a trough. It is no surprise to anyone that the rate of profit rises and falls periodically. The movement of the profit rate combines both long-term tendencies and short-term cyclical variations due to the business cycle. Once the data is extended to the crisis of 2008, we see that profit rates failed to mount any sustained recovery after 1982. The period cannot be seen as "one of an extended upturn in profitability" unless the data is "selected" to prove this.[15]

McNally's book made an additional argument, namely that it was not acceptable to compare the "neoliberal boom" period with the long boom that followed the Second World War. In my review of his book I explained at some length why I disagreed, basing myself on changes to

---

15: McNally, 2012, p184. See Kliman, 2012, pp104-105, for a critique of this kind of "cherry picking" of data.

capitalism over the past century.[16] McNally has chosen not to argue the point. But, for what it's worth, a paper by Simon Mohun presents the long-term US profit rate, and seems to show a higher trend rate through much of the 1890s and 1900s than during the long boom (figure 3).[17]

Figure 3: Long-term trends in profitability
Source: Mohun, 2012

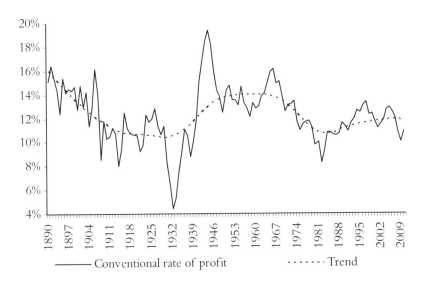

——— Conventional rate of profit   · · · · · · Trend

One final point about the figures. McNally claims that I "simply [declare] the rising trend in profits to be 'fictitious'".[18] On the relevant page of my review the reference to "fictitious profits" is me *citing McNally* who writes that from 2001 the profit data should be treated with caution "given the *widespread phenomena of fictitious profits* based on financial manipulation and accounting fraud".[19]

Causes and consequences
So much for the trend itself. McNally's response to my review sets out

---

16: Choonara, 2011, pp165-167.

17: Again, I don't endorse Mohun's method, but this is essentially a long-term version of the sole graph of profit rates presented by McNally. See McNally, 2011, p49.

18: McNally, 2012, p184.

19: McNally, 2011, p49 (my emphasis). I do not believe this is restricted to the period post-2001.

three causes for his perceived rise in profitability: attacks on workers' living standards, rising productivity levels and the creation of global production chains.

On workers' living standards he says that I "backhandedly grant this point" by citing Shaikh's recent article. I would go further. In my review I fully endorsed that argument. Many other authors in this journal—Chris Harman and Guglielmo Carchedi among them—have made similar points prior to McNally's book. We all said that the increased rate of exploitation helped to put a floor under profit rates from the 1980s. However, now I am not so sure.

Here Kliman's new book makes a genuinely heretical claim: that the total compensation (wages, salaries, and health and pension contributions) going to US employees, as a share of new value, did not change dramatically in this period. It is true that in the 1970s wages stopped rising as rapidly as they had in the 1950s or 1960s, but so did the new value created. The slowdown in the growth of compensation was a consequence of the "relative stagnation of capitalist production".[20] Unlike McNally, Kliman presents a carefully argued case. Far from "heresy hunting" I am convinced that his case should be taken seriously.

On McNally's second point, he wants to argue not just that a rise in productivity cheapens "subsistence goods", thus lowering the value that capitalists must grant workers to reproduce their labour power, but also that it "makes possible the capture of productivity gains by capital".[21] Marx's argument is that in the short term the introduction of new techniques might boost the amount of surplus value attracted by a particular firm or even a particular nation. But in the long run the replacement of living by dead labour leads to the tendency for the rate of profit to fall. Marx writes that "the progressive tendency of the general rate of profit to fall is...just *an expression peculiar to the capitalist mode of production* of the progressive development of the social productivity of labour".[22] In other words, a rise in productivity, if brought about by expanding the means of production harnessed by living labour, is perfectly consistent with a falling rate of profit.

Perhaps McNally means that the depreciation of constant capital raises profitability—one of the tendencies counteracting the falling rate of profit that Marx discusses in *Capital*. Again Kliman makes a compelling case that technological changes over recent decades have led to a substantial increase

---

20: Kliman, 2012, p124.
21: McNally, 2012, p180, n10.
22: Marx, 1971, p213 (emphasis in original).

in the rate of moral depreciation, through which the means of production lose value as they become obsolete, especially in computing.[23] However, this affects both the value of fixed capital *and* the amount of profit realised by capitalists. Kliman ultimately estimates that the overall effect on profit rates is to *reduce* the actual rate relative to that indicated by the graphs such as figure 2.

McNally's third underlying factor seems to rest mainly on the growth of China, an undisputed reality, which is described in an earlier article in this journal.[24] It is also clear that Chinese growth has been premised on the rapid expansion of a low-wage workforce. McNally agrees that this growth is contradictory and unbalanced and may not continue. Apparently the question is whether "something more has been going on than a 'long downturn' in the system".[25] I agree that a section of the capitalist economy has grown rapidly in the context of relative stagnation of the world system. As I wrote, "Capitalism retained strong *tendencies* towards stagnation that coexisted with the dynamism produced as those presiding over the system competitively reorganised their capitals and sought new areas of the globe into which to expand".[26] Indeed, I would argue that it is precisely this contradiction that is placing such a strain on China's expansion.

Because it is utterly unheretical to say that China has grown dramatically in recent years, it is also important to avoid unnecessary hyperbole. McNally is unhappy that I have decried his use of data as selective. The vertical line in figure 4 shows the year that McNally "selected" to show that China was the biggest recipient of foreign direct investment (FDI)—completely failing to mention that it is the only year for which such a claim could plausibly be made. Again I leave it to the reader to decide if there is a problem with McNally's choice of data—and, if there is, what it says about the strength of his argument.

Chinese growth may be real, but that does not mean that it compensates for the weakness of the global economy as a whole or has reversed the long-term decline in profitability at the core of the system. As Kliman shows, the "rate of profit [of US multinationals] on their foreign investments also fell and failed to recover. To be sure, the share of profits that US multinationals receive from their foreign operations has risen markedly. Yet their fixed assets located abroad have risen even more markedly as a share of their total fixed assets".[27]

23: See Kliman, 2012, pp140-148.
24: Budd and Hardy, 2012.
25: McNally, 2012, p182.
26: Choonara, 2011, p168.
27: Kliman, 2012, p78. See the graph on p79.

Figure 4: Annual flow of FDI into selected economies 1991-2007 (US$ in billions at current exchange rates and prices)
Source: Unctad

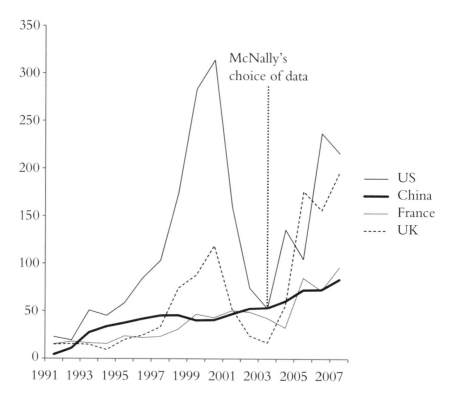

If the underlying causes of the "great boom" of 1982-2007 are suspect, as is the reality of the boom, at least as regards profit rates, what of the perceived consequences? On growth rates, McNally accuses me of hypocrisy because I criticise him for using Angus Maddison's data on world GDP growth, data also used by Robert Brenner and Alex Callinicos (and me, for that matter). This is not my gripe. I have exactly the same reservations about such GDP data as Brenner and Callinicos. These do not rule such data out of order if they are used carefully and with awareness of their limitations.[28] My criticisms are over how McNally uses the data.

28: Although Maddison's estimates of Chinese GDP are far higher than those generally used—he estimates the Chinese economy at 94 percent the size of the US economy in

McNally claims that the world economy tripled in size from 1982 to 2007. The data shows that it did not. He claims to present a table showing that the compound growth rates of GDP for 1982-2007 are favourable compared with every phase of capitalist history apart from the long post-war boom. Actually his table does not give data for 1982-2007; it ends in 2001. If these are converted to per capita growth rates, the period is far from impressive (see figure 5).[29]

Figure 5: My estimates of the annual average compound growth of global GDP per capita, based on Maddison's data

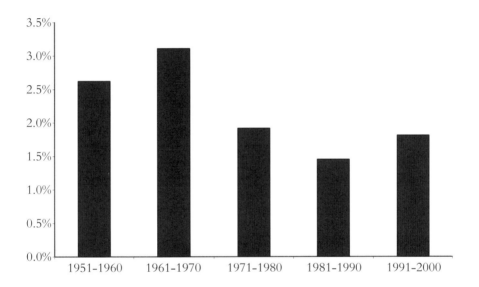

Conclusion

Why does any of this matter? First, because I think McNally mischaracterises the period from 1982, seeing capitalist strength where I see weakness. Second, because this seems to be grounded in a misunderstanding of Marx's method, undermining our understanding of the current crisis and

2008. See Kliman, 2012, p52. If we accept recent Chinese growth rates as accurate, this would mean that China is already the world's largest economy.

29: If World Bank data is used instead of Maddison's, the rise in 1991-2000 relative to 1981-1990 is even less evident.

capitalism generally. Third, because I think that the expansion of the financial system, particularly the growing dependence on debt and the creation of asset-price bubbles in the run-up to the crisis, is rooted in the underlying weakness of capitalism.[30]

Fourth, I do not believe that the decline in the rate of profit is an irreversible trend. But I do believe that restoring profitability will require a far greater destruction of capital than has thus far taken place. As I made clear in my review, such destruction faces more substantial obstacles in contemporary capital than it has in the past. This implies a protracted period of economic and political instability, recurrent crises and revolutionary explosions. On this ultimate point at least, despite our ill-tempered exchange, McNally and I can hopefully agree.

References

Choonara, Joseph, 2011, "Once More (with Feeling) on Marxist Accounts of the Crisis", *International Socialism* 132 (autumn), www.isj.org.uk/?id=762

Hardy, Jane, and Adrian Budd, 2012, "China's Capitalism and the Crisis", *International Socialism* 133 (winter), www.isj.org.uk/?id=777

Kliman, Andrew, 2012, *The Failure of Capitalist Production: Underlying Causes of the Great Recession* (Pluto).

Marx, Karl, 1971 [1894], *Capital*, volume 3 (Progress), www.marxists.org/archive/marx/works/1894-c3/

McNally, David, 2011, *Global Slump: The Economics and Politics of Crisis and Resistance* (Spectre).

McNally, David, 2012, "Explaining the Crisis or Heresy Hunting? A Response to Joseph Choonara", *International Socialism* 134 (spring), www.isj.org.uk/?id=802

Mohun, Simon, 2012, "The Rate of Profit and Crisis in the US Economy: A Class Perspective", chapter in forthcoming book.

Shaikh, Anwar, 2011, "The First Great Depression of the 21st Century", *Socialist Register 2011: The Crisis This Time* (Merlin).

30: McNally does not respond to my arguments on the relationship between finance and the wider capitalist economy, preferring to restate his own position (which, of course, does not involve an account of the relative stagnation of production).

Clutching at straws? Some mainstream accounts of the crisis

Brian O'Boyle

A Review of Gillian Tett, **Fool's Gold: How Unrestrained Greed Corrupted A Dream, Shattered Global Markets and Unleashed a Catastrophe** *(Abacus, 2009), £8.99; Paul Krugman,* **The Return of Depression Economics** *(Penguin, 2008), £9.99; and Joseph Stiglitz,* **Freefall: Free Markets and the Sinking of the Global Economy** *(Penguin, 2010), £9.99*

The crash of September 2008 was no ordinary event.[1] Within days financial markets crumbled as asset values plummeted and credit slowed to a virtual standstill. For a moment some feared that the global financial architecture might not survive. But the ruling classes soon steadied themselves for the job at hand. Aggressive interest rate cuts, forced nationalisations, blanket bank guarantees, ongoing recapitalisations and unlimited liquidity quickly became the hallmarks of monetary policy around the globe. The United States and China also synchronised fiscal packages to coincide with more modest measures from Britain and the European Union.[2] Collectively, the core capitalist states backstopped the financial sector to the tune of over $14 trillion, making it clear that this was far from the limit of their commitment.[3] These tactics staved off the immediate threat of financial catastrophe. However, they also accentuated a whole series of secondary difficulties—crises of sovereign debt, the fiscal system, investment and employment—while

---

1: I would like to thank Alex Callinicos and Joseph Choonara for their comments on an earlier draft.

2: See Roubini and Mihm, 2011, pp162-163, for more details.

3: According to Stiglitz, 2010, p110, the US alone gave guarantees of some $12 trillion.

leaving the deeper causes of the crisis unresolved. Since then the system has been in virtual stagnation. What began as a financial crisis has now become the Great Recession of the 21st century.

As with any epoch-making event, accounts have varied, with commentators struggling to fit the new reality into the framework they previously espoused. The difficulties for economists who vigorously championed the superiority of the market are obvious. But for many of those with outlooks influenced by Keynesianism, this crisis has been a textbook case of financial hubris triumphing over the real economy.[4] John Maynard Keynes once remarked that "speculators may do no harm as bubbles on a steady stream of enterprise. But the situation is serious when enterprise becomes the bubble on a whirlpool of speculation".[5] Speculative excess has undoubtedly been a feature of the current crisis, and each of the authors I consider here has, in their own way, attempted to situate the crash of 2008 in the "financialisation" of the past 30 years.

Gillian Tett is currently the US managing editor of the *Financial Times*, having previously spent time as the capital markets editor in London. Tett's articles often give useful insights into the complex world of finance. Paul Krugman and Joseph Stiglitz both won Nobel Prizes in economics and both challenge the market fundamentalism of the mainstream. Krugman is a proponent of the "neoclassical synthesis", meaning he marries a version of Keynesian macroeconomics with the microeconomic foundations of neoclassical theory. Historically this position was quite reactionary.[6] But within the stultified arena of US academic economics, Krugman now appears as a critic of the dominant paradigm. His weekly column in the *New York Times*

4: Krugman, 2008, p101.

5: Keynes, 1997, p159.

6: The central message of Keynes's *General Theory* was that the demand side of the economy mattered. Prior to this orthodox economics had assumed that supply creates its own demand and that changes in the price mechanism would always bring the economy back to equilibrium. Keynes argued that in a monetary economy driven by expectations of future profits, situations may arise in which capitalists could not be persuaded to invest at any price, leading to deficiencies in overall demand. However, Keynes explicitly accepted the idea that the macroeconomy was built on millions of rational decisions made by individuals and firms about how best to allocate their scarce resources. There were three distinct mainstream responses to the *General Theory*. The first, adopted by many older economists who Keynes criticised (such as Alfred Pigou), was to basically ignore it. The second, taken up by many of Keynes's younger supporters (such as Joan Robinson and Nicholas Kaldor) was to try to complete the revolution against neoclassical theory. The final approach, which dominated until Keynes's ideas fell out of favour in the 1970s, was adopted by many post-war US economists (such as Paul Samuelson and Robert Solow). This sought to assimilate the key ideas of the *General Theory* into neoclassical economics. Krugman belongs to this tradition.

has made him an influential commentator. Stiglitz originally made his name by challenging the informational assumptions underpinning general equilibrium theory. However, he is better known today as the "insider" who turned against the International Monetary Fund (IMF). Stiglitz, once the chief economist at the World Bank, produced a trenchant critique of his experiences of policymaking during the 1990s and has since further hardened his position. In a sense, Krugman and Stiglitz represent two attempts to rescue the market by humanising it.

Perspectives and approaches

Although each of the books under review attempts to grapple with similar material, there are differences in emphasis and perspective. Tett originally trained as an anthropologist and her approach adopts techniques she honed while studying marriage rituals in rural Tajikistan. Like other social systems, investment banking has its own language, mores and moral norms.

Tett works hard to break into this world and the results of this endeavour convey both the strengths and the weaknesses of her approach. On the positive side, *Fool's Gold* is meticulous in its explanations of financial concepts that have been bandied about since the start of the crisis. By the end of the book complex terms such as collateralised debt obligations, securitisation, derivatives contracts and special purpose vehicles are significantly illuminated.[7] But the book's narrow focus also leaves significant gaps. The first is in the broader economics of the crisis. Although Tett refers to bad corporate governance, loose monetary policy and lax regulation, she never explores any of these issues in great detail.[8] Instead the reader is left to infer the importance of these "background conditions". The second gap is political. Tett's eagerness to develop a narrative from the participants' perspective means that she is extremely soft on them. The book follows the exploits of senior bankers at JP Morgan and, much like the feeling one gets when watching *The Godfather*, it is tempting to side with them. But this would be to forget the scale of the damage they caused. According to David Harvey, Wall Street banks colluded with the IMF and the US Treasury to thieve upwards of $4.6 trillion from some of the poorest in the world.[9]

Krugman made his name in the area of international trade and *Depression Economics* often reads like a primer in globalisation theory. Unlike Tett, Krugman is anxious to establish the credentials of his own perspective,

---

7: These issues will be taken up in the section on complex finance below.

8: Tett, 2009, p xi.

9: Harvey, 2005, p162.

and his book simultaneously tries to outline the policies he believes would stabilise the global economy. The book begins on a triumphant note, proclaiming that all of the really debilitating economic problems have effectively been solved. Policy mistakes during the Great Depression have now been largely corrected. Krugman argues, "Capitalism and its economists [have] made a deal with the public: it will be OK to have free markets from now on because we know enough to prevent any more Great Depressions".[10] But while Krugman maintains that a dollop of "good old-fashioned demand-side macroeconomics still has a lot to offer in our current predicament", he is also aware that something must have gone drastically wrong.[11] The title of his book is, after all, *The Return of Depression Economics*, and its central thesis is that the Keynesian compromise no longer holds in a globalised economy.

To make this case, the book considers the crises that have afflicted the global economy since the early 1980s. The analysis is cursory but relatively clear and gives a sense of the pattern of boom and bust that has accompanied global neoliberalism.[12] Concepts such as the balance of payments, current account deficits and exchange rates are interwoven into the narrative and some of the best parts of the book describe the tensions in simultaneously trying to maintain fixed exchange rates and discretionary monetary policy in the face of international capital movements.[13] However, Krugman massively overextends the analysis by pinning all the problems of the past 30 years on the policy constraints imposed by globalisation. Having filled in important gaps left by Tett, the book fails to identify the class dynamics of the neoliberal period. Indeed, *Depression Economics* never moves beyond the confines of technical policymaking.

Stiglitz's book is far better in this regard. From the outset *Freefall* attacks the naked class abuse of the past 25 years. Instead of merely arguing for a novel set of economic policies, Stiglitz is looking for a new vision for the organisation of the economy.[14] Capitalism is now characterised by "economic colonialism", "corporate welfare" and a massive increase in inequality.[15] He engages in a trenchant critique of the "ersatz capitalism"

10: Krugman, 2008, p102.
11: Krugman, 2008, p183.
12: Neoliberalism is a catch-all term applied to capitalist restructuring since the early 1980s. Often summarised by the ideals of market liberalisation, privatisation and stabilisation, it is best understood as a class offensive designed to reassert the power of capital in the face of falling levels of profitability.
13: I consider these issues below.
14: Stiglitz, 2010, p36.
15: Stiglitz, 2010, pp195, 220, 294.

(neoliberalism) that has grown up since the 1980s.[16] Like Krugman, Stiglitz defends a form of Keynesian interventionism and he works hard to dissociate capitalism proper from financial interests. Stiglitz contextualises the 2008 crash in the bad governance, lax regulation, loose monetary policy and financial innovation of the period.[17] But his rejection of neoliberalism means that his analysis is generally fresh and interesting. Alan Greenspan's monetary policies are described as responses to tax cuts by the Bush administration, deregulation is seen as the triumph of the bankers and financial innovation is, quite rightly, conceived as a predatory move to rob working people of their savings.[18] Stiglitz pulls no punches. His treatment of what he calls the "Great American Robbery" is, along with his critique of globalisation, a highlight of his book. Unfortunately, his critique is not matched by any of his solutions. Stiglitz believes we can establish a "new set of social contracts based on trust between all of the elements of our society".[19] This is either hopelessly naive or just plain hopeless.

Neoliberal globalisation

The epicentre of the 2008 crash was so obviously in finance that even staunch neoliberals were momentarily forced onto the back foot. In considering the role of finance, it is best to start with the policy analysis in *Depression Economics*. According to Krugman, economic managers ideally want three things. The first is discretionary monetary policy to fight recessions and curb inflation. The second is stable exchange rates so that business is not faced with too much uncertainty. The third is international capital flows to allow the private sector to generate wealth.[20] Unfortunately all of these cannot be secured simultaneously. Fixing exchange rates automatically reduces discretion, while allowing capital flows is incompatible with strict management of the national economy. Previously countries imposed capital controls and/or gave up on discretionary monetary policy. But today the overwhelming policy consensus is that flexible exchange rates and free capital movements are the best combination for economic success:

> Today we live in a world that has relearned the virtues of free markets, is suspicious of government intervention and is particularly aware that the more things are prohibited the greater the scope for bribery and cronyism…

16: Stiglitz, 2010, pp135, 200, 296.
17: Stiglitz, 2010, p154.
18: Stiglitz, 2010, p175.
19: Stiglitz, 2010, p208.
20: Krugman, 2008, p108.

[Globalisation has] removed hundreds of millions of people from abject poverty…and…capitalism could with considerable justification claim the credit… Rapid development was possible after all—and it had been accomplished not through proud socialist isolation but precisely by becoming as integrated as possible with global capitalism.[21]

Capital flows allow developing economies to access resources that would otherwise be unattainable. However, they also bring attendant dangers in the form of currency speculation and increased volatility. Allowing hot money in necessitates allowing it back out again. And this makes individual economies vulnerable in the face of sudden shifts in mood. Krugman writes of the dangers posed by unscrupulous hedge funds and predatory specula-tors.[22] But by far the most severe concerns are those associated with capital movements under normal conditions. There are a number of prerequisites for economies to integrate into the global market. The first is liberalised capital markets, but there must also be secure property rights, labour market flex-ibility, privatisation and (frequently) a currency peg to guard against inflation.

Once these supports are in place, foreign capital can start to flow in, and Krugman highlights the centrality of mobile capital in initially fostering economic booms. One consequence of massive inflows of foreign capital is that the country begins to run a current account deficit.[23] This means that there are more resources flowing in than flowing out. This can be caused by foreigners investing, foreigners lending (to the government or private sector) or exports being less than the value of imports—or by some com-bination of these. In many of the most devastating crises it was the sheer volume of foreign investment that led to these current account deficits and, as far as Krugman is concerned, this suggests that "market sentiment" rather than "market fundamentals" eventually undermine peripheral economies.[24] In theory, investment from abroad should be viewed positively as it signals

21: Krugman, 2008, pp108, 27, 28.
22: Krugman, 2008, chapter five, deals with these issues in some detail.
23: The balance of payments is a record of a country's international transactions. The current account captures all visible and invisible trade (imports and exports of goods and services); the capital account captures those items such as foreign direct investment which will yield returns over many years. If a country takes in more foreign capital than it sends abroad, it runs a capital account surplus by borrowing from private investors. This necessarily means running a current account deficit in order to achieve a balance of international payments. In normal times this would not cause any real concern. However, jittery investors often look at a current account deficit as a sign that a country is "living beyond its means". If this becomes market sentiment, it can trigger a run on the currency and/or massive capital flight.
24: Krugman, 2008, p109.

that private investors have confidence in a country. The problem though is that capital moves with a herd mentality and, having grabbed the lion's share of the productivity increases, exuberant capital continues to spill in until a bubble begins to form. Price increases take over from rising productivity and eventually market participants judge the situation to be unsustainable. When this happens, the bubble bursts and capital rushes for the exits.

At this point governments should in theory use their monetary discretion to stimulate spending. This is what happened in the US in 1975, 1982 and 1991.[25] But in the face of recent crises in the developing world, the policies prescribed by the IMF and the US Treasury were diametrically opposed to those the US had previously devised for itself. The cynic might argue that the class interests of US capital were also opposed in the different cases. But for Krugman the key villain is the power of international capital in an era of deregulated globalisation.[26] Unlike the US, peripheral nations have to work extremely hard to win the confidence of the markets, and once a rush to the exits occurs it becomes imperative to slash the deficit no matter what the social costs. It doesn't really matter whether a country has sound fundamentals. What matter are *perceptions* and the overriding market orthodoxy is that governments must engage in significant austerity coupled with raised interest rates to hold whatever capital remains. This causes widespread social misery while driving the economy further into recession. But such is the power of global investors that "governments have to show their seriousness by inflicting pain on themselves…because only thus can they gain the trust of the markets".[27] Once capital becomes global, national governments must trade economic sovereignty for economic development. Krugman is undoubtedly on to something when he highlights the advantages for mobile capital in a system framed around national priorities. But this still does not explain how capital gained so much power in the core of the system.

Financialisation in the US
To answer this question *Depression Economics* shifts from the periphery to the core. Krugman begins by recounting the godlike status that Greenspan enjoyed during his 18 years at the helm of the US Federal Reserve.[28] When markets were stagnating, Greenspan could rally them. When markets were booming, he wasn't afraid to keep them booming, and "for investors the

---

25: Krugman, 2008, p102.
26: Krugman, 2008, p103.
27: Krugman, 2008, p116.
28: The Federal Reserve is the central bank in the US.

Greenspan years were heavenly as…stock prices on average rose more than 10 percent a year".[29] Greenspan's philosophy was basically to "make hay while the sun shined", cleaning up any problems after they arose. While the periphery was suffering a series of devastating crises, the US economy entered what Ben Bernanke, Greenspan's successor, termed the "Great Moderation". Unemployment fell to levels not seen since the 1960s, inflation remained persistently low and the two recessions that did occur were brief and relatively painless. But beneath the surface things were not as healthy as they first appeared. Countercyclical intervention in the economy allows policymakers to intervene when things are overheating. This is an important tool in the central banks' armoury, and by refusing to use it Greenspan became the first chairman in Fed history to oversee two massive bubbles—first in stocks, then in housing.

The housing bubble was, according to Krugman, actively encouraged. Immediately after the dotcom crash in 2001 Greenspan slashed interest rates, keeping them historically low for almost a decade. This made house-buying particularly attractive.[30] According to Krugman, "Greenspan had succeeded only by replacing the stock bubble with a housing bubble".[31] But why had he allowed the dotcom bubble to originally emerge? Krugman never addresses this question. The obvious answer is a lack of a strong motor in the productive economy. If the second bubble was necessitated by a lack of any real alternatives, it stands to reason that the first bubble must have been necessitated for similar reasons. Greenspan's monetary policy was thus a pragmatic response to a general malaise in the productive economy, and his easy money and deregulation were *designed* to facilitate the building up of asset bubbles.

Innovations in complex finance
Capitalism is the first economic system in history to be geared almost entirely towards the market. In previous times people generally produced to satisfy human needs, but under capitalism production is for profit and needs are satisfied through commodity exchange. Capitalists must purchase raw materials, machinery and human labour power before producing commodities. This obviously takes time and on occasion some of the accumulated profits can be held in reserve (savings). All of this makes a functioning financial system extremely important. Exchange can only be generalised through a universal medium, which the financial system

---

29: Krugman, 2008, p140.
30: Stiglitz, 2010, p88.
31: Krugman, 2008, p152.

provides through its supervision and distribution of the currency. Banks also promote exchange by allowing capitalists to buy and sell on credit. Producers give credit to wholesalers, wholesalers give credit to retailers and retailers give credit to consumers. Finally, the banking system facilitates economic growth by recycling resources that would otherwise lie idle.

Without these financial supports the flow of goods and services would grind to a halt, investment would be severely disrupted and mortgages would become all but impossible to obtain. These are just some of the reasons that financial institutions are often deemed to be too important to fail. And yet the irony is that banks can be the very institutions most likely to fail. Lending is a risky business, and doing so with other people's resources makes it even more precarious. Banks create credit from the deposits they receive and this makes them more vulnerable than other capitalists to a crisis of confidence. Financial institutions face the possibility that some of their loans may eventually turn bad. This is exacerbated by the problem of "borrowing short" and "lending long". Banks accept deposits and other liabilities on short time horizons. They must be able to return assets at a moment's notice. But they can rarely impose this condition on the people to whom they lend. Banks traditionally gain their returns over many years. Even if loans are performing, there is still a mismatch between the liquidity of their liabilities and the liquidity of their assets.

These difficulties are inherent in banking. But what if innovative ways could be found of dealing with them, unleashing a wave of capital into the economy and making those who developed these innovations extremely wealthy?[32] This was the problem confronting the group of "cerebral young traders" at the heart of *Fool's Gold*. Their first innovation was to take the idea of a derivative contract and apply it to corporate loans. Derivatives, as the name suggests, *derive* their value from the asset being insured and versions of derivative contracts have been around for centuries.[33] Key to the contracts is that those who buy and sell them are each making a bet on the future value of the asset.[34] If a commodity owner wants to guarantee her income, she may try to agree a *future* price for her commodity. Alternatively she may pay a nominal fee for the *option* to sell at some future date. There are numerous ways to configure these deals. But the essence of derivatives contracts is that they always allow commodity owners to trade the risk of a loss on their assets. The bankers at JP Morgan understood the benefits of

---

32: Tett, 2009, p24.

33: Tett, 2009, p11.

34: Tett, 2009, p11.

derivatives, so why not create contracts allowing banks to trade the risk that a bond or corporate loan might go sour?[35] If ways could be found to insure against the threat of default, banks could reduce their capital reserves and risk could be matched up with those who were more willing to accept it.

Credit default swaps (CDSs), which pay out if a debtor defaults on a loan, helped to solve the problem of picking winners. These were joined by a novel way of increasing liquidity. The idea was known as "securitisation". Thousands of potential sources of revenue (bonds, corporate loans, etc) were bundled together before being "sliced and diced" and sold on to investors. This enabled the banks to solve their "maturity mismatch" by turning illiquid streams of revenue into immediately saleable commodities (collateralised debt obligations, CDOs). Those investing in these streams of debt could even be sold a CDS as well. As investment banks receive their fees from fixing contracts, there was a strong incentive to continually find parties to both CDO and CDS deals.

Given the complexity of this system an example might be useful. Suppose IBM wants to borrow $100 million from Bank of America (BOA). BOA is happy to lend the money, but knows this will tie up resources for years and that it will not receive a big return. So BOA writes a derivatives contract moving the risk of default onto a third party, say American Insurance Group (AIG). This would then allow it to hold less capital in reserve, freeing up money. In addition BOA could bundle the $100 million loan up with other such loans and create assets out of them. If the total value of the loans is $40 billion BOA may try to sell them on for around $41 billion. Instead of receiving a steady stream of payments they have sold this stream to an investor. This investor now assumes both the risk of default and the longer time horizon, in exchange for the extra revenue that gradually comes in. BOA may finally arrange with AIG to give insurance to the investor to guard against the threat of default. This will be done for a fee (both for AIG and BOA) and it supposedly lets everyone assume the levels of risk they are comfortable with. If AIG started to worry about its level of exposure, it could simply write another contract with Barclays Investment Bank to offload some of the risk. Anyone can buy a derivative, and pretty soon these contracts can be so far removed from the original asset that both the complexity and the ability to gamble have massively increased.

Writing in his 2002 Annual Report for Berkshire Hathaway the investor Warren Buffet described derivatives as "financial weapons of mass destruction". The shift that proved him correct was the application of both

35: Tett, 2009, p24.

securitisation and derivatives contracts to mortgage markets. Mortgages are notoriously difficult to assess for risk. Those taking out a mortgage are unlikely to have a track record in repayments and the problems were compounded by the explosion of the "subprime" mortgage market. By 2005 over 50 percent of US mortgages were to people with a poor credit history and a lack of sufficient resources.[36] To make matters worse, the conveyor belt of home loans that developed left nobody with any incentive to reduce the risk of these mortgages defaulting. Brokers granted mortgages that they never intended to hold. Investment banks bundled these mortgages into CDOs before getting them rated for risk, creating CDSs against them, and selling them on to unwitting investors. Investors assumed that any product rated as "triple A" by rating companies could never turn sour.[37] At every stage the incentive was to maximise the quantity of mortgages, while assuming property prices would continue to rise. When house prices began to fall, all hell broke loose.

Problems of effective demand

Any underlying weaknesses in the economy were masked but only so long as financial innovations were driving the economy. Financial innovation was extremely lucrative for the capitalist banks.[38] But it was the cheap credit that they helped to unleash that really sustained the Greenspan mirage. For example, according to Tett: "In 2005 US households extracted no less than $750 billion of funds against the values of their homes...of which two-thirds was spent on personal consumption, home improvements and credit card debt".[39] Stiglitz argues that it was closer to $1 trillion.[40] As a Keynesian, Stiglitz is highly attuned to the problem of "effective demand", and at a number of points informs readers of the rising inequality that has accompanied financialisation.[41]

36: Tett, 2009, p112.
37: Triple A rated products are of a sufficiently low risk that they are supposedly suitable for risk-averse actors such as pension funds. The agencies that rate these products (Standard and Poor's, Moody's, Fitch, etc) are supposed to increase market efficiency by providing information for market participants. In reality they became highly reliant on the investment banks that they were supposedly rating.
38: According to Stiglitz, financial institutions were claiming almost 40 percent of all corporate profits in the years preceding the boom. This was up from around 15 percent in 1965 and it shows just how reliant capitalism had become on debt-fuelled asset bubbles. See Stiglitz, 2010, p7, for more details.
39: Tett, 2009, p146.
40: Stiglitz, 2010, p2.
41: See Stiglitz, 2010, pp xxi, 2, 193, 284.

America like much of the rest of the world faces growing income inequality, but in America it has reached levels not seen for three quarters of a century... the global economy needed ever-increasing consumption to grow, but how could this continue when the incomes of many Americans had been stagnating for so long? Americans came up with an ingenious solution: borrow and consume as if their incomes were growing... [This then led to] an unsustainable bubble. Without the bubble, aggregate demand...would have been weak, partly because of the growing inequality...which shifted money from those who would have spent it to those who didn't.[42]

Cheap credit essentially replaced falling real wages. Without the innovations the economy would have stagnated. If Stiglitz is correct: "Many Americans have wound up paying 40-50 percent of their incomes to the banks".[43] This conveys an important truth about the latest round of financial products missing from *Fool's Gold*—they were never about improving services but about robbing as much as was possible. Useful innovations should reduce what economists call "transaction costs" at the same time as providing products that consumers can rely on. Instead, Wall Street ramped up the transaction costs (their own fees), while preying on vulnerable customers with all manner of teaser loans, Ponzi schemes and predatory lending.

Stiglitz's challenge to Krugman's analysis

Krugman's *Depression Economics* would leave the reader assuming that capital, while far from virtuous, is basically benign. When it comes to the IMF's role, Krugman writes:

Because speculative attacks can be self-justifying following an economic policy that makes sense in terms of fundamentals is not enough... Now, consider the situation from the point of view of those clever economists who were making policy in Washington. They found themselves dealing with countries whose hold on investor confidence was fragile...the overriding policy objective must therefore be to mollify market sentiment... It became an exercise in amateur psychology in which the IMF and the Treasury Department tried to persuade countries to do things they hoped would be perceived by the market as favourable.[44]

42: Stiglitz, 2010, pp193, 2, 18.
43: Stiglitz, 2010, p103.
44: Krugman, 2008, p113.

In stark contrast to Krugman's apologetics, Stiglitz charges those who run the economic system with being far more interested in protecting the interests of Western banks than with protecting the lives of the people of the Global South.[45] The Washington Consensus (liberalisation, privatisation, stabilisation) was designed to open vulnerable countries to a host of disastrous measures. Stiglitz writes of a central banker who told him that "the country would have to be on its deathbed before ever returning to the IMF" and in many parts of the developing world the Bretton Woods institutions came to be seen as instruments of post-colonial control.[46] Structural adjustment was little more than a ruse to increase exploitation and, for Stiglitz, it is once again the particular brand of neoliberal capitalism that has left the poor so dangerously exposed:

> In the end the programmes of the "Chicago boys" didn't bring the promised results. Incomes stagnated. Where there was growth, the wealth went to those at the top… Free market ideology turned out to be an excuse for new forms of exploitation. "Privatisation" meant that foreigners could buy mines and oilfields in developing countries at low prices. It also meant they could reap large profits from monopolies and quasi-monopolies, such as in telecoms. "Financial and capital market liberalisation" meant that foreign banks could get high returns on their loans, and when the loans went bad, the IMF forced the socialisation of the losses meaning the screws were put on entire populations to pay the foreign banks back.[47]

These insights show how disillusioned Stiglitz has become with neo-liberal capitalism. The extent to which the Federal Reserve has been at the forefront of the corporate bonanza poses, for Stiglitz, serious questions about the nature of American democracy:

> One of the reasons why the Fed was able to get away with what it did was that it…didn't need to get congressional permission for putting at risk hundreds of billions of taxpayer dollars. Indeed, that was one of the reasons why the administrations turned to the Fed; they were trying to circumvent democratic processes knowing they had little support.[48]

45: Stiglitz, 2010, p xvi.
46: Stiglitz, 2010, p220.
47: Stiglitz, 2010, pp220-221.
48: Stiglitz, 2010, p142.

The impossibility of the Keynesian compact

Stiglitz's conclusion is that "the current crisis has uncovered fundamental flaws in the capitalist system, or at least, the peculiar version of capitalism that emerged in the latter part of the 20th century".[49] This makes his account far superior to Krugman's. But while the strengths of Stiglitz's book flow from his challenge to neoliberalism, his unwillingness to break with capitalism more generally means that there are also significant weaknesses. Perhaps the most glaring is the mismatch between the book's critique and its prescriptions. Stiglitz's call for a "New Capitalist Order" is both utopian and uninspiring.[50] Like Krugman, Stiglitz champions a reversion to a traditional form of Keynesian interventionism. But Krugman's "Keynesian compromise" is decisively undermined by the twin realities of globalisation and the easy money policies of the Fed. Despite all the requisite know-how, peripheral governments are unable to intervene, while the US government has no interest in intervening, unless it can be squared with saving the banks. Nowhere is income redistribution on the cards. The idea that we can somehow revert to a more caring version of capitalism is extremely implausible.

Contrary to popular myth, the global restructuring associated with neoliberalism was never about replacing a benign state with the vicissitudes of the market. Rather it was about reorienting the state to support the new requirements for capital to accumulate. From a high point in the 1950s, profit rates fell steadily until the early 1980s,[51] and this necessitated a new form of state intervention. How is the system now to be remoulded? Elites have, after all, used the crisis to reassert their political dominance. Far from compromise, ruling classes have increased their attacks, and as the system continues to degenerate it is extremely unlikely that wealth can be redistributed without massive working class resistance.

There is another, more basic reason why it is problematic to argue for a more caring version of capitalist society. Put simply, there can be no compromise with the class of exploiters. Rather than arguing for some form of "capitalist utopia", the real message of the crisis should be the need to emancipate ourselves from every form of class exploitation. Stiglitz never gets close to asserting this. But unlike *Fool's Gold* and *Depression Economics*, it would be hard to finish his book without realising that some form of social(ist) transformation is exactly what is needed.

49: Stiglitz, 2010, p xxi.
50: The title of chapter seven of Stiglitz's book.
51: See Moseley, 1997, 2000; Duménil and Levy, 2001, 2002; Brenner, 2006; Harman, 2007; and Shaikh, 2011, for more details.

References

Brenner, Robert, 2006, *The Economics of Global Turbulence* (Verso).

Duménil, Gérard, and Dominique Lévy, 2001, "Imposing the Neoliberal Order: Four Historical Configurations (US, Europe, Japan and Korea)", www.jourdan.ens.fr/levy/dle2001h.htm

Duménil, Gérard, and Dominique Lévy, 2002, "The Profit Rate: Where and How Much did it Fall? Did it Recover? (USA 1948-2000)", www.jourdan.ens.fr/levy/dle2002f.htm

Harman, Chris, 1996, "Globalisation: A Critique of a New Orthodoxy", *International Socialism* 73 (winter), www.marxists.de/imperial/harman/global-e.htm

Harman, Chris, 2007, "The Rate of Profit and the World Today", *International Socialism* 115 (summer), www.isj.org.uk/?id=340

Harvey, David, 2005, *A Brief History of Neoliberalism* (Oxford University).

Keynes, John Maynard, 1997 (1935), *The General Theory of Employment, Interest and Money* (Prometheus), www.marxists.org/reference/subject/economics/keynes/general-theory/

Krugman, Paul, 2008, *The Return of Depression Economics* (Penguin).

Moseley, Fred, 1997, "The Rate of Profit and the Future of Capitalism", www.mtholyoke.edu/~fmoseley/

Moseley, Fred, 2000, "The Decline of the Rate of Profit in the Postwar US Economy: A Comment on Brenner", www.mtholyoke.edu/~fmoseley/Working_Papers_PDF/HM.pdf

Roubini, Nouriel, and Stephen Mihm, 2011, *Crisis Economics: A Crash Course in the Future of Finance* (Penguin).

Shaikh, Anwar, 2011, "The First Great Depression of the 21st Century", *Socialist Register 2011: The Crisis This Time (Merlin)*.

Stiglitz, Joseph, 2010, *Freefall: Free Markets and the Sinking of the Global Economy* (Penguin).

Tett, Gillian, 2009, *Fool's Gold: How Unrestrained Greed Corrupted a Dream, Shattered Global Markets and Unleashed a Catastrophe* (Abacus).

Grappling with the united front

Ian Birchall

A review of John Riddell (ed), **Toward the United Front: Proceedings of the Fourth Congress of the Communist International 1922** *(Brill, 2012), €199.00*

Why, 90 years on, study the detailed proceedings of the Communist International (often known as the Comintern)?[1] Many years ago, when I was young, it was common to find orthodox Trotskyists who claimed they based their politics on "the first four congresses of the Comintern". (You can probably still find such people in the remoter reaches of the Trotskyist blogosphere.) A position that made some sense in the 1930s, when Trotskyists were insisting that there was a clear break between Lenin and Stalin, became less and less relevant as both capitalism and the working class went through enormous changes.

But if such a scriptural approach to the Comintern is misguided, so too is the opposite position, summed up in George Galloway's famous warning that we should stop talking about "dead Russians". The years following the Russian Revolution represented the highest level of working class struggle and organisation yet seen, and if we study them carefully, without trying to read off simple slogans or directives, they can be of great value.

So we should be very grateful to John Riddell and his team of collaborators for making available, for the first time in a full English version,

---

1: A (relatively) cheaper paperback edition will be published later this year by Haymarket Books at $55. References in brackets are to this book.

the minutes of the Fourth Congress of the Comintern.[2] Probably few people, other than dedicated reviewers, will read this volume cover to cover—it's a bit like reading the collected scripts of a soap opera with a bewilderingly large cast. But for anyone seeking to understand the history of the 20th century it will be an invaluable work of reference, and no library with pretensions to serious historical coverage should be without it.[3]

The Fourth Congress took place from 5 November to 5 December 1922. To understand its wide-ranging and sometimes heated debates it is necessary to place them in historical context.[4] The International had been founded in 1919, amid hopes that the Russian Revolution would spread rapidly to other countries in Europe. But short-lived Communist regimes in Hungary and Bavaria were crushed, and capitalism was beginning to stabilise itself. The failure to seize revolutionary opportunities was beginning to exact a heavy price. As RH Tawney pointed out, onions can be eaten leaf by leaf, but you cannot skin a live tiger paw by paw. And if you do try to pull a tiger's claws out, it gets very angry indeed.

So by 1922 the ruling class was on the offensive. It wanted to reverse the gains made in the preceding years and, even more important, to reassert its political hegemony and to frighten the working class into subjection. In Yugoslavia Communist publications were banned and Communists jailed; French strikers were shot down in Le Havre. In Germany employers were determined to extend the working day from eight to ten hours (reversing the one real gain of the 1918 Revolution). Just days before the congress Mussolini had become Italian prime

2:   Riddell has previously published a number of volumes on the roots and development of the Comintern, in particular the proceedings of the First and Second Congresses—Riddell, 1987; Riddell, 1991. The publication of the proceedings of the Third Congress has unfortunately been delayed "for technical reasons beyond our control" (p58), but hopefully they will be available soon. Riddell's work is based on high standards of scholarship, but his interest is not purely historical; he is an activist historian, as can be seen from his website (http://johnriddell.wordpress.com/) which contains many pieces relating the experiences of the Comintern to current situations, notably in Latin America.

3:   Unfortunately more and more institutions of higher education are abandoning such pretensions by dropping the study of history. Any culture that fails to study the past is doomed to misunderstand the present—a point neatly summed up in a Doonesbury cartoon a few years back. Two US soldiers in Afghanistan are talking. The older one remarks that the situation is becoming more and more like Vietnam, to which the younger responds: "I don't know; we didn't do history at my college."

4:   For a short overview of the Comintern see Hallas, 1985; there is a vivid account by a participant in Rosmer, 1971. The best history of the Comintern, showing the strengths of its early years while not glossing over its weaknesses, is Broué, 1997. Hopefully this will be available in English before too long.

minister after the March on Rome. France, having imposed an intolerable burden of reparations on the defeated Germany, was preparing to occupy the Ruhr region.

So the delegates who assembled in Moscow (after an opening ceremony in Petrograd to commemorate the fifth anniversary of the Russian Revolution) faced a grim prospect, but one that was not without hope. Capitalism was still in deep crisis and it seemed as though revolutionary hopes had merely been temporarily postponed.

There is much about the congress that can appear very remote—the long set speeches, often employing a rather abstract rhetoric that belongs to a different age. But this was not a wholly stage-managed conference, as is clear from various clashes and confrontations. Minority positions within various parties were put before the congress. And there is a familiar feel to the way the chairs were constantly trying to keep to the agenda and prevent speakers going on beyond their time limit. When told that his time was up, the delegate from the Dutch Indies (Indonesia), Tan Malaka, simply replied, "I come from the Indies; I travelled for 40 days," and went on speaking.[5] Sometimes the optimism of the delegates seems excessive, as when Zinoviev (the Comintern's president) declared, "What we are now experiencing is not one of capitalism's periodic crises but *the* crisis of capitalism, its twilight, its disintegration".[6] But we should beware of the "condescension of posterity". These delegates were tough women and men who had lived through an exceptionally demanding decade. If they believed that success was still within their grasp, then we should not let our retrospective knowledge of impending defeat make us dismiss that testimony.

The delegates were well aware of the seriousness of the situation, and that their decisions could make all the difference between victory and catastrophic defeat. There was no place for either fatalism or voluntarism. As Clara Zetkin reminded them, the Bolshevik conquest of power in 1917 had been based on a wager, with no guarantee of success. So she urged them, "Weigh the situation carefully, to be sure, but, in the process of weighing, do not forget to wager. Weighing must be the basis and preparation for wagering".[7]

And in a later speech she anticipated chaos theory in urging the delegates to see what bold action could achieve:

5:   Riddell, 2012, p264.
6:   Riddell, 2012, p120.
7:   Riddell, 2012, p311.

Society is objectively ripe, indeed overripe, for capitalism to be swept away and overthrown... But, sisters and brothers, this historical situation is like a landscape in the Alps, where great masses of snow lie stored on high peaks, which have defied all storms for centuries and seem ready to defy the influence of sun, rain, and tempests for several hundred years to come. Yet, despite all appearances, they are hollowed out, brittle and "ripe" to come cascading down.

It may be enough for a little bird to move its pinions and touch these snows with the tip of its wings, to bring the avalanche into motion and bury the valleys down below.[8]

The congress brought together around 350 delegates from 61 countries, an indication of how the movement had grown in the five years after 1917. That the congress was politically dominated by the Russians is scarcely surprising—they were the only ones who had successfully made and maintained a revolution, though Zinoviev was perhaps excessively confident of his ability to pronounce on all aspects of the Comintern's work. Many delegates confined themselves to what they knew, their own local situation, and thus failed to address the questions of overall strategy that confronted the movement.

But there were delegates who showed that the movement was accumulating experience and a capacity for judgement. Alfred Rosmer from France (who would be expelled from the French Communist Party two years later) spoke with passion moderated by sober realism. Clara Zetkin showed herself to be the most level-headed member of the young and divided German party.[9] The Jamaican-American poet Claude McKay attended and spoke, and Lenin's wife, Krupskaya, contributed thoughts on methods of agitation. Antonio Gramsci was present, but unfortunately, given some of the confusion about the Italian situation,[10] did not speak. He was a member of a commission on Egypt, and was elected to the Comintern's new Executive Committee.

There is one notable absentee—JV Stalin. It may seem surprising that in this bulky volume of over 1,200 pages there are just *two* references

---

8: Riddell, 2012, p851.
9: Nowadays Zetkin tends to be remembered only for her important work on the organisation of women. But her contribution was far broader than this. It is hoped that a future issue of *Revolutionary History* will be devoted to the full range of Zetkin's contribution.
10: As Zinoviev put it, "Among the Italian comrades, there is now a debate on what has happened in Italy: a coup d'état or a farce. It could possibly be both"—Riddell, 2012, p106.

to Stalin. But Stalin always despised the International and took little or no part in its activities.[11]

The congress covered a range of topics, among them economic perspectives, the impact of the Versailles Treaty, the oppression of women, black workers in the US, cooperation with Muslims and attitudes to Pan-Islamism, trade union work and the internal difficulties of the French and Czechoslovak parties. The Comintern was still largely limited to Europe, and it had only just begun to develop organisations in Africa and Asia, still largely subjected to European colonialism. The advance of Communism was not assisted by the fact that in North Africa Communist organisation tended to be dominated by settlers of European origin who at times espoused openly racist positions.

Thus a Tunisian postal worker, Tahar Boudengha, quoted at some length from a resolution adopted by a settler-dominated Communist conference in North Africa, which stated:

> The native population of North Africa can only be liberated by the revolution in France. The native masses have been subjugated for centuries in a status of half-slavery. They are fanatical and fatalistic, patient and resigned, oppressed and imbued with religious prejudices. At this time, they still cannot imagine their liberation... It is entirely unnecessary to publish calls to rebellion in our press or distribute Arabic-language leaflets.[12]

But the central theme of the congress, which recurred under various headings, was the united front. Since it had become clear that the first revolutionary wave would not lead to victory, the Comintern had recognised the need for a more defensive strategy. And that meant unity in action with the reformist organisations that still retained the loyalty of the majority of workers in most countries.

The united front was not spun out of the skulls of the Comintern's leaders. It was born of the experience of workers in Germany: in late 1920 Stuttgart metal-workers had formulated defensive demands taken up in early 1921 in the "Open Letter" of the German Communist Party to other workers' organisations.[13] Already the Third Congress in 1921 had begun the turn towards the united front strategy with the slogan "To the

---

11: Marie, 2001, p457.
12: Riddell, 2012, p703. On this see also the response by Robert Louzon, who had launched the first Arabic language Communist daily paper, which was promptly banned—Louzon, 2012.
13: Broué, 2005, pp468-473, and Riddell, 2011a.

masses", and later that year the Comintern Executive had adopted the policy of the united front.

But it was not an easy turn to make. Many Communist parties had come into being only a couple of years earlier from splits in mass reformist organisations. Such splits had of necessity often been lively and acrimonious affairs. It was not always easy to convince militants who had just been through such a split that they should seek united action with those they had so recently been denouncing. There were obvious dangers of opportunism on the one side and sectarianism on the other; as the German delegate Edwin Hoernle put it, "I would like to compare the united front with a narrow mountain ridge. I tell you that it is slippery and the way is narrow".[14]

Hence there were many opponents of the united front strategy—on the one hand ultra-lefts for whom proclamation of the Communist ideal was all that was needed, but on the other right wing elements who had their own factional reasons.[15] As Richard Schüller of the youth international pointed out, there was an old slogan in the movement: "First clarity, then majority".[16] Some Communists were reluctant to abandon this principle and move on to the task of winning the masses.

So the congress was still grappling with the problem of the united front. It is this that makes some of the debates so interesting: the strategy was not encapsulated in a neat formulation, but was rather a matter of experience to be approached through trial and error.

Some basic principles stand out very clearly. The united front depended on the close interaction of economic and political struggle. As Radek had put it in 1921, workers must "unite at least for the struggle for bare existence, for a crust of bread".[17]

Although unity at the grass roots was paramount, a united front could not be purely from below. Many, if not all, members of reformist parties stayed in those organisations because they still had some degree of confidence in their leaders. So no approach to rank and file reformist workers could succeed without some form of dialogue with their leaders. As Radek explained, rank and file Social Democratic workers, who still had some faith in their leaders, would ask why the Communists were not talking to them:

14: Riddell, 2012, p457.
15: Rosmer, 1971, pp229-232, gives an account of opposition to the united front in the French party.
16: Riddell, 2012, p784.
17: Riddell, 2012, p146.

Should we reply by telling them that Scheidemann is a traitor? If they agreed with us in this judgement of Scheidemann, we would not have to preach to them about that; they would be with us. But this judgement is precisely what divides us. That is why, despite this opinion, if we want a united front, we must negotiate with the leaders of the Second International.[18]

Yet here too there were difficulties. Some of the congress statements seemed to undermine this principle. Zinoviev declared fiercely that "reformism is our main enemy",[19] and even that:

The ideology of Fascist syndicalism...is a petty-bourgeois ideology that is actually not as far removed from that of Social Democracy as is sometimes thought. The ideology is fundamentally the same, but in a different form... It is no accident that the [Italian] reformists...ally themselves with the Fascists.[20]

One can see his point. The betrayal by the Second International at the outbreak of war in 1914 and the complicity of the German Social Democratic leaders in the murder of Luxemburg and Liebknecht were still fresh in the minds of delegates. Nonetheless some of Zinoviev's formulations are all too reminiscent of the language of the German Communist Party before Hitler's seizure of power, when Social Democrats were labelled "social fascists". There was a slippery slope here, and it is not clear that Zinoviev was fully aware of the dangers.

There were more difficulties with another implication of the united front—the question of the so-called "workers' government". What attitude should Communists take if governments composed of (reformist) workers' parties were elected? This was a new problem for the movement—apart from some Labour governments in Australia there was no experience of reformism in power.[21] (Nowadays we have all too much.)

There was considerable confusion about the question at the congress. Some delegates stated openly that they were unclear about what was being argued. And it was made clear that a workers' government was only one of a

---

18: Riddell, 2012, p394. Scheidemann was right wing leader of the German Social Democratic Party.
19: Riddell, 2012, p1047. Of course, things are different when the reformists are in power. During the Iraq War Tony Blair was indeed the "main enemy", though it would have been inaccurate and stupid to call him a fascist.
20: Riddell, 2012, p1052.
21: A (minority) British Labour government was formed a year later, from January to November 1924.

number of possible ways in which a revolutionary situation could develop; in Radek's words, "The workers' government is not inevitable, but possible".[22]

The essential problem was what could be demanded of a government which might claim to represent the working class, but which was working within the framework of the existing state.[23] Quite rightly the congress resolution argued that the key question was mass involvement—nothing could be expected from a workers' government without mass struggle on the ground, and mass struggle, not the particular form of a government, was always the determining factor:

> A workers' government is possible only if it is born from the struggles of the masses themselves and is supported by militant workers' organisations created by the most oppressed layers of the working masses. Even a workers' government that arises from a purely parliamentary combination, that is, one that is purely parliamentary in origin, *can* provide the occasion for a revival of the revolutionary workers' movement... Even an attempt by the proletariat to form such a workers' government will encounter from the outset most determined resistance from the bourgeoisie. The slogan of the workers' government thus has the potential of uniting the proletariat and unleashing revolutionary struggle.[24]

Obviously there are echoes here of situations in our own world and there is much to be learnt from a study of these debates. But I remain sceptical as to whether detailed formulations from 1922 can be applied to the world of the 21st century.[25]

The other major question that flowed from the debate on the united front was that of fascism, already taking power in Italy. And the congress recognised that "the danger of fascism now exists in many countries: Czechoslovakia, Hungary, almost all the Balkan countries, Poland, Germany (Bavaria), Austria, the United States, and even in countries like Norway".[26]

22: Riddell, 2012, p399.

23: For a discussion of the whole question see Harman and Potter, 1977. They point out that the Comintern's position must be radically rethought in the light of subsequent experience: "Unfortunately, 55 years of bitter experience have shown that reformist governments without the participation of the bourgeoisie are quite possible without capitalism crumbling, and have often been used to strengthen its rule."

24: Riddell, 2012, p1160.

25: See for example the discussion of Bolivia in Riddell, 2011b, Riddell, 2011c, and Webber, 2012.

26: Riddell, 2012, p1154. If this seems melodramatic, it should be remembered that 20 years later all these countries except the US had pro-Nazi regimes.

Yet there was no clear understanding of the enormity of the danger. Ever since the massacre of workers in the overthrow of the Paris Commune in 1871 the socialist movement had faced violent repression; the fact that fascism was something qualitatively different would take time to understand. Bukharin was moving towards a recognition of this when he said, "Fascism is not merely an organisational form that the bourgeois had in the past; it is a newly discovered form that is adapted to the new movement by drawing in the masses".[27] But Italian Communist leader Bordiga still insisted, "Fascism does not represent any new political doctrine".[28] Perhaps he learned something of its novelty in 1926 when he found himself in one of Mussolini's jails.

There was eventually, however, some honest accounting about the failures of the Italian Communists in relation to the anti-fascist struggle. When a mass campaign against fascism had developed in the form of the Arditi del Popolo (a non-aligned organisation),[29] the Italian Communists had stood aside in a sectarian fashion, not willing to take part in a united front of which they themselves were not at the centre. As Zinoviev mocked:

> It was said: "Should we really get involved with such confused people? They have not even read the third volume of Marx's *Capital*." That is very true. Perhaps they had not even seen the first volume, let alone read it. But, nonetheless, these were people who were ready to fight against Fascism.[30]

The Fourth Congress was Lenin's last. He was too ill to make more than one intervention, but he was received with evident affection and enthusiasm. Whether anyone was actually listening to what he said is less obvious. Referring to the resolution on organisation carried at the Third Congress, he savagely attacked the mentality according to which the Russian experience could be applied mechanically in different circumstances:

> The resolution is too Russian; it reflects Russian experience. That is why it is quite unintelligible to foreigners, and they cannot be content with hanging it in a corner like an icon and praying to it. Nothing will be achieved that

---

27: Riddell, 2012, p212.
28: Riddell, 2012, p413.
29: See Behan, 2003.
30: Riddell, 2012, pp1053-1054.

way. They must assimilate part of the Russian experience. Just how that will be done, I do not know.[31]

And he appealed to the delegates to "study...in order that they may really understand the organisation, structure, method and content of revolutionary work".[32] Lenin clearly saw that, just as he had had to rethink basic principles in order to seize the opportunity offered in 1917, so now new thinking was again required to face new problems.

Clearly some delegates had been busy with something else during this speech. Presenting a report on the reorganisation of the Comintern Executive, Eberlein promised a "strictly centralised world party" and "much stricter discipline".[33] And by 1924, freed from Lenin's watchful eye as the latter's health declined, Zinoviev launched the so-called "Bolshevisation" of the parties of the Comintern—in effect a purging of many of the best revolutionaries, a mechanical reorganisation, and a process which paved the way for the total subjection of the Comintern to Moscow control a few years later.[34]

There was much that was positive in the Fourth Congress and the delegates' hopes were not unrealistic. But they did not prevail. Capitalism was stabilising itself and getting much more vicious in the process. At the same time, as yet unremarked by most, the revolution was degenerating from within. Riddell's excellent "Biographical Notes" show the subsequent fates of the participants in the congress: acquiescence in Stalinism by many, isolation, demoralisation and even betrayal by others, and for those who remained true to their principles, persecution and sometimes death. Of the five Russian leaders who gave reports to the Congress (Lenin, Trotsky, Zinoviev, Radek and Bukharin), only Lenin died in his bed.

As Lenin urged, study this congress, but study it in historical context.

31: Riddell, 2012, pp304-305.
32: Riddell, 2012, p305.
33: Riddell, 2012, pp925-926.
34: In Pierre Broué's words, by 1924 the Comintern had "a single, centralised and disciplined apparatus of professional militants, reproduced on the model of the Soviet party, led from Moscow and in conformity with Soviet foreign policy"—Broué, 1997, pp384-385.

References

Behan, Tom, 2003, *The Resistible Rise of Benito Mussolini* (Bookmarks).

Broué, Pierre, 1997, *Histoire de l'Internationale Communiste* (Fayard).

Broué, Pierre, 2005, *The German Revolution 1917-1923* (Brill).

Hallas, Duncan, 1985, *The Comintern* (Bookmarks).

Harman, Chris, and Tim Potter, 1977, "The Workers' Government", *International Discussion Bulletin* (Socialist Workers Party), www.marxists.org/archive/harman/1977/xx/workersgov.htm

Louzon, Robert, 2012, "A Disgrace", *Revolutionary History* 10/4 (2012).

Marie, Jean-Jacques, 2001, *Staline* (Fayard).

Riddell, John, 1987, *Founding the Communist International: Proceedings and Documents of the First Congress—March 1919* (Pathfinder).

Riddell, John, 1991, *Workers of the World and Oppressed Peoples Unite! : Proceedings and Documents of the Second Congress, 1920* (Pathfinder).

Riddell, John, 2011a, "The Origins of the United Front Policy", *International Socialism* 130 (spring), www.isj.org.uk/?id=724

Riddell, John, 2011b, "Progress in Bolivia: A Reply to Jeff Webber", *Bullet* (9 May), http://johnriddell.wordpress.com/2011/05/05/progress-in-bolivia-a-reply-to-jeff-webber/

Riddell, John, 2011c, "How Clara Zetkin Helps us to Understand Evo Morales" (18 September), http://johnriddell.wordpress.com/2011/09/18/how-clara-zetkin-helps-us-understand-evo-morales/

Riddell, John (ed), 2012, *Toward the United Front: Proceedings of the Fourth Congress of the Communist International 1922* (Haymarket).

Rosmer, Alfred, 1971, *Lenin's Moscow* (Pluto).

Webber, Jeffery R, 2012, "Revolution against 'progress': the TIPNIS struggle and class contradictions in Bolivia", *International Socialism* 133 (winter), www.isj.org.uk/?id=780

ALIENATION
An introduction to
Marx's theory
by Dan Swain

The young German radical
Karl Marx began to diagnose
the phenomenon of alien-
ation in the early 1840s, and
remained pre-occupied with it
throughout his life. He sought
to explain how capitalist production, with all its dynamism,
only took us further away from
control over our lives.

   This accessible guide to a
central aspect of Marx's philosophy takes the reader through
the development of the concept from its roots in the Enlightenment through Marx to later debates and controversies.

Dan Swain is a postgraduate researcher in philosophy at the
University of Essex. He is on the editorial board of International Socialism.

ISBN: 9781905192922 Price: £5
Available now direct from Bookmarks, nationwide from March

BOOKMARKS
PUBLICATIONS

Bookmarks the socialist bookshop,
1 Bloomsbury Street, London WC1B 3QE
020 7637 1848 | mailorder@bookmarks.uk.com

Book reviews

It's hard to be a saint in the city

Dan Swain

David Harvey, **Rebel Cities: From the Right to the City to the Urban Revolution** *(Verso, 2012), £12.99*

David Harvey has established himself as one of the most significant and influential thinkers in contemporary Marxist thought. Recordings of his reading groups of Marx's *Capital* have been viewed by tens of thousands of people online, while last November he filled Friends Meeting House in central London when giving the Isaac Deutscher Memorial Lecture. Harvey has contributed in particular to developing the influence of Marxism within the field of geography, focusing in particular on the role of space and location within the dynamics of modern capitalism. In doing so he has contributed towards extending the scope of both geography and Marxism itself.

This book is a continuation of an argument for the importance of urbanisation, the production of the modern city and its suburbs that Harvey has been developing over a number of years. It is, characteristically, extremely clearly written and easy to understand, free in the main of the kind of jargon that dominates many academic Marxist writers. Harvey is as concerned with destroying capitalism as he is with understanding it, and, he argues, grasping urbanisation is crucial to both. His argument is that much of the existing and

traditional left has failed to understand its significance. Urbanisation has played and continues to play a role in both capitalism's development and its crises. The creation of vast cities, through, for example, huge investment in building projects, has been, he argues, crucial to absorbing the surpluses created by capitalism. At the same time housing markets are a frequent trigger for crises, of which the recent sub-prime mortgage crisis is a clear example.

Because of the central role of the city in capitalism, Harvey argues that the left ought to take movements which are focused on the city far more seriously. This is the "right to the city" referred to in the title. This is not a narrow, individual property right of the sort which prevail under capitalism, and which is, for many, the only kind we can imagine. It is "to claim some kind of shaping power over the processes of urbanisation, over the ways in which our cities are made and remade, and to do so in a fundamental and radical way". The argument goes that, by focusing either on entirely excluded groups or on the traditional working class, the existing left has ignored the importance of such struggles, and that this has to stop. Urban movements and organisations, including demands for citizenship and rights of access to public services and public space, have to be seen as central to the struggle to overthrow capitalism.

It is difficult to disagree with much of Harvey's conclusions. This, however, is not always a strength, since it is difficult to disagree in part because the conclusions are somewhat vague and imprecise. To a certain extent this reflects a sincere and welcome modesty; Harvey does not know all the answers, any more than anyone else (least of all the British left!), and it is to his credit that he does not pretend that he does. However, there remains a frustrating vagueness about Harvey's arguments, a feeling that he, perhaps, intends to say something more controversial and radical than he actually does.

Harvey argues for a rethinking of anti-capitalist struggle along urban lines. In particular, he offers a number of "theses" for urban revolution. One of these is that "work-based struggles, from strikes to factory takeovers, are far more likely to succeed when there is strong and vibrant support from popular forces assembled at the surrounding neighbourhood or community level". This is something it is hard to disagree with, and it is not clear who would. Another, however, is trickier: "the concept of work has to shift from a narrow definition attaching to industrial forms of labour to the far broader terrain of the work entailed in the production and reproduction of an increasingly urbanised daily life." On the one hand, this looks like an important argument for the extension of the concept of work and working class into all those who produce, not merely the stereotypes of a traditional factory worker. This is, once again, hard to disagree with. However, it also seems to mask important differences. It is not always clear who Harvey means to include in this category. So sometimes it seems to be producers of value in the traditional Marxist sense, other times it appears to include almost everyone in the city.

One problem with this is that not all reproducers of the city, in Harvey's terms, are equally powerful, equally capable of undermining capitalism or stopping it from functioning. So, for example, Harvey notes, "Thousands of delivery trucks clog the streets of New York every day. Organised,

those workers would have the power to strangle the metabolism of the city." This is an important observation about the potential power of a particular group of workers, but not everyone within the city has such power. Similarly with the British electricians' struggle of last year, an example which Harvey does not mention. These protests showed the power of a militantly organised group of workers in an urban environment. The nature of their work meant their action could be astonishingly effective, and ultimately victorious, yet this kind of power does not exist in everyone who produces and reproduces the city. Furthermore, it is not clear to me exactly how seeing them primarily as producers of the *city* would have changed either the approach of the sparks themselves or of those who delivered solidarity to them.

Although we are hardly the main target, the Socialist Workers Party (SWP) does get a direct mention, so it is worth responding to it. Harvey, repeating a comment made at the *Historical Materialism* conference in November, argues that the SWP "led the successful struggle against Thatcher's poll tax in the 1980s". This is a claim that gives us far too much credit, and will perhaps surprise those who were present. It is also indicative of the vagueness surrounding Harvey's claims. This is intended as a sort of "gotcha" moment. The implication is "You guys go on about factories and workers, but actually your most successful historical intervention was over an issue of citizenship and tax". Yet it is unclear where this criticism is supposed to land. For one thing, it suggests a certain ambivalence about what counts as truly urban, since, as comrades where I live in East Anglia never tire of telling me, the poll tax revolt was hardly limited to the urban metropolises. On the other hand, it shows that the "traditional left" might have been rather better at identifying the class character of this kind of issue than Harvey maintains.

None of this is to ignore that Harvey is grappling with serious questions, probably the most important of which is how to organise a vast and diverse working class, for many of whom organising within the workplace (if they even have one) is extremely difficult. Here the idea of city-wide organising has a genuine appeal, and should not be ignored. Nor is it to demand from Harvey a new manifesto or roadmap for the future. Obviously that would be too much. But I was left wanting more, much more. This is compounded by the final two chapters, one a short commentary on the London riots and one a hymn of praise to Occupy Wall Street, which feel (and I assume were) bolted on. In these chapters the detailed questions of class and production fade out, in favour of generalisations about broad coalitions of the oppressed and exploited. This is out of keeping with the rest of the book, and it would be a shame if this is where Harvey's compelling analysis ends up.

Consuming culture
Bea Leal

David Campbell and Mark Durden,
Variable Capital *(Liverpool University Press, 2008), £28.50*

The starting point for *Variable Capital* was an exhibition of the same name held at the Liverpool Bluecoat gallery in 2008. The book is not a catalogue though. It takes a selection of pieces, mostly by artists who took part in the exhibition but not all, and uses them to discuss various themes, for example, Hollywood, sex and recycling. Each theme is a chapter a couple of pages long, and most are illustrated by one artist's work. An introduction sets out the wider

topics the authors want to deal with: consumerism or "cultures of consumption", how artworks work under capitalism, and how artists can (or should) deal with this.

Within these categories, the attitudes of the artists vary widely, as do the artworks. Some are photographs, picking details of everyday life related to consumption, while some reuse commodities themselves as artworks. Some use the visual language of adverts, making their "products" look as appealing as possible; others focus on tatty and rejected objects. Other pieces create situations where things or people are presented as commodities in unexpected ways. The authors are especially interested in two possible artistic responses to modern capitalism. One is to turn the experiences of producing, desiring or consuming products—described using the covering term "commodity culture"—into artworks. The other is to focus on the material results and remains of the process: excess consumption or waste (p9).

These themes repeat throughout the book, but on the whole the text does not flow from one chapter to another. We are given a general impression of the authors' interests, not an ordered story or definite argument. This means the text sometimes poses questions that are left unanswered. On the other hand, they are not questions easily answered, and the primary purpose of the book seems to be to raise them, and provoke readers to think of their own answers.

For example, one recurring point is how artists take part in commercial relationships themselves, potentially commodifying or exploiting their subjects, and whether this is a legitimate strategy for highlighting these processes in wider society, or is simply unethical. For example, the Common Culture collaboration—of which the authors are members—hired comedians to perform their sets to an empty stage, and bouncers to stand in a gallery as living artworks. In both cases, people normally seen as confident and tough could be seen as vulnerable, and manipulated. The performances were intended to show that these qualities (confidence or toughness) have been made into commodities. They also give the uncomfortable impression of reducing the individuals who took part in the performances to these qualities, which again, as the artists point out, is what the labour market does (p55).

The implication is that these methods are appropriate because the purpose of the artwork is to make a point specifically about exploitation. On the other hand, the authors are very critical of Boris Mikhailov's *Case History*, in which he paid homeless Ukrainian people to pose naked. They describe his attempt to justify this as "phony humanism", which it does in fact sound like, and define him as "part of the 'non-ethical' capitalist art market" (p37). This poses the question of what an ethical version would look like, or whether it is even possible (this left unanswered). Where is the line drawn between exploitative art, and art about exploitation? Does it depend on the intentions of the artist—or their ability to come up with a good explanation—or on the finished result?

Although the introduction defines the last 50 years as key for such "critical" art (p5), comparisons can be made with pieces predating this period. Common Culture's *Binge* series may be motivated by different intentions to Hogarth's *Gin Alley* (or not), but the appearance is similar. Hogarth composed "modern moral subjects", satirising and exposing aspects of 18th century society, and several of the works in the book are apparently based on similar ideas. However, there is a risk of this blurring into actual moralising, in the sense of judging the people depicted. Some of the

photographic pieces use their subjects, for example a woman collapsed after a night out or a family eating fast food at a grubby bus stop, as visual shorthand for generalised experiences or conditions. Although the accompanying texts discuss the images in terms of these wider messages, the photographs themselves can appear critical of the individuals.

Going back further in time, some of the ideas discussed, for example artworks as objects of conspicuous consumption by the ruling class, are arguably as old as class itself. Nevertheless, the authors are justified in saying that it is only fairly recently that artists have become so fascinated with using the problematic status of artworks and the work of art-making as the subject of their work.

As that tangled-sounding definition suggests, this is a rather self-obsessed subject, art *about* art. The book is critical of the "utopian and transcendental" status art is sometimes given (p147), and for this reason focuses closely on the negative aspects of the "global culture industry" (p146). This tends to downplay the value (in a human sense) of art, which persists despite commodification. However, that would probably need another book to discuss, and in terms of analysing the negative side, *Variable Capital* is very successful.

Lastly, the book looks good, which might sound either obvious or irrelevant, but for a discussion of mainly conceptual artworks, dealing with heavy theoretical issues, this is quite an achievement. The theoretical writing is largely in the introduction, and is dense but clearly written, giving potted summaries and references of various writers on popular culture. In the rest of the book, the text does not overwhelm the pictures. Finally the variety of the artworks selected means there is probably something to catch every readers' interest.

Capital ideas

Sarah Young

Sasha Lilley (ed), **Capital and its Discontents** *(PM Press, 2011), £14.99*

This book is a collection of interviews with left wing intellectuals conducted by its editor Sasha Lilley. One of its strengths is that Lilley is constantly concerned with what the left should be doing and how the ideas of those interviewed can be married with radical action. There are interesting discussions of the roots of the crisis and the role of the state from the likes of Ellen Wood, Leo Panitch and David McNally, among others. However, there are, I would argue, two major problems: the lack of a clear discussion of organisational form and the failure to adequately grapple with the nature and legacy of Stalinism.

The focus on theory and practice throughout the collection would have benefited greatly from dealing with the question of organisation more robustly. Generally throughout the book there is the attitude that "vanguardist" or Leninist parties are a problem for the left today. Lilley in the introduction, while not ignoring the question of organisation, argues that we need to move beyond the notions of the "old left".

This idea manifests itself in a number of ways throughout the book. So, for example, Andrej Grubačić argues that Marxism is the theory and anarchism, particularly "prefigurative politics", the practice, reducing Marxism to a merely contemplative tool.

David Harvey says that he would ask of those in parties "in what ways does your organisational form actually have the capacity to address what is the global problem of finding an alternative to capitalism, that can feed, and shelter 6.8 billion people adequately in a way that is sensitive to all sorts of cultural variety?" (p75).

In fact, revolutionary Marxism theorises the role of organisation not to "prefigure" a new world in the shell of the old or to develop a blueprint for a future socialist society, but rather to most effectively unite those who want to settle accounts with the whole rotten system in common action.

John Sanbonmatsu argues that the left needs to develop a long-term strategy and says one of the weaknesses of the left today is that it just comes together to react to issues as they arise in a way that would have been anathema to Gramsci and Rosa Luxemburg. What is missed (by, for example, not recognising that both Gramsci and Luxemburg were both members of communist parties) is that revolutionary organisation is vital to developing the kind of strategy that would allow the left to do more than simply react.

Sanbonmatsu's contribution deals with the legacy of postmodernism on the left and argues that one of its greatest failings is that it obscures the social totality and so does not offer us a way to really fight the whole system of capital. His contribution is reflective of the overall nature of the book: it offers some partial insights and it has a commendable focus on the need for strategy, but it falls short of offering an alternative strategy or discussing how one ought to be developed.

A further thread running throughout the book is the legacy of Stalinism, which Lilley sets out as a key obstacle for the left today. If postmodernism obscured the social totality and directed people away from struggle, the foundations for this were laid by the Stalinist regimes. However, the only chapter that deals explicitly with the class nature of the Stalinist states is Mike Davis's chapter on

Deutscher. Davis hails Deutscher as the "key to understanding 1989" due to his "dialectical" understanding of the nature of the Soviet Union as encapsulating both top-down reforms and working class struggle from below, which together could revert these states back to socialism.

The idea of the former Communist states as being somewhat socialist—rather than as a form of bureaucratic state capitalism—is repeated throughout the book. A lack of a serious engagement with the *class* nature of these regimes is a significant weakness in these discussions: they rightly raise the legacy of Stalinism as an obstacle to the recomposition of the left but offer no coherent way to deal with this.

Overall, the book is an accessible overview of many influential thinkers of the radical left today. However, while it attempts to deal with key questions facing the left, it does so in a manner that raises more questions that it attempts to answer and leaves you unsure where to go next.

Dark mirror
Jack Farmer

SS Prawer, **Karl Marx and World Literature** *(Verso, 2011), £16.99*

In a letter to his daughter Laura dated 11 April 1868, Marx wrote, "You'll certainly fancy, my dear child, that I am very fond of books, because I trouble you with them at so unseasonable a time. But you would be quite mistaken. I am a machine, condemned to devour them and then throw them, *in a changed form*, on the dunghill of history." [my emphasis]

In *Karl Marx and World Literature*, first published in 1976 and recently reissued, SS Prawer shows decisively that literature played a central role in the development of Marx's ideas. References to plays, poetry and novels are the constant companions of his materialist arguments. This is of more than antiquarian interest. It should affect our understanding of Marx's critical method, the better to renew it today.

Prawer chases down every reference he can find to a work of imaginative literature in Marx's writings, sifting through many passages to reveal different layers of meaning that emerge from Marx's allusions. He shows just how broadly Marx read and how deeply embedded imaginative literature was in his thinking. Literary references do more than simply illustrate and justify important arguments—they help to form them.

At times Marx plays on broader meanings he expects his readers to infer from quotations, at others he is content to rip them out of context, extracting an isolated point. Shakespeare looms large. Timon crouched in his cave provides evidence for the levelling effects of money: "[Gold] will make black, white; foul, fair;/Wrong, right; base, noble; old, young; coward, valiant". Shylock regularly appears as the archetypal miser and hoarder; as capital personified, craving laws that allow the rampant exploitation of children; and as the voice of the worker haunted by the prospect of losing his means of subsistence: "You take my life/When you do take the means whereby I live". Shylock proves especially useful in *Capital*, because he can represent a world where money has replaced God and human suffering is guaranteed by laws written to protect the owners of wealth. Tellingly, when Goethe's Mephistopheles appears, he takes a devilish pleasure in the power of money without expressing the wracking doubts of Shylock or Timon.

Marx uses specific characters as short-hand for clusters of characteristics that he attributes to historical figures and contemporary opponents. Prometheus, the ultimate rebel, crosses paths with Falstaff, who appears as a clown, but also a recruiting sergeant and knowing cynic. Marx is happy to alter the passages he refers to if it suits his purpose. Misquoting Hamlet, he claims that *"everything* is rotten in the state", while in a famous passage from the *Communist Manifesto*, Marx reverses the roles in Goethe's poem "The Sorcerer's Apprentice" to make it the master-sorcerer (*hexenmeister*), not the apprentice, who has lost control of the spells he has summoned. It is the bourgeoisie's apprentice, we must infer, who holds the power to tame capitalism's manic magic. Prawer convincingly argues that the *Communist Manifesto* is a palimpsest of world literature, each reference peeling away to reveal further layers of meaning.

Marx never produced an extended work setting out his views on literature as such. Instances of literary criticism tend to be partial, incidental, or subordinated to other aims. Prawer does not set out to comment on what a Marxist "theory of literature" might be but in the course of surveying Marx's literary sources, he does draw out some important points about Marx's attitude to literature in particular and culture in general.

Marx famously used a spatial metaphor—"base" and "superstructure"—to describe the relationship between culture, philosophy, aesthetics, the legal and political systems and religion on the one hand and the economic structure of society on the other. Marx has since been charged with suggesting that the base fully determines the superstructure, rather than merely "in the last instance", as Engels put it.

It's true that Marx's phrasing in some places lends itself to mechanical interpretations—that the superstructure is merely a passive reflection of social relations at the base. But if culture reflects economic relations it does so in a mirror, darkly. The image of society visible in culture is one altered, conditioned by artistic form itself. Like the legal and political systems or religion, culture grows from the economic base of society but is not reducible to it. That Marx was sensitive to the complex interaction between the "base" and "superstructure" is evident from his insertion of qualifications and his preference for organic metaphors when describing this relationship.

Marx's understanding of culture affected the way that he wrote his economic and political theory. In 1865 he told Engels, "Whatever shortcomings they may have, the merit of my writings is that they are an artistic whole, and that can only be attained by my method of never having them printed until they lie before me a as a whole." The alternative method, of sending parts of a manuscript to the printers before the whole work is complete, is "more suited to works not dialectically constructed". Even as he describes the shape of history in *The Eighteenth Brumaire of Louis Bonaparte*, Marx reaches for literary genres—"tragedy" and "farce". Time and again complex ideas emerge first as literature.

In art, Marx sees an image of unalienated labour—in the *Grundrisse* he argues that the relation between capitalists and workers develops "in a manner all the more pure and adequate in proportion to the extent that labour loses its character of art". Art implicitly criticises a world dominated by exchange-value.

Marx felt compelled to pepper his work with literary quotations and allusions, but in doing so he changed them, extracting and elaborating on their best insights to feed his growing understanding of capitalism. Literary quotations and allusions are deployed as more than mere ornaments, but as material from which he can begin to construct theory. An awareness of the importance of the literary sources that originally nourished Marx can help us to renew the living tradition of revolutionary Marxism today.

Liberalism: theory and practice
Marieke Mueller

Domenico Losurdo, **Liberalism: A Counter-History** (Verso, 2011), £22

The Oxford English Dictionary defines liberalism as the "support for or advocacy of individual rights, civil liberties, and reform tending towards individual freedom, democracy, or social equality". In his book *Liberalism: A Counter-History* Domenico Losurdo opposes the view that liberal philosophy from the 18th century onwards (represented by Locke and others) was part of a gradual transition towards political freedom and equality. Slavery, repression of the emerging working class, limits to political freedom and mass extermination of indigenous populations are not, as Losurdo shows, curious by-products of a general progress towards democracy but phenomena intrinsically bound up with the development of liberal ideas and with the reality of countries claiming to be "liberal".

Throughout the book, Losurdo argues that there is an "entanglement of emancipation and dis-emancipation" inherent in liberalism (p391). He questions whether the established thinkers of liberalism, such

as Calhoun, Locke, de Tocqueville, Sieyès and Montesquieu, can be called liberals at all. His answer tears apart the standard teachings of textbook philosophy. Locke was not only a shareholder in the slave trade but his writings more fundamentally legitimised the emerging chattel slavery at the time. Liberalism and racial slavery are the products of a "unique twin birth" (p35). Montesquieu, who comes closest to a refutation of slavery, does not oppose it on the grounds of human equality. Instead he argues the "uselessness of slavery" in Europe (p44), relegating slavery from the metropolis but justifying it in the colonies. Losurdo's book does not simply condemn liberalism, but tries to work out its contradictions. Adam Smith for instance saw that "the freedom of the free was the cause of the great oppression of the slaves", but proposed a despotic government as a solution.

This close analysis of a liberal ideology which goes hand in hand with slavery (and other limitations to equality and democracy) is vital for an understanding the history of slavery. But Losurdo is not only concerned with ideas. In his short methodological preface he declares his intention to write about liberal ideas and their expression in reality. But he often does more than that: rather than just seeing history as an expression of ideas, he often shows the dialectical interaction between ideas and history. He notes for example the important role played by the masses in the 1848 revolutions. Losurdo shows that it is the spectre of socialism that leads liberal thinkers to adopt a language of individualism and that provokes de Tocqueville to criticise the 1789 French Revolution.

Losurdo also emphasises the resistance of the oppressed, for instance the slave rebellion in Haiti, and the shock it caused the ruling classes in Europe and America. In reaction to the failure of the American and

English liberal models, he argues, a radical strand of thought (eg Diderot) began to identify with the oppressed and revolution from below. It is this radical thought that was inherited later by Marx and Engels. Whether or not it is always useful to distinguish between liberalism and radicalism, Losurdo makes a very valuable contribution in describing how more radical thought emerges out of the contradictions of liberalism.

Losurdo asks whether 18th and 19th century England and America can be identified as liberal countries. He reveals the American Revolution as a movement for independence—and for the right to own slaves, expressed in the American Constitution. Subsequently, the American settlers adopted a racialised notion of slavery, while in England a spatial definition of slavery emerged, like Montesquieu's, which relegated it to the colonies. At the same time, the court which ruled that England was a territory whose air was "too pure for a slave to breathe" (p48) expressed its own form of racism. The lack of political freedom and the effect of slavery even on whites in America, and the slave-like conditions of workers in England and Scotland, leads Losurdo to dismiss these countries as being liberal.

Losurdo defines the political system in America as a "master-race democracy", a term defined as "democracy which applied exclusively to the master race" (p107). Because of the key role racism played also in the North, the term, being based on white supremacy, is also applied to those states. This exemplifies very well that democracy was available only to a very small minority in America, to the caste of whites. Losurdo insists that the division along race lines "was conducive to the development of relations of equality within the white community" (p107). The prevalent ideas of the community of the free whites may have led

poor whites to identify with the ruling class. However, an analysis of class interest would have made it clear at this point that *objectively* the poor white shared a common interest with slaves and poor black people.

England after the Glorious Revolution is also termed a "master-race democracy", on the basis that the category is not understood in a merely ethnic sense. It is opened up to the situation of indentured servants, the dehumanisation of wage-labourers, and the harsh sentencing of the poor. The merit of this analysis is that it shows the ways in which liberalism excludes great numbers of people from the enjoyment of its supposed values. From this point of view it is unproblematic that the analysis is not based on a theoretical differentiation between race and class. Losurdo demonstrates precisely the conflation of race and class in liberalism itself. But if we want to move on to think about the possibilities of self-emancipation of the various groups excluded from freedom, we are in need of additional tools that help us understand the difference between them.

At points the book would have benefited from a clearer definition of the term "liberalism", and therefore the reason for the choice of authors discussed is not always obvious. *Liberalism* for instance includes Locke, but not Hobbes. Losurdo frequently references Burke in his analysis, a thinker who the defenders of liberalism would arguably exclude on account of his being a conservative. The choice would be perfectly justified if liberalism was treated as the ideology of the ruling class, or an element of it. But this is never spelt out. Instead, the term "liberalism" is sometimes used in a confusingly broad way, for instance when Losurdo disagrees with Marx (with whom he also has many agreements) on the definition of the revolutions from 1688 to 1848. Losurdo calls these "liberal revolutions", rather than bourgeois ones. By blurring class and ideology the book at this point is too vague about the definition of its very subject matter.

But this does not detract greatly from the aim of the book: to show the contradictions of liberalism and the way in which it inherently excludes great numbers of people from its own values, both in theory and in practice. Losurdo has produced a very useful book which brings together elements of the history of liberalism often presented as disconnected by bourgeois thought. He shows the close connection between the ideology justifying slavery, the racism of the Jim Crow laws and a racialised vision of the community of the free. Without fear of being provocative ("Roosevelt can thus be calmly approximated to Hitler"—p338), he argues that the horrors of the 20th century were by no means an inexplicable exceptional event. The book is highly relevant beyond its immediate historical subject. It will not only be useful to anyone interested in liberal philosophy. It is also a significant contribution at a time of revolutions and "humanitarian" interventions pose again the questions of the so-called "democratic world" and the self-emancipation of the oppressed.

Ethnic dissension
Shirin Hirsch

Prodromos Panayiotopoulos, **Ethnicity, Migration and Enterprise** *(Palgrave, 2010), £58*

Academia is constantly filled with new buzzwords. In the last decade, transnationalism has become a prominent new concept with numerous conferences and journals emerging that attempt to deal with this supposedly new phenomenon. In the wake of Seattle and the protests which marked the World Trade Organisation meetings, scholars began to turn their attention to ways of organising and networks of people framed beyond the nation state.

Panayiotopoulos's book responds to this new "transnational theory" through a number of case studies exploring different migration experiences. He powerfully shows the weaknesses of the theory, arguing that the political-institutional framework is central to an understanding of how racial and ethnic groups are ranked for exclusion or inclusion in systems of immigration control. Ideas of "deterritorialisation", which are central to transnational theory, stand at odds with the international refugee system, with increasingly strengthened border controls. According to Panayiotopoulos, the nation-state is central to analysing migration.

The book continues to trace the structural framework in which to understand patterns of migration. While much of refugee literature and broader studies of multiculturalism tend to focus on particular cities and neighbourhoods, Panayiotopoulos is keen to stress the importance of enterprise and the workplace on migrants. One study he references is illuminating here, focusing on a recent migrant group employed in London's low-paid sectors. Researchers found that respondents conveyed the distinct sense that racism within the locality was not a major problem.

Their main concerns were about racist practices in the labour market with many stressing that they felt "excluded from professional and white collar jobs" despite holding relevant skills and qualifications. Responding to this exclusion, Panayiotopoulos focuses on specifically migrant enterprises. His work shows that far from taking jobs from native workers, immigrants are in fact creating large numbers of jobs in particular sectors and localities. Ethnic minority enterprises are a highly visible phenomenon in the transformation of many inner-city neighbourhoods and run-down suburbs.

Panayiotopoulos's opening chapter is a defence of the conceptual use of the term "ethnicity". He strives to show that while ethnicity is not a natural "primordial" category, it has real influence as an associated condition of class. Rather than ignoring the term altogether, he argues that in work there is a real "ethnicisation" of particular trades and occupations. For example, one in seven Pakistani men in Britain is a taxi driver.

However, there is little discussion over how these ethnic categories are used in a top-down manner to divide class solidarity. Eric Wolf notes that the allocation of workers to invented ethnic categories is doubly effective in this respect, first by ordering the groups and categories of labourers hierarchically with respect to one another and secondly by continually producing and recreating symbolically marked "cultural" distinctions among them.* At times Panayiotopoulos stresses too much the cultural difference between ethnic groups as a real phenomenon shaping labour relations, rather than something created to divide people into different groups. Indeed, not only is the class system structured by race, but it is also fractured by conceptions of ethnicity.

Rather than a fixed and stable division, the relationship between race and ethnicity is messy and confusing and needed further discussion in this work. The exploration of Hispanic migrants in the US is a useful example. While Hispanic migrants are often categorised as one group, and the term "Hispanic" is used both as an ethnic and racial category, the class divisions are unavoidable, most noticeably between the success of the Cuban Hispanic community in Miami and the Mexican and Central American Hispanic grouping, which often serves as a reserve army of labour.

The term ethnicity also does not give adequate space for any wider migrant solidarity movements or resistance within "ethnic" enterprises. Panayiotopoulos notes the largest mobilisation in the history of the US in 2006, when more than 2 million immigrants and their supporters demonstrated against the anti-immigration bill, a proposal that would have criminalised all 12 million undocumented immigrants in the US. These demonstrations showed the power to change the very nature of migrant employment. In California the protest had the aspect of a state-wide general strike and in Los Angeles alone an estimated 1 million people marched under the banner "A Day Without Immigrants". At the height of Bush's state racism policies, the movement was able to defeat the anti-immigration bill.

More in-depth research on some of these compelling moments of resistance could perhaps have enriched the book and offered a potential way out of the ethnically divided workforce. However, the book remains a valuable resource that provides a wide-ranging overview of key debates surrounding migration and enterprise.

* ER Wolf, 1982, *Europe and the Peoples Without History* (University of California), p380.

Revolution revisited

Julie Sherry

Stephen Eric Bronner, **Socialism Unbound: Principles, Practices, and Prospects** *(Columbia University Press, 2011), £20.50*

In this second edition of his book *Socialism Unbound*, Stephen Eric Bronner argues that liberalism cannot provide answers to the continuing problems of capitalism, and that "socialism remains on the agenda". He states that "abstract definitions from times past no longer make sense" and that he aims to free socialism from "its authoritarian and parochial shackles".

Starting with the "democratic legacy of Karl Marx and Frederick Engels", Bronner traces this legacy through its influence on Karl Kautsky and Eduard Bernstein during the growth of social democracy and reformism. He then pits this against Leninism, which he claims has "surrendered". After following the "abject failure of the communist experiment" through to the collapse of the Stalinist regimes, Bronner places Rosa Luxemburg as representing "another tradition...bound by a spirit of revolutionary humanism and libertarian socialism".

He identifies three opposing strands of how Marxism has been interpreted and applied since its birth: reformist social democracy; revolutionary authoritarianism; and a revolutionary democratic politics that rejects both reformism and authoritarianism.

Bronner insists on his intention to "not throw the baby out with the bathwater". His mission is to look thoroughly at this history, and clarify the strands he deems necessary for a socialist perspective today.

He usefully places Marx's and Engels's contributions in the context of the limits of the bourgeois revolutions, which he describes as "the unfulfilled promises of the Enlightenment and the French Revolution". By the second half of the 19th century, Bronner says, "The bourgeoisie was no longer capable of leading a revolution. Its time for radical democratic values had passed." He explains how the most radical ideas of the once revolutionary bourgeoisie "now came to inspire another class: the workers".

This chapter essentially celebrates the significance of Marx's and Engels's revelation that the working class were "the key to the riddle of capitalist production". Bronner argues that their ideas represented a breakthrough, providing those struggling to fight for economic equality and democracy with an understanding and a confidence that they could win. But he describes Marx's use of the term "dictatorship of the proletariat", to express the need for workers to seize power from the bourgeoisie, as irresponsible. This is reflective of a wider argument Bronner develops throughout the book in his rejection of the Bolshevik method as anti-democratic.

In his analysis of Karl Kautsky, Bronner accepts the negative role Kautsky played in opposing the Russian Revolution, failing to effectively oppose the war, and selling out European workers. He also says these critiques "do not exhaust the importance or the relevance of Karl Kautsky's contribution". At the turn of the century, Kautsky stood as a giant of the Second International. He came to prominence as a theoretician in the period that followed the brutal crushing of the Paris Commune, but before the 1905 Russian Revolution, when capitalism was advancing exponentially, and along with it organisations of the working class such as trade unions and social democratic parties.

Leon Trotsky described Kautsky's "principal theoretical mission as the reconciling of reform and revolution". Bronner echoes this, showing Kautsky's weaknesses as rooted in a particular interpretation of Marxism. Unlike other contemporary leading figures in the German Social Democratic Party, Kautsky believed revolution was at some point necessary, but he saw Marxism as a rigid stagist theory of history. He felt bound by these politics to condemn the Bolshevik seizure of power as "premature".

Ultimately Bronner argues that Kautsky became an "embarrassment to both major political organisations of the working class in the postwar period". Social democrats saw him as "dogmatic", while communists saw him as a class "traitor". Trotsky summarised this contradiction remarking, "How savagely the dialectic of history has dealt with one of its own apostles!"

Bronner places Kautsky's contribution as an attempt to straddle the contradiction of reformism and revolution. He shows Eduard Bernstein's politics as more consistent. He assesses Bernstein's aim as "to distinguish between the scientific and utopian forms of socialism with an eye on eliminating the latter". Bernstein argued that "the movement is everything, the end goal is nothing", and believed that socialism would be brought about gradually through capitalism, not by overthrowing it.

But Bronner describes Bernstein as having been proven blatantly wrong in his "assumption that capitalism had overcome its crisis character", identifying Bernstein's evolutionary socialism theory as stemming from this notion. He places responsibility at Bernstein's door for the "political identity crisis that has plagued the labour movement for the second half of the 20th century", linking this back to the revisionist impact in rendering "class power irrelevant". Bronner concludes this chapter highlighting the importance of the lessons contemporary socialists can take from an analysis of Bernstein's politics in their attempts to challenge its legacy today.

The chapter titled "Leninism and Beyond" is the most telling. While making his condemnation of Lenin immediately clear, Bronner says it is still worth asking "whether the entire undertaking could have turned out differently". He does not crudely equate Leninism to Stalinism. He concedes that "if not necessarily in theory, then certainly in practice, a sharp and decisive break took place between Leninism and Stalinism". But he is unwilling to concede that there was a theoretical break.

This is despite admitting that Stalin "transformed" world communism's "former commitment to international class struggle" with an "unqualified preoccupation with national interest". This would seem to most like a pretty fundamental theoretical break. He describes the party under Stalin's control as changed from one of "professional revolutionary intellectuals" to one of "fawning bureaucrats and thugs". Under the leadership of Trotsky or Nikolai Bukharin, things would have turned out differently, Bronner argues. He likens their understanding of the party to Lenin's, and contrasts the fact that their arguments were always conducted politically, with Stalin's "use of power to settle grudges".

Although the notion that the seeds of Stalinism were sowed under Lenin's leadership is alluded to a number of times, Bronner does not offer up a clear argument that pinpoints this. He focuses on exploring alternatives within Russia without acknowledging how significant the international context was. It is interesting to study the possibilities had Trotsky followed Lenin, and it is important to establish the extent of the Stalinist distortion of the party. Besides, this helpfully undermines Bronner's flippant allusions to Lenin's "responsibility" for Stalinism. But Trotsky's leadership alone could not have overcome the Russian Revolution's isolation and the impossibility of real socialism in one country.

Bronner's overall general argument is not crude like many histories of Leninism. Yet the element he does not accept—the Bolshevik model of revolutionary organisation—is the very ingredient that could have transformed the world situation and in turn prevented the distortion, and then suffocation of the Russian Revolution. Had such a party existed in the countries where workers were in revolt, the struggle could have been directed and developed to the point of seizing power.

The 1918 German Revolution failed, Britain came close to revolution in 1919, and Italy saw a wave of workers' councils grow out of factory occupations in 1919 and 1920. But lack of revolutionary leadership meant this resistance was not generalised.

A rooted revolutionary party could have shaped these struggles towards victory—as the Bolsheviks had done in Russia. The capitalist ruling class are organised. They have foresight, a strategy and tactics, and a dynamic ability to readjust in order to maintain their system of oppression. Without a workers' organisation developed and shaped by workers' experiences and

that consciously works to overthrow capitalism, the other side will catch us out in these crucial battles.

The book lacks a chapter that could look critically at these missed opportunities and the weakness of the western European left. These experiences offer vital lessons for what kind of organisation was needed, and how it could have transformed world history.

Bronner helpfully points out the problems of reformism, but he does not provide an alternative. He sets Rosa Luxemburg apart from both reformism and the authoritarianism he ascribes to Lenin. The chapter is a useful exploration of her theoretical contributions to Marxism. He also places her pamphlets *Social Reform or Revolution*, and *The Mass Strike, the Political Party, and the Trade Unions* as crucial interventions against the "immediate danger" of reformism.

She is described as "scathing in her criticisms of vanguardism" in relation to Lenin, and Bronner also notes Lenin's criticism that Luxemburg was "too soft on the need to break with the social democrats and the creation of a new organisation". But in most of the examples he gives to accentuate the political differences between Luxemburg and Lenin, Bronner admits that she had not grasped the desperate concrete situation facing the revolution.

Luxemburg enthusiastically embraced the Russian Revolutions, both in 1905 and 1917, though she did not uncritically accept every decision the Bolsheviks took. But unlike Bronner, Luxemburg placed the Bolsheviks' use of coercion, in the face of extreme pressures, in the context of the "failure of Western social democracy to meet its international revolutionary obligations".

Contrary to his own intentions, Bronner does throw the baby out with the bathwater, as he renders revolutionary parties null and void. While celebrating the legacy of Marx in showing we can transform the world, and critiquing reformism, he fails to actually offer a coherent strategy towards socialism.

A citizen of whose world?

Jamie Pitman

David Held, **Cosmopolitanism: Ideals and Realities** (Polity, 2010), £15.99

History will tell whether David Held is best remembered for his role in developing the London School of Economics' intimate relationship with the Gaddafi regime in Libya or for his voluminous body of work advocating a global turn towards "cosmopolitanism". Modern cosmopolitanism has come to be defined as a supplement to globalisation that seeks to emphasise the moral obligations human beings owe to one another, over and above allegiances to nation, race, gender, religion or political affiliation (class is often the elephant in the room in cosmopolitan thinking). This stress on liberal ethics, individualism and universalism is designed to smash the forcefield of nationalism, aided by a raft of more familiar measures including human rights, a universalised legal framework and the improvement of our existing democratic structures.

The supreme twist of irony at the centre of Held's connection to the Gaddafi regime was that so-called "humanitarian interventions"—where "no-fly zones" become a euphemism for Western fighter

jets to kill with impunity—are a central plank of the new cosmopolitan agenda (a register of whose thinkers include Martha Nussbaum, Jürgen Habermas, Mary Kaldor and Ulrich Beck). But there is (theoretically at least) a sizeable gap between Held's own conception and the hawkish realities of the Washington security agenda. Held's more nuanced position is succinctly summarised by his occasional co-author, Daniele Archibugi, who (condemning the Afghan war) states, "a criminal act is not enough to justify the unleashing of brute force... What we need is democratic management of global events, not high-tech reprisals."

Held takes another step in this direction by refusing to abstract Al Qaeda from Western foreign policy, instead emphasising the symbiotic relationship between military adventurism and global terrorism. Yet Held's road map for his own cosmopolitanism remains largely normative. It relies on: (a) institutional reform; and, (b) globalisation forcing the transnational ruling class into making the collective decisions necessary to combat climate change, terrorism, nuclear proliferation, global poverty, etc.

But this optimism is both unsatisfactory and ahistorical. First, Held treats globalisation as "a thing in itself", a runaway, irreversible process divorced from capitalism rather than the effect of neoliberal policy-making and an internal logic that strives "to batter down all Chinese walls", as Marx put it. Secondly, there is little historical evidence that merely staring into the abyss will provide a sufficient fulcrum to divert global leaders from the dangerous trajectories that they have locked us into. The failure of successive climate change conferences and the creeping return of the mutually assured destruction narrative as Iran and other nations pursue nuclear programmes testify to this as surely as the failure of the Millennium Development Goals—to name but a few examples of Held's own choosing.

Held's argument that our "overlapping communities of fate" provide a springboard to overcome shared global risks naively hangs upon the idea that global elites will suddenly discover a hidden store of good will down the back of some collective sofa. In a world of combined and uneven development, where historic advantage is built into the system and underwritten by military power, betting the farm on "cooperation" when all the other players are so bent on "competition" seems a bet too far, especially with stakes this high.

Despite that, many Marxists will find it difficult to simply dismiss this work with well-rehearsed "reform or revolution" arguments. Held's critique of the concentration and entrenchment of economic, political and military power on the world stage is as commendable as his stated desire for social justice. Held does not shy away from connecting climate change to neoliberal dogma or the same dogma to the current economic crisis, even if he incorrectly attributes the crisis to "light touch" regulation rather than a structural crisis of overaccumulation and profitability.

This naturally leads to the question of what is the bulwark that prevents largely decent analysis from shaping a deeply flawed end product? The answer to this paradox lies in the underlying theory and assumptions that inform Held's work.

It was Immanuel Kant, the 18th century critical philosopher, who first outlined a fully formed cosmopolitan theory. The material motivation was provided by the aim of constituting harmony between sovereign states so that the massive expansion in global trade under way at the time could continue unabated. The idea was that travellers (read: traders) would be extended every courtesy when they crossed national boundaries. Kant's mistaken belief that a fledgling capitalism could act as an instrument of "perpetual peace" has been hollowed out both in theory (notably in the analyses of Lenin, Nikolai Bukharin and Karl Kautsky) and in practice, underlined by the experience of the two bloodiest wars in history.

Despite these glaring shortfalls in the Kantian heritage, the mistakes of the past continue to be writ large on much of the new cosmopolitanism, mostly activated by the uneasy combination of capitalism and idealism. We can see the echoes of Kant's radical liberalism in Held's (albeit reserved) advocacy of military interventionism; a clunking moral economy and a belief in a universalism that will reconcile people's conflicting interests—despite the fact that any real universalism has continually evaded the liberal tradition (slavery and colonialism historically end any arguments in that arena). Human rights are another Kantian import that, uncoupled from any socio-economic context, can all too easily become an instrument of oppression and a philosophical justification of the market. Taking a panoramic view, the potential for ambiguity within cosmopolitan programmes means that it is impossible to identify any consistency within it. This explains Held's adoption of what he terms a "layered cosmopolitan approach". Such an approach (termed "hermeneutic") means Held fully expects any framework he develops to be "interpreted" rather than strictly followed, dependent on a whole nexus of variables such as class, race, sex, culture, location and so on (and it is in no way clear how any of this would impact on already persecuted national minorities).

Effectively this leaves us with two potential outcomes: either the whole project